NO ONE
gets there
ALONE

DR. ROB BELL

Disclaimer and FTC Notice

ISBN 978-0-9899184-6-6 (Hardback)
ISBN 978-0-9899184-5-9 (Paperback)
ISBN 978-0-9899184-7-3 (E-book)

Book Design: Gurtowsky Graphics

Published by: DRB Press

BASED ON WORLD LEADING MEDICAL AND SPORTS SCIENCE BACKED BY PROVEN RESEARCH, SOS IS THE ONLY
HYDRATION DRINK FORMULATED BY A DOCTOR AND TWO FORMER PRO ATHLETES.
SOS® IS COMMITTED TO THE HIGHEST QUALITY FROM THE FACTORY TO BEYOND THE FINISH LINE.
WE ARE ORGANIC, NON GMO, LOW CALORIE, AND CERTIFIED BY INFORMED CHOICE.
"sourced from nature designed by science"
www.ineedsos.com

A special thank you to the sponsor of the book.

SOS HYDRATION - ineedsos.com

ALSO BY DR. ROB BELL

Mental Toughness Training for Golf

The Hinge: The Importance of Mental Toughness

NO FEAR: A Simple Guide to Mental Toughness

Don't "Should" on Your Kids: Build Their Mental Toughness

50 Ways to Win: Pro Football's Hinge Moments

Follow NO ONE Gets There ALONE At

 www.facebook.com/
TheImportanceofmentaltoughness/

 #NOONE
@drrobbell

www.drrobbell.com

Advanced Praise

"NO ONE Gets There Alone is a read with a lot of helpful thoughts, techniques, and practices that we can all apply to our lives. None of us can have success without the help of others and our interactions can make or break success for ourselves and those we encounter. I recommend that everyone reads this book at least once."

— Joe Skovron, PGA Tour Caddy

"NO ONE Gets There ALONE is the mental toughness book for people who want to not only improve themselves but everyone around them. When you pick this up, you'll find it impossible to put down."

— John Brubaker,
Author of *Stadium Status*

"Life is NOT a Race, It's a journey. It's you vs. you and it matters who you help along the way. Dr. Rob gets it."

— Jesse Itzler,
Author of *Living with a Seal*

"A coach's greatest gift is to positively create echoes you'll never hear to transform lives beyond the game. This book hammers home that message and much more."

— Reed Maltbie,
Author of *Echoes Beyond The Game. TEDx Speaker*

TABLE OF CONTENTS

TABLE OF CONTENTS

TABLE OF CONTENTS

NO ONE Writes ALONE

This book would not be possible without the support of my wife, Nicole Bell. Thanks to all of the experts who contributed their invaluable experience, strength, and hope into it. Please visit their sites for more detailed strategies and techniques.

Rich Allen	ProThree
Jason Allred	
Frank Bell	
John Brubaker	CoachBru
Jonathan Byrd	
Andrew Curtis	Fuelvm.com
Will Drumright	
Sam Engel	
Jack Frisby	Optimizeselling.com
Robert Garrigus	
Philip Haid	PublicInc.com
Jennifer Hahn	JVA Volleyball
Rebekah Keat	Rebekahkeat.com
Shawn Keith	
Rusty Kennedy	Leavener
Susan Legacki	TrainingPeaks.com
Mike Lingenfelter	Munciana Volleyball
Allie Nicosia	
Ollie Matthews	Body Catchers
Megan Melchiorre	
Tyler Miller	Force Barbell
Jason Minnick	
Darrell Mitchell	
Jerred Moon	End of Three Fitness
Shannon Mulcahy	Shannonmulcahy.com
Mike Ricci	D3 Multisport
Neil Richmund	Neil Richmund.com
Devin Riley	Hoffackerfitness.com
Mary Ann Sedor	Intentlife.com
Dave Sicklesteel	

Corey Smallwood
Dr. Kevin Sverduk
Derek Tow
Mary Towe
Mitch Towe
Bill Van Valer

Dr. Barbara Walker
Zac Vidic
Josh Zaffino

Go Performance
Paramitacoaching.com
thesouth40.com

Elements Massage

"If you want to go fast, go alone. If you want to go far, go together."
— African Proverb

Thank you Glenn Maenhout and Brian Rismiller for stopping to help!
To my wife Nicole, and my children, Ryan and Porter.

NO ONE GETS THERE ALONE

"You can get everything in life you want if you will just help enough other people get what they want." — Zig Ziglar

Journey (Definition): Noun- An act of traveling from one place to another.

Race (Definition): Noun- A competition between two or more to see who is the fastest covering a set course.

...

It was May 7th, on a Saturday evening at home, my kids were five and seven years old at the time, so this was sort of a relaxed Disney movie night.

I was checking my email after putting them both to bed and one of the emails was for a nearby ½ Ironman. I hadn't considered racing a ½ Ironman, and while it was on my bucket list, it was not on my immediate radar of things to do.

Besides, this race was in exactly **two weeks!**

1.2 mile open water swim, 56 mile bike, and then a 13.1 mile run = ½ ironman.

I laughed it off at first, but was intrigued at the same time. I felt the need to check my schedule for the next two weeks and see if I was even going to be in town during the race day.

The oddest part was that I didn't even own a bike and had not ridden one in over 10 years. The reason I hadn't signed up for these types of races previously is because of the biking. I do run and swim and strength train at least five days a week, but with no immediate goals. Frankly, I was also not in any type of "racing" shape.

How was I going to complete a race of this distance with no training and no bike?

The decision to commit to the race made me examine my past, present, and future self. Did I have the confidence I needed to sign-up?

One of my strengths in my past has been the ability to set a goal and reach it. I have run in a number of races before and have trained extensively for these, but these felt like another lifetime ago. Some of my meager, yet personal accomplishments that gave me confidence included a sub 20 minute 5k, a 3:20 marathon, a tough mudder, and a few marathons and 10k. I also managed to break 1:00 barrier in the 100 Freestyle.

One of the toughest things is coming up with a vision of who we want to become. Not what, but who? I want to become someone with no regrets and don't want to sit on the sideline of life and not go for it. I also have an extreme love for my kids; I want to model the importance of having a vision and the mental toughness to execute it for them.

Most importantly, examining who I want to become in my future self became the biggest driving force for me signing up. I signed up for the race on May 21st with less than two weeks to train and prepare for a ½ ironman.

No one gets there alone!

My friend Bill Van Valer provided a bike for me to race and train on for the two weeks. I obtained the services of a mental coach John Brubaker to help with my focus and confidence strategies. I prepared by doing two-a-day workouts either biking, running, or swimming. I rested two days before the event and was as prepared as I could be.

However, this race would be life changing.

The swimming portion of the race went fairly well, but at mile 32 on the bike portion, I was beginning a climb on a very small hill. The race was outside Indianapolis and this was the only hill on the course, and probably in all of Indiana.

The bike I was borrowing for the race had GatorSkin® tires, which are the ultimate in tire protection, so I need not worry about a flat tire. This was a relief because my bicycle maintenance was certainly not up to snuff for I had not biked in ten years.

Near the top of the hill, BAM! My back tire went flat!

I had none of the necessary materials needed to change the tire. No bike tube, cartridges, levers, or fix a flat, nothing! The Boy Scouts were probably turning over in their graves for my lack of preparation.

I assessed the damage and panic set in. I needed to re-focus, prioritize the issue, and find a way to fix the tire. A house was nearby, which I ran to borrow their phone and call the race team, director, somebody, anybody. I was not in a good spot.

I returned back to the side of the road. All the while, bikers were cresting the hill and passing me: I felt so helpless and stupid. Where I was stopped, however, on top of the hill, meant that every biker was at his or her slowest pace. If I had blown a tire on a flat stretch or a downhill with speed, the ending of this story may have been different.

After waiting for about ten minutes, a biker actually stopped at the top of the hill. He saw my plight and asked me if I had anything to change the tire, and I sheepishly answered him that I didn't. He handed me his tube, levers, and cartridge to fix the flat.

The racer #215 who gave me the changing tools, Brian Rismiller, continued on, and I told him I would find him and get him his stuff. It felt like a Disney movie scene where he is riding off and I am yelling, "I'll never forget you." The first issue was solved, but how long would it take me to change it? Under these conditions, this was the worst possible time to try out my tire changing skills.

Just then another biker stopped and asked me if I knew how to change the tire. In my most honest voice, I said "No sir!"

He dismounted his bike and said, *"Well let's get you fixed."*

The saint who stopped to help change the tire was named Glenn Maenhout. He was a complete stranger in his own race, who stopped to help out a dumbass who was ill-prepared. It took a ton of mental toughness for him to stop his entire race to help out a stranger. WOW!

I thanked him so many times, as I watched him fix the tire. The entire ordeal took about 20 minutes, and unfortunately, the clock doesn't stop. If I had to do it myself, it would have taken me *at least* another 20 minutes and much, much more stress, which would have affected my overall performance as well.

If it weren't for these two guys, my race probably would have finished on top of the hill, because I am not sure I could have changed it and still completed the race under the allotted amount of time.

Even though the ½ Ironman was an individual event, no one gets there alone.

Over the next few days, as I continued my keynote speaking and told the audience and other coaches, athletes, and friends about Brian and Glenn, a strange thing occurred. I realized the greater impact of the generous, kind, and selfless acts that they performed. I knew it was a huge moment, but after sharing the story, the impact sets in.

I then began to ask myself, "Rob, would you have stopped?"

Now it is your turn to answer; Would YOU have stopped?

In the journey of real life, I feel like I am generous, kind-hearted, and willing to help others. But, my racing side is different. If we are playing Ping-Pong, or Trouble, or chess, I am trying to win. I know my competitive side and it has tons of benefits, but it also has a bit of a dark tint to it. I was taught long ago and still practice doing whatever it takes to win and finding a way out of no way to succeed. That does not mean cheating, but it does mean pushing oneself past our own limits in practice and competition; basically, leaving everything out on the field, office, pool, etc.

In the racing environment, I would always cheer on other racers and offer encouragement but I was not privy to stopping and helping others out, especially at my own expense. I could not honestly have said, "Yes, I would have stopped."

However, after that event, I have re-examined my own priorities and if I am on a journey or in a race. Can I be on a journey with others and instead of racing against others, race with others? This incident became the reason I had to write this book because no one gets there alone.

DR. ROB BELL

FROM JERUSALEM TO JERICHO

"Life is not a competition. Everyone is on their own journey." —
Eleven52

In 1973, researchers John M. Darley and C. Daniel Batson conducted an experiment on people's propensity to help others in need.[1]

They recruited 40 students to participate, but these were not ordinary students, they were theological seminary students — those in the life sphere of service. Participants of the study were asked to prepare a talk to give to a class across campus. Before they went to the class, each student filled out a questionnaire in one building before walking over across campus to speak. A variable was added to the study, participants either spoke on a regular topic or on *The Good Samaritan*.

The Good Samaritan parable was from the Bible about a wounded Jew on the side of the road in need of assistance. A priest and Levite both passed him by without lending helping hands. However, even though Samaritans and Jews disliked each other, the Samaritan stopped to help the man, hence the Good Samaritan.

The researchers also added a variable of time and hurry to the study. Before each participant left the questionnaire to go speak, they were either told, "You're late, they were expecting you a few minutes ago." or "It'll be a few minutes before they are ready for you, but you might as well head over."

On the way over to the building to speak, each student then passed a man slumped over, groaning and coughing. The experimental question was, who would stop and offer help to the man?

Results of the study revealed that it did not matter the topic that the students were speaking of, they were only influenced by the amount of time each had. Those that were in the hurried condition only stopped 10% of the time. While those who were not in a hurry stopped to help 63% of the time.

Regardless of the type of students, or that they were primed to help because they read about the Good Samaritan, time was considered the biggest factor in these studies.

WOULD YOU STOP?

"So it's definitely not just a sport, it's a lifestyle." — Evie Tate

The biggest factor on whether or not they stopped in the study was if they perceived they were in a hurry. The purpose of research is that results are generalizable to the greater population of people. Chances are that we (you and I) would not stop as well. If this was a more modern day study, then the only difference may have been we would have been looking at our phones instead of even noticing the person.

Now, almost everyone wants to be part of the 10% of people who stopped even though they were in a hurry, no one would readily admit to being part of the 90% of people who would not stop.

In life, whether we stop or not has little to do with our overall character, and more to do with the perception of time and if we are only focused on ourselves. But, let us face it, we are all busier now than ever before. Unless we are made aware that no one gets there alone and that we are all in a greater race together; the human race, chances favor that we will act like most of the participants in the study. We will pass on by.

Sure, two amazing people stopped their own race to help me, but this was an amateur event. In high-level sporting examples, would people under stress and time constraints and pursuing their own performance rewards stop to help a fellow competitor?

...

One of the best moments at the 2016 Olympic Games in Rio involved two runners in the 5000M who didn't even know each other.

With one mile to go in the 5000-meter race, New Zealand's Nikki Hamblin tripped and fell, causing USA runner Abby D'Agostino to fall over her. They were the only two runners affected in this pack. With the event unfolding, before Abby D'Agostino continued, she stopped and helped Nikki Hamblin back up on her feet.

As they both started to again run, Abby fell to the ground as her knee buckled. This time it was Hamblin who stopped and helped D'Agostino continue.

Both runners eventually finished the race, even though D' Agostino had torn the ACL in her knee. What took place with the memorable scene embodied the human spirit and the Olympic Games.

...

Chrissie Wellington was one of the best Ironman Triathletes of all-time, winning the coveted Ironman World Championships at Kona four times and winning the championship as a rookie in 2007.

In 2008, as Chrissie Wellington defended her title as the favorite in Kona, she had a five minute lead on the bike portion of the race when difficulty struck. She suffered a punctured tire at the 55k mark of the 180k bike. Now, these events often occur and the top racers are prepared for these mishaps. However, as she attempted to inflate the tire, her replacement air cartridges failed. So, she was stuck on the side of the road as other riders passed her, unable to continue or accept any outside help from non-competitors.

After ten minutes or so of waiting while the race continued, Australian Rebekah Keat actually stopped and gave fellow competitor Chrissie Wellington her own air cartridge. Chrissie ended up still winning the championship and later commented how winning wouldn't have been possible if not for Rebekah Keat, herself a multiple ironman and half-ironman champion throughout her career.

...

Justin Wadsworth, a Canadian National cross-country ski coach simply had an awful day at the 2014 Sochi Olympic games. The entire team was prepared and favored in many events, but there were some technical issues with the skis early on in the games and his athletes were eliminated. This was a difficult situation for a coach, having prepped endlessly for four years only to have all aspirations dashed.

He was on the course in the Coach's area during the Men's sprint event and as he watched the leaders finish, something happened.

Russian Anton Gafarov came over a hill, but was visibly struggling. Although he was an early medal favorite, he crashed in the race and had broken his ski. He was struggling to move, yet alone finish, because of the damage.

With little hesitation, Wadsworth ran onto the course with a spare ski and clipped in Gafarov so he could finish the race "with dignity." Here was the Canadian Ski team coach who was crestfallen himself because of his own athlete's performance helping out the local athlete at the Russian games. When asked why he helped out this athlete, he answered, "I honestly don't know, I didn't think about it."

...

Thirteen-year-old Natalie Gilbert won a singing competition during half time of a Portland Trailblazers basketball game. Her prize was the opportunity to sing the national anthem for the opening home playoff game of the Portland Trailblazers vs. Dallas Mavericks.

Unfortunately, during the day of the national anthem, she had battled the flu and a 104º F temperature.

As she began to sing, she started to struggle with the words at "Twilight last gleaming" and completely forgot where she was in the song. She stopped singing and the crowd was silent. It was a situation you wouldn't ever wish on anyone.

Just 25 feet away, Trailblazers head coach, Maurice Cheeks walked over immediately and put his arm around her. He began to sing the words with her. In a few seconds, the entire crowd of 21,000 joined in and she finished the song. For the former NBA player turned coach who specialized in assists, this was one of his greatest.

People have forgotten the words to the National Anthem before, but this instance became a national story.

Why did Maurice Cheeks walk over to help? He answered, "I honestly don't know."

...

These selfless and caring acts reveal a truism in life.

NO ONE gets there ALONE!

The skill set of a professional athlete requires many hours of training, years on end, which is only accomplished through sacrifice and extreme time management. Most of their outside life comes secondary to their preparation and competition. Their dedication lives in the world of selfishness and borders on obsessiveness because it is frankly what it takes to reach the top level. It is why if parents actually knew all that it took to be a professional athlete, they would never have their kids sign up.

Evie Tate confirms the sacrifice and dedication it takes. A Division I Cross-country runner at Clemson University, she stated, "Every decision I make is made based on whether or not it's going to make me faster or a better runner. So it's definitely not just a sport, it's a *lifestyle*..."

During the 2016 ACC championships in cross-country in North Carolina, Madeline Adams from Boston College crested the final hill and was about 20 yards from the finish line when she collapsed. Her legs just completely gave out under her and she was unable to even get up. As she fell, Clemson runner, Evie Tate, stopped and put Madeline's arm around her shoulder and started to drag her to the finish line. A few moments later, Rachel Pease from Louisville stopped and helped carry Madeline Adams across the finish line.

Even though Evie and Rachel finished 127th and 128th in the one hundred and thirty one person field, the entire Boston College team hugged them both at the finish line. They both were awarded the ACC Sportsmanship award and the video of this event went viral overnight.

When Evie was asked why she stopped, she replied, "I was in the moment, and it was one of those moments that's *bigger than myself.*"

...

We are moved when we witness these events take place during competition and stressful circumstances. These people sacrificed their own race for the greater journey. They sacrificed for another competitor, someone who they didn't even know, and in doing so, made the greatest show of love possible. We witnessed in real life basically the same 10% of people who stopped during the Jerusalem to Jericho research study.

In these professional instances, these athletes and coaches acted during highly competitive and stressful environments. There was little if any time to comprehend what they would do or not do. And they seemed to all answer the same way when asked about why they helped out, "*I don't know.*"

These individuals did not hesitate and just acted without motive. They had no idea the results of their actions. Their response was one to simply act.

Would you have stopped?

...

The USS Juneau was a battleship that was sunk in the naval battle of Guadalcanal during World War II. Over 680 United States sailors were killed during the initial sinking of the ship and the days afterward. Of deeper implication of the sinking were that five brothers were all killed in action. The five Sullivan brothers all joined the service at the same time and served on the same ship and their collective legacy shaped significant U.S. War Department policy.

The United States government in an attempt to protect families from similar incidents thus enacted the Sole Survivor policy. It basically stipulated that no family members were to simultaneously serve during wartime. It extended that if a family member re-enlists or voluntarily extends their active duty beyond the requirement, then other family members automatically become ineligible.

The Sole Survivor policy seriously took hold during the Vietnam War. Johnnie Ash joined the United States Marine Corps directly out of high school in 1965. He was deployed to Vietnam in 1966. Johnnie Ashe was the younger brother of Arthur Ashe, who was stationed at West Point after having graduated from the ROTC program at UCLA. Arthur Ashe won both a NCAA championship and team national championship in tennis at UCLA and was a top ranked junior player.

When Johnnie Ashe returned from his tour of duty in Vietnam in 1967, Johnnie knew that enough service time remained Arthur that he could be sent to Vietnam. He also knew that the possibilities for Arthur Ashe because of tennis and believed that "I always thought Arthur had a destiny far above the norm."

Knowing exactly the situation he was headed back into, Johnnie volunteered to serve an additional tour of duty in Vietnam. By voluntarily going back, it ensured that Arthur would not have to Vietnam. He never told Arthur of his decision until later in life. It was his sacrifice for his brother that ended up changing history.

In 1968, while Johnnie served another tour in Vietnam; Arthur Ashe won the U.S. Open at Forest Hills becoming the first African American to win the illustrious event. Arthur Ashe went on to win the Australian Open and Wimbledon. He also became the first

African American to be inducted into the Tennis Hall of Fame in 1985.

However, it was Arthur Ashe's platform that enacted change for social justice. Arthur Ashe became one of the greatest educators, humanitarians, and activists in the world. He was a tireless advocate for worldwide civil rights, US foreign policy on refugees, health care for minorities, American Heart Association, and AIDS.

If not for Johnnie's own sacrifice and being the hinge for his brother, Arthur's legacy and impact may have been entirely different.

DR. ROB BELL

THE HINGE

"True heroism is remarkably sober, very undramatic. It is not the urge to surpass all others at whatever cost, but the urge to serve others at whatever cost." — Arthur Ashe

Every door has a hinge. A door without a hinge is a wall, it just doesn't work. The Hinge is any one moment, event, or person in our lives that will make all of the difference. It connects who we are with who we become!

Have you ever noticed when we look back upon any important game or contest that there was usually one play that decided the outcome? It is these pivotal moments that make all of the difference.

These moments provide proof that no one gets there alone. A fallen Olympic runner helping another get back up, an ironman triathlete tossing her own air cartridge to a competitor, or a crestfallen Olympic coach providing a ski for an opposing athlete during competition. There are going to be thousands of events and people in our lives, and within these, there will be a few significant moments or people.

The hinge connects opportunities and people. We have the expertise and skills, but we need to know and be in front of the right people who make a difference: who helped us get our break; whom did we get the special idea from; Who connected with us and served as our mentor, our coach, or our adviser.

How do our lives intersect and connect with others at critical moments?

John Tumpane was walking in downtown Pittsburgh at three o'clock in a summer afternoon to umpire a Major League Baseball game between the Pittsburgh Pirates and Tampa Bay Rays.

As he walked across Roberto Clemente Bridge, he noticed a woman who was trying to get on the other side of the railing. This caught his attention and he hurried over to her just as she successfully got herself on the other side of the railing eighty feet above the Allegheny River.

He put his hand on her shoulder and then both arms around her, as she asked him to let go so she could jump. He said, "I won't let go."
    She told him that no one cares and even he would forget about her. He told her "I'll never forget you my whole life."

Emergency personnel arrived in time, but if it weren't for the actions and timing of John Tumpane, this 23-year-old woman would have committed suicide.

...

All of us will experience these hinges at various points in our lives; a specific person or moment that connects and shapes our future. We can't connect the dots in our lives looking forward; we can only connect the dots looking backwards. It is only after reflecting and seeing how the dots connected are we able to see the impact and significance. We often don't or can't know the impact of the hinge until weeks, months, or even years later.

Here is the rub; we can't predict the future, we can only prepare for the unpredictable. Since we cannot know who or what these will be, our role is to be prepared.

Because it only takes one and we have no idea who or what are the important ones, every person we meet or interact with can be a possible hinge. Thus, EVERY person and moment is the most important one.

It only takes one!

The real importance is that no matter how bad things are in our lives, or how mediocre we feel, or even how bad we messed up, it only takes one event or person to turn everything around. One contact, one person, or one opportunity is what we are getting ready for. One chance is all you need!

You may be thinking of what have been some of the hinge moments or people in your life. You will see them. So how do you prepare and make these hinge moments connect?

In order for the Hinge to connect, we need to give ourselves as many opportunities as possible. It is simple mathematics actually, if we meet 100 people, then the chances increase of connecting with the difference maker of whom we need to.

However, it is ineffective to approach people in a selfish manner. If we approach like we are mentoring, networking, making sales, or doing performance self-seeking, then it is like we are cold calling. Cold calling simply means connecting with someone else in terms of "How do I get this person to hire me or buy something from me?" It is much more productive to ask yourself, "What are this person's needs and how can my skills help him or her?"

Modern day self-seeking cold calling on LinkedIn is connecting with someone and asking, "Hey, can you introduce me to your top 5 clients?" How does that even work? Instead, as sales trainer and coach, Jack Frisby simply states, introduce someone to another person first before asking for an introduction.

In basketball, the headfake gets the defender moving one way and then the ball handler goes in the opposite direction. Here is the headfake about making your hinge connect: if you help enough people reach their goals, then you will reach yours.

Since no one gets there alone, the way we make the hinge connect is by approaching situations and people like, "Who can I be the hinge for?" or "How can I connect someone else with who they need to meet?"

Our hinge moment will manifest itself when we become the Hinge for others.

PLANT TREES YOU WILL NEVER SEE

"Sweep the sheds." — The All Blacks

James Kerr wrote an amazing book titled *Legacy*. The book details the success of the All-Blacks New Zealand National Rugby team. The All Blacks are one of the sporting teams having achieved the most success in all of history; they have won almost 80% of their matches across 68 years. They do so by design, not default. [2]

One of their purposes is that *"better people make better all-blacks."* In that, if every teammate focuses on leaving the jersey better than how they found it, then long-term, sustained success can be obtained.

It is by recognizing those individuals who came before you and those that will come after that awareness is born. The results from that awareness are actions consistent with better intent for the team instead of self. A legacy is created when we prepare and play with a sense of a higher purpose.

One of the actions on display from the culture of the All-Blacks is to sweep the sheds. After their home games, the veteran players, who just performed in front of thousands and received the praise and adulation from their nation, sweep their own locker room after everyone has left. Their culture is by design, not by default and they act consistent with their message of leaving the jersey in a better place than how they found it.

...

We don't know which planted tree will be the one that provides the shade for others, but if we don't plant a tree, there will be no shade. Since a tree takes so long to grow and develop, much like the hinge, we can't know what will be the results from our actions.

The best time to plant a tree was twenty years ago, the next best time is today.

...

In 2009, photographer, Jitu Kalita was exploring a barren river island in India named Majuli Island. What amazed Jitu was that after miles of desolate space, he came across something strange; a massive dense forest. He met a man during his exploration, Jadav Payeng, who single-handedly planted and cultivated the forest, which was now larger than the size of Central Park.

As a kid, Payeng found hundreds of dead, curled up snakes that had been washed away by flood rains and massive erosion with no shade to protect them. From this hinge moment, the 16-year-old boy simply began planting seeds on this island. Jadav Payeng began planting trees in 1979 on the island that housed approximately 150,000 people.

Jadav, over the course of 40 years, tirelessly created a vast forest than spans over 1300 acres. Today, the island houses over one hundred elephants, a hundred deer, five Royal Bengal tigers, wild boars, several species of birds, including vultures and pelicans, many one-horned rhinoceroses, and of course snakes.

Jadav Payeng became known as the "Forest Man of India" for his continued effort. [3]

Jadav's work and passion for his daily routine transformed his entire environment. Most of us will not follow in his footsteps, but we can still plant trees that no one will see, by how we treat other people.

...

Every transaction we have with someone has the potential to be transformational. We don't know which acts or gestures will be the hinge, so every person and transaction is important.

We may not develop a transformational encounter with someone at the cash register, but of course, isn't it really nice when we enter a store and they know our coffee order or remember our name. In those cases, our transactions did become transformational.

On the simplest level, we each have the potential in our lives to positively impact everyone we encounter.

If we allow someone else to merge into traffic, wave to someone, or hold the door for others, it makes a connection. This simple transaction establishes the possibility that the beneficiary of your kindness will extend it further to someone else. Of course, someone probably did the same for you at some point in your life - a gesture long forgotten. While it is impossible to know the impact of even these simple, generous acts; the effect is invaluable. However, if we hold back and do not extend to connect with those around us, then there can't be any positive impact.

What is fascinating is why others do not wave back.

What if WE are the non-waver? The thought process is usually "Why should I wave, if they don't even acknowledge it?" If we wave enough to a neighbor and they never look up or wave back, it strains our own self-worth. If it happens enough, we may even cease acknowledging that person altogether and we stop planting trees.

We actually want to plant trees that we will see and enjoy ourselves. Planting trees that we will never see, means doing actions because it is the right thing to do, not because of the reaction or non-reaction we get from someone else. If we wave, acknowledge, support, and are generous to enough people, then we eventually will receive the reciprocation.

People do not wave back, allow others to merge, or help others, not because of you, but because of themselves. I try to wave as often as I can, but there are times when I do not wave. In my neighborhood, if someone driving through does not stop at the sign, or drives way too fast, or blasting their music, I probably won't wave. But there are also times where I just haven't initiated the wave. At that exact moment of someone driving, I was probably focused too much on myself and my own problems.

A theme echoed in this book is that we give away the mindset that we possess ourselves. Our preparation toward improving ourselves and improving others makes capturing these moments possible.

There is no way that those mentioned in this book could have known the results of their actions. We need to be that hinge for others.

EVERYONE IS AN ATHLETE, OUR OFFICE IS DIFFERENT

"Accept that some days you are the bug, some days, you are the windshield." — Jill Shalvis

I was caddying for one of my golfers at a PGA Tour event at The Greenbrier in West Virginia. During a practice round, we played with Tom Watson for the entire day. What a treat! As we were walking down one of the fairways, he put his arm around me and said, "This is such a nice office."

I have been borrowing that line ever since because it is true.

...

Everyone is an athlete our office is just different. Some of us are corporate athletes, sales athletes, or entrepreneur athletes. Being an athlete is an attitude and awareness. It means looking through our own lens of life as an athlete.

First, as an athlete, we compete.

Competition has always been part of humanity, ecology, and biology and at its basic level, competition for space or resources. We learned early on that there is only one captain, one head cheerleader, one starting spot, or one class president. Some are drawn toward this type of competition while others often shy away from it.

Too often competition is only viewed as an "I win and you lose" concept. This viewpoint of competition has been easily perverted into trying to beat someone else, which turns into a mindset of scarcity — which is a belief that there *can only be one winner*. We misread competition as being only against some other opponent and thus create a mindset of scarcity, fear, and isolation.

With the "I win, you lose game" the opponent can become anyone outside of ourselves, even our own teammates or co-workers. Scarcity mindset is born from: there can only be one promotion, one president, one *winner*, so it must be me. The scarcity mindset can be seen on the majority of athletic teams, law schools, orchestras, etc. Most any life or business situation where there is a winner can breed scarcity.

However, true competition is me vs. me.

Competition against ourselves isn't easy. It is easier to focus on beating others and doing what it takes to win rather than competition against ourselves. Competing against ourselves is much slower and deliberate. We are quick to improve our circumstances or our situation, but not ourselves. Competition against ourselves is the most difficult part of being an athlete because we already know everything about our opponent.

We compete in all that we do. We can compete in our job, our relationships, and our physical endeavors. We can compete in being a friend, a spouse, father, mother, teacher, etc. We do not always compete against others, but against a much tougher opponent, ourselves. Competition is about challenging ourselves about how good we can become.

It becomes a competition against ourselves if we refuse that piece of cake or get that workout in or wake up when our alarm goes off or help out someone else.

Competition against ourselves operates from an abundance mindset. We can always get better, everyday, in every way. So instead of scarcity and beating others, we focus on being the best at getting better.

When we focus on becoming the best version of ourselves, it means that there are setbacks, pain, adversity, suffering, struggle, and learning. However, there will also be growth, joy, thanksgiving, satisfaction, and true success.

Second, being an athlete means being in shape.

When we show up to our office, we need to be conditioned. Yes, there is some physical fitness to our lives, and our overall well-being. But, it doesn't mean that we all need to be able to play 90 minutes of a top-level soccer game.

Being well-conditioned means that we show up early, are able to be present, deal with others in effective manners, commit and contribute to the overall mission, and simply be focused on others.

Third, as an athlete, we are always training, practicing, and preparing.

A funny thing about competition and practice is that we will practice *way* more than we will ever actually compete.

How many tennis balls have a Wimbledon champion hit in their entire life? How many mountain climbs has someone completed before a successful first ascent? How many range balls or simple practice rounds have a Masters champion finished, or how many practices has an NCAA Volleyball champion done?

Athletes competing in the Olympics will have just one event or at most, maybe a couple events. Thus, 99% of their time invested in the previous four years has been in preparation.

We will practice more than we will ever actually perform. Thus, our preparation is in many regards more important than our actual competition because when our moment arrives, it is too late to prepare. We will need to be ready because we do not know what or who will be our hinge moment.

DR. ROB BELL

TRUE SUCCESS

"It is one of the most beautiful compensations of this life that no man can sincerely try to help another without helping himself."
— Ralph Waldo Emerson

Duke basketball fans have earned the right to be called the Cameron Crazies. The students epitomize passion, organization, and wittiness. They even camp out in Krzyzewskiville for three months prior to games, hand out cheat sheets for the student cheers, and were actually the ones who coined the now famous *air-ball* chant.

So, can you imagine that the Cameron Crazies once actually cheered for an opposing player?

It happened!

During one game in 1995, Joe Smith of the Maryland Terrapins was unstoppable. He scored 40 points, 18 rebounds, and had a tip-in basket as time expired to beat the Duke Blue Devils, 94-92.

At the end of the game, after Duke lost, they applauded the opponent, Joe Smith!

...

True success means rooting for everyone.

The 1989 Ironman championships in Kona became known as the Iron War. Dave Scott and Mark Allen had a rivalry that culminated in the closest Ironman finish ever. They raced side by side for the entire 8 hours through a 2.4-mile swim, 112-mile bike, and 26.2 mile run. Both men crushed the ironman record and only finished 58 seconds apart. [4]

It was one of the most epic races ever in any sport, because both individuals were at their BEST. Yes, one man lost the race and the other won, but it was the epic competition that made the history.

When we compete, we are focused on winning which means there has to be a loser. That is true in most sports, but not always in life. But, let us say there are indeed direct competitors and a winner and loser. We often want to win at any cost, which again is fine, but too often, we focus on our opponent and want them to make mistakes, so we can get an advantage. It makes sense, since that is competition.

Rooting for everyone simply means we want to beat others at their BEST. Those rivalries throughout history and close match-ups are so great because two teams, people, or companies were at their absolute best, gave it all they had, and in doing so made each other better.

At the 2017 PGA Championship, Rickie Fowler completed his final round and temporarily enjoyed the clubhouse lead at -5, but there were several players still out on the course. He had played exceptional golf on the back nine and was interviewed for his play. He was asked if he thought his score would hold up and possibly make a playoff. He replied that he didn't know, but quickly added that he wasn't rooting against anybody. He wanted the other players to play great golf.

We in fact NEED others at their best because it is the way we make ourselves better. All historic rivalries were based on two greats performing at their best. Ali had Frazier, Hertz had Avis, Nicklaus had Palmer, Coke had Pepsi, Magic had Bird, FedEx had UPS, Ford had GM, Coe had Ovett, Federer had Nadal, Navratilova had Evert and so on.

Rooting for everyone does not mean that we do not want success for own team or ourselves. However we do not have true success because even in non-direct competitions, we often feel threatened by others having success. Somehow, we perceive another's success, as we can't be successful too. The scarcity mindset...

If you ever watch a professional golfer make a hole-in-one, everyone in the vicinity high-fives each other! They are happy because they witnessed a significant feat and just because someone made an ace does not mean we can't do the same.

In fact, we actually need others to succeed so we know what we have to do in order to improve. A funny thing happens when others around us have success. It cements the belief in ourselves that it is possible to reach the next level. If everyone around us was mediocre, what models do we have to get better?

The only way we can root for others, as a competitor is when we are confident. It shows that we are secure enough to actually wish the best for others. That is true success!

When this philosophy is posted, questions arise like, "I have to root 'even for the Yankees?'" No, it doesn't mean in our fandom, that we have to cheer or root for teams or people to actually win. It is just a reminder that close contests are much more fun because they bring out the best in both.

...

In 2010, Chris McCormack was leading the Ironman championships in Kona when he was caught during the marathon run at mile 22 by Andreas Raelert. The race of 140.6 miles would be decided in the last four miles. Both struggled in the extreme heat, their endurance tested as they ran the next three miles together. At one point however, Chris McCormack used a sponge to cool down and then handed it to Andreas to use as well. In the middle of the race after almost 8 hours of racing, the competitors even shook hands after that sponge exchange.

NO ONE gets there ALONE!

DR. ROB BELL

A BETTER US MAKES A BETTER YOU

"Success is infinite. Someone else getting their slice of the pie doesn't mean there's less for you." — Dr. David Holmes

Professional soccer player, Sergio Aguero, an Argentinian and a striker for Manchester city, had a slight dilemma. He was one of the highest goal scorers of non-European decent in the Premier League. However, as he aged, Manchester City signed a younger forward, Brazilian, Gabriel Jesus. Doubts thus emerged about Aguero's future with the team, especially after he was benched for Jesus during a stretch of games.

To add to the dilemma, future Hall of Fame coach Pep Guardiola typically only played one striker at a time in his system. It was also suggested that coach thought the Argentinean was too individualistic for his collective system of play.

Intra-team competitions for playing time can sometimes turn ugly, and in the least do not add to the overall team chemistry. It has the potential for the players involved to be individually focused instead of team focused.

In one of the home openers vs. Liverpool in a Premier League game, both strikers actually started the game and the relationship amongst these two strikers was revealed. Sergio Aguero scored early in the contest to put Manchester City ahead vs. Liverpool 1-0. With his goal, he became the Premier League's all-time highest ever non-European goal scorer.

Jesus scored the second goal to lead Liverpool 2-0.

Later in the match, with both strikers having scored one goal apiece, Aguero received a great pass and had a one-on one with the goalkeeper and an almost assured goal. However, he deftly passed the ball to his left and fellow striker and heir to his position, Gabriel Jesus easily put the ball away.

Aguero put his team and his teammate ahead of his own wants. After the game in which Manchester City won, Pep Guardiola said, "I don't say to the striker pass the ball, I say score a goal please,' *[But] it means a lot to me, what Sergio did. A lot.*" 5

...

In basketball, hockey or soccer, an assist is a statistic measured and tracked along with scoring. An assist is any pass to the player that results in a score. The assist in sports is an altruistic measure of teamwork. The assist requires communication, anticipation, and execution from team members. Assists also reflect increased team maturity; that is why one won't see too many assists in youth leagues compared to more experienced teams.

Sergio Ibanez and colleagues sought to examine the most important statistics in basketball and the differences between successful and unsuccessful teams. The researchers looked at statistical data from two entire seasons (870 games) of professional basketball. Three in-game statistics revealed that one offensive category and two defensive categories determined the overall success of a team. These statistics were assists, blocks, and steals. Obviously, scoring and preventing the other team from scoring is ultimately what determines winning and losing, but it is the *how* a team scores and prevents scoring. 6

The assist, although statistically important for success, has an innate flaw. The assist is entirely reliant upon whether or not the recipient of the assist scores. All passes are not created equal. So, in basketball a pass to a teammate for a lay-up, is way different than a pass to teammate for an outside shot. In soccer, a pass to a teammate's foot in front of the goal is better than a cross into traffic of an opponent.

Thus, the assist requires trust of teammates. Teams that emphasize the assist are more dependent on each other than teams that rely on individual play. But, it requires an environment of team first culture.

...

Kenyan runners dominate distance running. With half of the country's population living in poverty, winning a small half-marathon and a check for $3000 is four times the yearly income. In Kenya, there is little farming, no factories, and many kids run barefoot to school. Running is the escape and means to a better life.

The best champions of the sport in Kenya train right alongside those merely trying to *make it*. All of these runners motivate one another to keep going and push one another, recognizing just how fleeting success can be. The success from Kenyan runners is without the *advantages* of modern elite distance athletes and they are denied access to the cutting edge technology and training methods.

Their assist to each other in an individual sport rests upon helping one another. The motivation to *make it* is a direct result from the environment of a better us makes a better you.

...

Who is your *us*?

Your *us* is your environment. It's your sphere of influence and the people involved in your interactions and relationships.

Is your *us* small or large? Is it your school, team, or business? Could it branch out into your community, industry, or conference? Does *us* include your country, or region, or perhaps the entire world of human kind?

Essentially, whomever you come in contact with and influence through your actions and practices becomes your *us*.

On a micro-level, how is the culture of your environment? Mary Kay Cosmetics® AdvoCare,® CrossFit,®, Jenny Craig,® and/or Alcoholics Anonymous® all rely on each other as the culture of how no one gets there alone. Each person's success and longevity depends upon others. They are all connected to each other.

We need to become other people focused, create assists for one another and a culture of improvement and excellence. That means, surrounding ourselves with people who can challenge us, support us, and make us better. It also reinforces that no one gets there alone.

STEP #1- OUR FOOTPRINT NEEDS A BLUEPRINT

"If you want to go fast, go alone, if you want to go far, go with others."
— African Proverb

Footprints represent where we were and what we have done. We often don't think about what we have done as footprints, unless our footprints in the sand or our carbon footprint.

Could you imagine how many steps it would take to leave footprints in stone?

Incredibly, it has been done, but, not alone.

The Tomb of The Unknown Soldier at Arlington National Cemetery has been guarded 24 hours a day, 365 days a year. Every second of every day since 1937, men and women followed the blueprint, guarded the tomb, and created these footprints in stone.

Service men and women of the 3rd U.S. Infantry Regiment (The Old Guard) make up the oldest active-duty infantry, serving since 1784. Only the elite soldiers, who volunteer, are qualified, and those that can pass the stringent requirements become guards. The Tomb Guard badge is the least awarded badge in the army.

Part of the requirements to guard the Tomb of the Unknown Soldier includes *trial* periods. Soldiers learn seven pages of Arlington National Cemetery history and must be recited verbatim. Three hundred memorable grave locations must be memorized. After several months of servicing, all tests on their manual of arms, uniform preparation, and their "walk" must be passed. Finally, the badge test must be passed with 95% accuracy, which includes 100 random questions.

The blueprint of service for others is how the footprints are created in stone. One has to think about and plan not only the sheer number of steps to create footprints in stone, but also the manner in which the steps are placed. It requires a blueprint of dedication, sacrifice, teamwork, and extreme precision.

The Old Guard "walk" in specific twenty-one step arrangements, the heel strike and toe push are so precise, that footprints are eventually created. There are twenty-one steps and 21 seconds in-between movements at the end of each walk. Twenty-one symbolizes the 21 gun salute which is the highest honor bestowed in the United States military.

The changing of the guard is where the blueprint gets riveting. Each changing of the guard is so precise that perfection is the goal and each sentinel is graded after every change. If there is a mistake, each guard will hear about it during review.

Tradition demands it and The Guard enforces it.

In order to leave a footprint, there must be a blueprint.

The footprint represents success; the blueprint requires repetition.

Their dedication to service of others is remarkable, exemplifies the highest form of selflessness and validates that a better us makes a better you.

Our preparation matches our commitment. If we are to take ownership of a better us, then we need to develop a blueprint.

Our tendency or inclination to help others reach their goals eventually results from the culture of our environment. The environment that we create is our blueprint and will become the deciding factor in helping others. If our blueprint is not by design, then it becomes by default, meaning we will waver in our approach toward places, people, and things. The culture of our environment needs to be intentional.

DR. ROB BELL

THE CULTURE OF YOUR ENVIRONMENT

"Culture eats strategy for breakfast and talent for lunch."
– Peter Drucker

Blake Mycoskie vacationed in the countryside of Argentina one year, learning both the positives and shortcomings of the country. He discovered a major issue in foot infection with children and adults across the country and most of these were preventable. He knew he needed to do something about it. So, in 2006, instead of developing a charitable foundation to assist, he created a shoe company.

The motto became for every shoe bought here in the United States, TOMS delivers a pair down there to a child. *"For every pair bought here, they donate a pair down there."*

You will find TOMS shoes everywhere across the United States and because of the massive impact it made, it has delved into seven-figure range. The rise of TOMS was so fruitful that it continued its mission of one for one into eyewear, safe birthing, clean water, and anti-bullying. For example, one for one, means that a sale of eyewear is used to restore eyesight in developing countries. A sale of coffee is used to provide drinkable water to a person in need. Handbag sales are used to provide assistance with birthing kits that help mothers practice safe childbirths.

Blake Mycoskie knew that no one gets there alone.

Culture occurs by default or by design. At TOMS Shoes, the employee culture is infectious. Basically, the norms, practices, and values of the people within the environment are what create the culture. The leadership in place then facilitates and leads from the front.

TOMS Shoes promotes flexible work schedules, no meeting Mondays, and Toms idea room, which is an online platform that encourages ideas from everyone. The result has been corporate training on leadership and business for its employees, eight weeks of paid maternity leave and an idea called *happy helping hour*. Once a month, a charitable organization visits Toms and engages employees in assisting the community through the organization.

...

Employers and coaches are almost always looking for a blueprint to motivate and keep their athletes engaged. Deci & Ryan (1985) discovered the solution. [7] They found three crucial components for successful motivating factors across all organizations. It is how we create an intentional culture.

When thinking about motivation, it is how moved we are to do something. The three components of successful motivation were competence, autonomy, and relatedness. If any of these basic and innate needs were missing, then motivation was compromised.

Competence — People have the inherent need to feel good at their position. Competence is confidence. There are innumerable examples about how being confident in a role increases their drive for success. We all like to do activities that we are good at. The secret is for leaders to instill, remind, and reinforce athletes *(we are all athletes)* that they are good at what they do.

Autonomy — People want to feel empowered to be able to make their own decisions. Think ownership rather than buy-in. For instance, a military general laying out battle plans must depend upon on field leaders to implement, but even the best plans can go awry. Hence the field leaders operate better when they can make immediate adjustments and decisions without having to seek permission. Horst Shulze, former president of Ritz-Carlton Hotels, created policies that encouraged autonomy. Front desk employees were all empowered to spend up to $2000 to serve guests and satisfy their customers needs if any issues arise. This created an intentional culture.

The opposite of autonomy is red tape and policies that restrict decision-making and require permission for most tasks. Deci & Ryan (1985) found that if a team is forced to operate in absolutes and act precisely in assembly line fashion than the lack of empowerment decreases their competence and vice-versa. It is far better to empower individuals and have them operate in terms of themes instead of absolutes. Of course people will still mess-up, but increased motivation occurs when people assume ownership.

The last component for effective motivation is aligned with the mission of this book. *Relatedness — People are motivated when they feel a part of something, an organization or cause larger than themselves.* What they do matters!

TOMS work environment fosters relationships amongst each other that simply builds stronger friendships. Disney calls every one of their employees cast members. Marriott's employees are all called associates as the average tenure for General Managers is twenty-five years.

Phillip Haid, CEO and co-founder of PUBLIC, integrates a model of relatedness, which is for companies to *profit with purpose.* Companies can create greater impact when they merge revenue with social change as opposed to the old model of keeping revenue and philanthropy separate. Making money and impacting society for the greater good can and should co-exist.

The concept of profit with purpose creates a structure of relatedness amongst employees, companies, and society. People are motivated when connected and participating in something larger than themselves. Relatedness means a better us makes a better you and a better you makes a better us.

...

What can I do to instill an intentional culture of being other-person focused into my environment?

That is precisely the point. Creating a blueprint of empowering people, fostering their confidence, and making them a part of something bigger than themselves is key.

The best cultures have people first and profits second. Process over product... Yes, results and successful outcomes are the ultimate goal, but the product can't come before the process of how we get there. It is like saying the goal is to win! Okay, but how do we get there?

A better us makes a better you begins with a commitment to focusing on others.

COMPARISON IS THE THIEF OF JOY, BUT CHALLENGES YOUR TALENT

"Our greatest weakness lies in giving up. The most certain way to succeed is always to try just one more time."
— Thomas A. Edison

One reason why years ago, I decided to run a marathon was that I saw the finishers. I was at the finish line watching people cross the line and complete the 26.2-mile race hours after the winners crossed.

These people were coming in at five hours or more. That was a long time to be out there running especially when these folks knew they were not breaking any records completing the race. In fact, they looked closer to death than celebrating. But as they crossed the line, their joy became obvious. You could tell it was a life-changing event for them. So my thoughts became "I want that feeling" and "If they can do it, so can I."

How do we know that we can do something — if they can do it, so can I.

Confidence is contagious! When we witness others having success, it ignites our belief in ourselves.

DR. ROB BELL

FOCUS ON THE SIMILARITIES, NOT THE DIFFERENCES

"If you ever find yourself in the wrong story, LEAVE." — Mo Willems

Alcoholism runs rampant in my family. My grandfather actually has the second longest living sobriety date of 54 years and counting in the U.S.

When I was younger, I wasn't an alcoholic. I mean I *only* fell off of an 80-foot cliff and was involved in a drunk-driving accident during college *in the same year.* Some people said I was lucky, some said I was very unlucky. Some told me that I was meant for much more in life. The tough part was that it had cost me playing baseball in college. I could have even hurt someone else, and I never wanted that, but I didn't think about those things.

After those mistakes, I got to attend the alcohol classes, meet regularly with a probation officer, perform 100 hours of community service, and attend Alcoholics Anonymous (AA) meetings. I remembered sitting in all of those AA meetings as an 18-year-old thinking that these other people had issues with alcohol, I wasn't *that* bad. I never drank mouthwash or drank in the morning. I believed I was different, which led me to focus on the differences between us, rather than the similarities.

However, even after those instances, for many years, I still drank. I thought I could control my drinking. I simply loved having fun and drinking beer was just a part of it. Games, concerts, parties, BBQ's, at the beach, after golf, during golf, at dinner, with friends, at the movies, hanging out, writing, chess, after runs, were all great times to have a cold one.

But, I could not drink like normal people. I am an all or nothing guy. If I have one, I am going to have two. A saying that resonated with me; *"One is too many and ten is never enough."* The problem wasn't the fourth or fifth drink, but the first. The only path for me was not having one.

Addiction has been in my life from early on. It was a way to both cope and celebrate, the cause and solution to all of life's problems. Addiction provided temporary pleasure and satisfaction, but with no fulfillment. The wake of it all affected my self-worth and my relationships with others.

It was only after I focused on the similarities between others and myself did I finally get help.

...

We all want to be special and unique, but oddly enough, no one wants to be special or different when it comes to surgery. Who wants their surgery or condition to be unique to a doctor? Everyone wants to be exactly the same as every other case.

We have more in common with one another than we do differences. But, we also focus on the differences more.

When we focus on the differences between us, we are in comparison mode, believing we are better than or less than someone else. That belief originates from a scarcity mindset, which ultimately leads to fear and a lack of confidence, which then isolates us. It is a negative cycle. We don't reach out to others because we do not want to burden them or bring them down.

When we isolate ourselves from others, we stop caring about ourselves. Perhaps, we are the one who has had a bad day, had issues at home, are lost and struggling, aren't feeling good, or are just beat from a long day. We are not able to give any energy to anyone else and we quit caring.

We have valid reasons why our moods sour. But it ultimately stems from a focus on ourselves and the differences between us. We look at others' lives and successes and it brings us down. Differences divide us. These differences can range from competitors, to school districts to imaginary boundaries in towns, parts of the state, parts of the country or parts of the world. Differences arise from varying ideologies to which teams we root for. Again, it's easier to focus on the differences than it is the similarities.

However, when we do focus on the similarities between us rather than the differences, we empathize, we care, we relate, we connect, we cooperate, we help, we humanize each other. We then see how our own experience can benefit others.

Think about the experience that we have at home sporting events where we celebrate the victories or suffer the defeats with our fellow fans. What about when watching a comedian and everyone in the audience is laughing? For that short time, we connect. We long for that feeling of relatedness.

However, the same reason why we focus on differences rather than similarities is why it's easier to criticize than compliment. It is simply easier. We feel insecure or inadequate, or our own self-worth is wrapped into someone else (our spouse, children, sports team) making his or her mistakes unacceptable.

We are also mentally wired that we either like someone or dislike someone in a matter of seconds. It is a defense mechanism that is intended to spot danger and prevent us from getting hurt. It is useful. But, in many life situations, focusing on the differences closes us off.

In life, we have much more in common with people than we realize. We need to remind ourselves to focus on the similarities rather than the differences. We are all dealing with some struggle that no one else knows about, and we are in need of someone else to help us get to where we want to go. No one gets there alone.

...

The Big Book of Alcoholics Anonymous was first published in 1939. It is considered one of the top 100 most influential books of all-time. The book's goal is to help the still-suffering alcoholic achieve true serenity and peace through the help of a higher power.

Alcoholic Anonymous cornerstone of recovery is based around the twelve steps which each have specific suggested actions.

The entire organization of Alcoholics Anonymous is about helping other alcoholics achieve sobriety and recovery. No one gets there alone. For instance the term "we" is mentioned in the Big Book of AA over 1,100 times in the first 164 pages. Even the steps of AA consists of plural "we" and "us." For instance, Step 1 is "we admitted that we were powerless over alcohol- that our lives had become unmanageable."

Alcoholics know that recovery depends upon having a sponsor. A sponsor is someone who can help another alcoholic and has gone through the process of recovery. Sponsors pass along their own story of what they were like before, what happened, and what they are like now.

Sponsors actually remain sober and recover by helping another person achieve sobriety. They give away the gifts of recovery so that they can keep it.

In Step 10, it is suggested that each person take personal inventory and when they are wrong in their lives, promptly admit it.[8]

Page 84 of the big book of AA provides three specific and life-changing action steps for Step 10: First, watch for selfishness, dishonesty, resentment, and fear. Second, when these crop up, ask God to remove them at once and discuss these with someone else immediately. The true secret lies in the third action. *"We resolutely turn our thoughts to someone we can help. Love and tolerance is our code."*

The only way out of our own heads and not focused on ourselves is to focus our thoughts on someone else.

...

As someone who struggled with addiction, I didn't think much of myself, but I was all that I thought about. Until I was willing to focus on others using my strengths was I able to get better. I was not able to do this myself, because if I could, then I would have, I needed help from others.

WE ARE ONLY AS SICK AS OUR SECRETS

"Help people even when you know they can't help you back."
— Anonymous

Yvon Chouinard was and still is an avid outdoorsman, climbing rocks, fishing and hiking across the Americas and Alps, and even spending as many as 200 days a year living outside. Early on, he made a living selling climbing gear out of his trunk.

He once bought a rugby shirt for his climbing expedition and loved its utility so much so that he ended up selling the shirt along with hats and gloves. His apparel company was then essentially launched. Chouinard named his company Patagonia ® and the mission became to build the best product, cause no unnecessary harm, and use business to inspire solutions to the environmental crises. The business started not as a means for people to buy stuff but to help sustain the environment. The company's entire existence has been focused on inspiring others to find solutions to the earth's environmental issues.

Chouinard donated 1% of all sales to support environmental grassroots projects. Patagonia ® even created Worn Wear in which people could trade in their used Patagonia, buy used and pass on older apparel instead of buying it new. In 2011, on Black Friday, the busiest shopping day of the year, Patagonia's full page New York Times Ad was *Don't Buy This Jacket*. It asked people to take a pledge to reduce consumption in an attempt to show consumers the environmental costs of their top-selling fleece. [9]

Patagonia built in public transparency as one can follow the Footprint chronicles, which outlines from birth to buy, the process of a product. In 2016, Patagonia also pledged 100% of Black Friday sales, which totaled 10 million dollars, to support environmental support groups.

A company's competitive advantage is often built from their Research & Design team discovering proprietary secrets.

However, Patagonia ® even changed the secrets game by sharing technological advances with other companies! Patagonia was one of the first companies to start using organic cotton and persuaded larger corporations to adopt the similar principles. In alignment with their mission statement, they are committed to making sure everyone benefits, even direct apparel competitors.

Patagonia not only shared their organic cotton practices, but also found alternatives to using petroleum-based wetsuits and started using natural rubber. It took ten years of research and development to create Yulex ® wetsuits, but Patagonia also released the technology and methods to produce the suits.

Patagonia realized at its inception the bigger mission and that the competition was against themselves.

...

We are only as sick as our secrets.

Is the culture of our environment one fraught with secrets or transparency?

When we hold onto a secret, do not provide credit to someone else, call out someone for a little mistake, or put someone else down, we create a culture of it in our surroundings.

Secrets perpetuate this notion of fear, scarcity, self-seeking, selfishness, and not helping others. Although keeping secrets is easy, communicating the truth is more difficult.

The number of secrets we have inside of our *us* indicates our overall health. The fewer; the better. The notion of secrets isn't also advocating that we need to tell everyone everything. Is it even possible to be completely honest with another person? We often conceal our own issues or insecurities so we can continue to act in specific ways. And it isn't so much the secret as it is about the story we need to tell ourselves about the secret. We need to believe in the narrative so we can continue the secret.

However, when we hold onto secrets, they hold onto us. It is like not bathing, but putting on aftershave or perfume to cover it up.

The degree of trust with one another is a large determining factor of success. Information and best practices get shared more, credit is freely given, and the culture of *us* becomes collective.

STEP #2- FOCUS ON OTHERS

"Time is what we want most, but what we use worst."
— William Penn

- If we use the bathroom 10 minutes a day, we will have spent over 6 months of our life just in the bathroom.
- The average person spends two hours a day watching T.V.
- We will also spend about 1 year of our entire life just cleaning.
- We spend over 2 years of our life merely waiting (traffic, lines in supermarket, etc.). Although, by being able to pre-order and avoid lines, on-line apps have now changed our entire behavior. This is cool of course, but doesn't help with our patience.

A transition is a process.

How can we devote time, energy, and resources toward becoming other-people focused?

Your transitions are the opportunity to focus on others.

We can have major life transitions, like changing careers, and minor transitions, like driving from the gym, waiting in the airport, cooking dinner, cleaning the house, pausing the TV during commercials.

We can maximize these transitions in our life, or they can maximize us.

Out of work? Focus on others.
Headed to the gym? Focus on others.
Cleaning your house? Focus on others.
On social media? Focus on others.
Planning out your day? Focus on others.

Jim Badger was a top-level executive who due to restructuring suddenly became out of work. During the first few months of this major life transition, the anguish and stress of finding another job resulted in nothing. This started a downward spiral of no results, which added more pressure, which caused self-doubt, and so on.

Then Jim changed his strategy from only focusing on finding a job to contacting his network of people and seeking out ways to help them instead. He reached out to dozens of people – friends, colleagues, and acquaintances – and simply asked about their current projects and goals and how he could help. That was it.

A funny thing happened. By not dwelling on his own struggles and becoming other-person focused, Jim's attitude changed. He felt good about himself because he was contributing to others. This made him feel productive, and in turn was no longer stuck. No coincidence, but by focusing on others, he found another job.

Obviously, we do not need to be out of work to focus on others, but we do often need to maximize all of our transitions to become other-person focused.

The key is to turn our thoughts towards someone else and then see if there are ways to help.

There are various degrees of turning our thoughts towards someone else, so try it now. Think of someone in your network who you don't normally reach out to and simply send him or her a message. Say something simple such as Just thinking of you, hope you are having a great day!"

Bam, done!

Keith Ferazzi in his first best-selling book, *Never Eat Alone*, coined this strategy *pinging*. He writes, "Life is less a quest than a quilt. We find meaning, love, and prosperity through the process of stitching together our bold attempts to *help others find their own way in their lives.*" [10]

This *pinging* strategy can be simple, utilized through email, text, messenger, a tweet, LinkedIn, or even a phone call. The key during your transitions is to focus on others. Reach out and contact a friend, coach, colleague, family member, or business associate.

Make connecting with others a goal of your transitions.

Ferazzi stresses the importance of not keeping score. This can not become a game of "I've done this, this, and this, *so you now owe me.*" These actions of focusing on someone else have to occur with no ulterior motives.

Indeed, focusing on others goes way beyond simple pinging. If you want to take this step further, send them an article relevant to their business or a hand-written note, or order them a gift or order them a book from Amazon.

CHANGE THE WAY YOU FEEL ABOUT SOMEBODY

"Resentment is like drinking poison and expecting everyone else to die."
— *Malachy McCourt*

Dr. John Gottman's research at the University of Washington examined successful and unsuccessful marriages. His initial study examined 95 newlywed couples across several years as he sought to find out predictors of divorce. Eventually, he completed over twelve longitudinal studies and 3,000 couples, even following one couple for over 20 years. He eventually predicted with over 90% accuracy, marriages that would end in divorce. [11]

He discovered an interesting thing about the communication between happy and unhappy couples. Successful couples had a 5:1 positive to negative ratio during conflict. In our most sacred relationships, the ones that we cherish and have invested in the most, five positive experiences were needed to every one negative one.

On the opposite end, unsuccessful couples had a .8:1 positive to negative ratio of interactions. The negative experiences carried greater weight as well. A put-down of a spouse in front of others felt much more hurtful than the warm feeling of a compliment. The bad outweighed the good and it took much more effort to correct a hurt.

Trust takes years to build, seconds to break, and a lifetime to repair. It is way easier to connect with those we know, like, and trust. It is much more difficult to relate to someone who you know, but don't like, nor trust.

If the 5:1 ratio is needed to be successful in our closest relationships, what is needed in our other relationships?

You may be thinking, why would I want to make connections with those types of people? Fair enough, but there are people in your office, on your team, in your networking group, or circle of influence that you must interact with.

Anger is labor intensive.

An interesting thing happens when we are angry at someone, we actually need to remind ourselves why we don't like this person. Maybe it is their quirkiness, issues, mannerisms, gossip, putdowns, they offer advice without being asked, they ignore us, or anything. We remind ourselves of the differences between us.

When we harbor this dislike or grudge, another transformation takes place. We are the one who actually suffers. Our thoughts become focused on someone else we do not like and they begin to occupy our own mind. Those thoughts stay there rent-free as well. These people aren't even bothered by us disliking them, they don't even know about it. We are the ones who are agonizing and reminded about our dislike.

This process is very sneaky as well. Our resentment, dislike, and hatred does not occur overnight. This scarcity mindset builds up over time until we suddenly realize that we have small issues with almost everyone. It is all the other people around us who are messed up. It eventually takes an emotional toll on us.

If we hold onto these thoughts, then that is what we are giving away. We can only give away what we have in ourselves.

Worse yet is that those who we care most about are the ones who are affected. We give away what we possess and thus share our irritability, discontentment, anger, and fear. If we do not receive a

5:1 ratio of positive to negative experiences, then it is much more difficult to give positivity away ourselves. Think about a simple random negative interaction with someone, such not getting a reply after saying *"thank you."* It has the possibility for us to now carry with us that negative experience.

If you want to change the way you feel about somebody, change the way you treat them.

Changing the way you treat someone takes commitment and action, and is far more difficult than just avoiding that person or holding onto the grudge. But, it is worth it. The only way to change how we think about others is through action. It is easier to act our way into right thinking than it is to think our way into right acting.

As a doctoral student, I provided mental training for a collegiate baseball team and really liked the coach. However, after some losses during the year, the season ended in unromantic fashion. To make matters worse, the coach failed to pay me the whopping sum of $500. This was difficult to deal with as a graduate student struggling with any sort of pay. I felt cheated, stupid, and angry. I realized the coach was simply never going to pay me, so I did what I had to do. I had to change the way I thought about him by changing the way I treated him.

I started writing Christmas cards to the coach. An interesting transformation occurred. Rather than reliving my hatred for the situation and feeling sorry about how I had been done wrong, this action allowed me to make peace with the situation. I couldn't write a Christmas card and bash him at the same time. This allowed me to let go of the resentment.

DR. ROB BELL

TEACH US HOW TO TREAT YOU

"We get what we tolerate." — *Anonymous*

Every so often, we all receive an important legal document and there is always a page labeled; *This Page Intentionally Left Blank.* Early on, I was puzzled. Why is this? If an important document had a printing issue and a page was blank, that wasn't meant to be, there might be serious consequences. It really means that the owners of the important documents you have received have accounted for every single page.

We teach others how to treat us basically the same way. We promote what we permit. If we do not respect ourselves, then we end up like Charlie Brown and Lucy with the football. At the very last second, Lucy pulls the football away and we end up on our back saying, "Good grief!"

...

We have to teach others to know which pages are intentionally left blank.

Let us say someone is always rude, criticizes us, dominates meetings, or simply tries to take advantage of us. These can be co-workers, employees, bosses, and the like that we have created resentment or contempt towards. If we do a poor job with our own boundaries, self-care, anxiety, and communication, then we need to improve how we treat others. We are in control of how we respond to the situation and the individual.

Oftentimes, we do not maintain these boundaries because we want to be liked or don't feel worthy and confident enough to coach others how to treat us. How will we respond when someone violates our boundaries or better yet, can we establish and maintain our own boundaries?

We create a better us when we hold others accountable for our own core values.

First, know that you are worthy of respect and self-care. If you are the boss or the person who everyone turns to for advice, or to solve the problem, how does that help *us*? You eventually get worn down and have little left for yourself or your family.

The funny thing about the people who serve on volunteer boards or "do" everything is that they are also the same people who continually serve. It is the same awesome people! These are usually incredible, kind-hearted people as well. This has nothing to do with service, it just begs the question: wouldn't a better boundary consist of asking others to serve and carry the burden as well?

Second, practice self-care. Be sure that your mental well-being and emotional needs are taken care of, because you will be no good to *us* if you are not okay with yourself. If our boundaries are too loose or dependent upon other people's moods, then we take on other people's problems and anxiety and our own stress builds. For instance, we continually do a job that stresses our own well-being, but we do it anyway because of the poor reaction we would get from someone else. So, we just assume someone else's role so we do not disappoint.

Third, say "no." Saying no means that you have focus. When Steve Jobs took over at Apple, he limited the product line from 350 to 10. The reasoning was that Apple had to say "no" to tons of mediocre products so they could focus on just the incredible products!

Saying yes to helping others is very cool, just as long as it is not at the expense of your own commitments and boundaries. Is it okay for your boss or a client to call you at 9:00 in the evenings? Do you drop what you are doing if a friend needs a ride even if you are already on your way to an event?

Setting boundaries means having enough love and self-respect of ourselves to say "no." We can't please people all of the time and we are going to disappoint others. But, it is better to disappoint someone rather than be resentful of them. We create resentment of others when we choose to do something in contrast to our boundaries. Resentment is a killer!

Fourth, talk about all stressful situations in non-stressful environments. Jeff Van Gundy, former head coach of the New York Knicks was adamant about this philosophy. During the stress of a game and near the end with little time remaining, he didn't want to decide who was going to be taking the last shot. Instead, he and his staff went over these scenarios the night previously in a non-stressful environment.

During an important meeting isn't the time to hash out issues or call someone out. These need to be communicated in non-stressful environments.

STEP #3- COACH OTHERS

"We need models to show us how they did it, coaches to teach us how to do it, and others around us trying to do it as well." — Dr. Rob Bell

This twenty eight year old female had a vision, but wouldn't achieve her goal until she was 64 years old. Her journey started in 1978, but it was not completed until 2013. She simply wanted to be the first person to swim the 110 miles from Cuba to The United States.

The greatest swimmers in the world had been trying to achieve this feat since 1950, and she had failed on her four previous attempts.

Before her fifth attempt, almost everyone, even those in her own team had said, *"It can't be done."*

Diana Nyad finally became the first person to accomplish this amazing feat of swimming from Cuba to Florida. It took her over 53 hours of continuous swimming, fighting off boxed jelly fish with the most deadly venom in all of the ocean, throwing up from all of the saltwater, and even hallucinating about seeing the Taj Mahal during the endeavor.

No one gets there alone. Her lead coach Bonnie Stoll was the one who Diana gives most credit for her finishing the goal. During the third morning, while struggling and barely hanging on, Bonnie pointed out the lights of Key West, and Diana then knew she *only* had about 15 hours of swimming remaining.

She commented how it didn't take her 53 hours of continuous swimming; it took her almost 40 years! She also said *"I didn't do it alone, WE did it."*

Even the most solitary, isolated feats like swimming from Cuba to the United States are not achieved without the help of others.

Everyone needs a coach in life.

...

Often times during hall of fame speeches by coaches or former players, the first person they give credit is to their significant other. I always thought it was a nice gesture, until I discovered it wasn't just symbolic, but a deep expression of sincerity, gratitude and truth. It is only after we realize how much sacrifice that our loved ones have made to help us that we remember that no one gets there alone.

Remember, even the Lone Ranger had Tonto.

A coach is someone who takes you somewhere you want to go. Just think of a stagecoach. A coach will provide support but also push you further than you could go on your own. All great professional and corporate athletes have a coach, and they do so to get better.

Coaches understand the commitment and struggle that it takes to succeed. In fact, coaches with experience also understand specific ways to challenge others and to get the best out of you.

When things go wrong for an individual, it is often because they didn't listen to the coach in their lives or allow themselves to be coached.

BECOME A BALCONY PERSON, NOT A BASEMENT DWELLER

"Everyone needs a coach." — Bill Gates

The balcony is the upstairs at a theatre or church or auditorium and those in attendance watch from above. Balcony people are able to look upon your life and recognize often what we can't see ourselves. They can point out our blind spots, our shortcomings, and simply look upon our own lives. Ultimately, balcony people encourage and challenge you to do and become greater.

Balcony people pull us up, not drag us down. Balcony people have specific qualities that we want. If we want to become better, then we need to find people that are more knowledgeable than us or have mastered what we are trying to do.

Maybe we have a few thousand friends on social media, but not one that we can call who can actually help us get better, rather than just make us feel better. Perhaps we struggle with fear, anxiety, restlessness, irritability, or discontentment. Maybe it is something professional or performance based in which we need help like fitness, health, or even sales training. Balcony people do not enable, they empower.

The biggest question is "who do we allow to become our balcony people?"

If we aren't coachable, willing to be honest, or want to be challenged, then it becomes more difficult to find someone that can pull us up.

Basement dwellers on the other hand, ugh! When we think of basement dwellers, they are those who figuratively still live with their parents and who wants sage advice from those people?

Basement dwellers are those toxic people who drag you down to their level. They discourage good habits, discipline, and goals, and encourage any activity that can undermine your own success and mental toughness. They can't help you achieve your goals because they aren't willing to make goals themselves. Since we give away what we possess, what they give away is not challenging you to be better.

There are far more basement dwellers than balcony people. Basement dwellers love to hang out with you of course, but that is chiefly all that they do. The difficult part is they become the people in our relationships who we like and even enjoy hanging out with. Unless we recognize who they are and are willing to make adjustments in our time with them, then we get stuck. I hung out with too many basement dwellers back in the day. I was just too focused on enjoying myself to realize they were in fact holding me back.

...

We are not intended to coach ourselves in life. We are meant to help others and allow others to help us. We can't be our own balcony person. Sure, we can walk up to the balcony and get a view before heading back down. Yes, even though there are times when we must coach ourselves, that act is accomplished because someone coached us first.

We need others in our lives. It is important to pick these people wisely.

We can have more than one balcony person as well. It is best to have people who have the positive qualities that you desire, to spend time with you, direct you, challenge you, and lift you up.

Every successful professional or corporate c-level athlete has had a coach.

...

Not only do I owe my finishing the ½ ironman to the two guys who stopped to help me, but I also owe it to my own coaches who helped me reach my goal.

Bill Van Valer, owner of Elements Massage, was one of my coaches. He completed a ½ Ironman previously and he trained with me and provided much needed support with the bike. It was his bike that I borrowed as well.

My other coach was a mental coach, Coach Bru, Jon Brubaker. There is power of being able to get our thoughts out of our own head. Being versed in the stressors, challenges, and excitement of competing, Coach Bru knew which direction the conversations should go.

We spoke at length about my *why*. We addressed pre-performance routines, confidence, and focus. There were many questions on contingencies, "what-if" scenarios, and anticipating the "worst" to happen.

Everyone needs a coach.

A BETTER YOU MAKES A BETTER US

*"Consider how hard it is to change yourself, and you'll understand
what little chance you have of trying to change others."*
— Jacob M. Braude

If anyone considers the greatest athletes of all-time, they always talk about stats and ultimately; the conversation veers towards the most important statistic, championships.

We always focus on the championships. One cannot be considered the best of all-time without having won a championship; it is a pre-requisite. All of the individual accolades, MVPs, scoring titles, or records mean very little if your team cannot win a championship.

Yes, one can be a hall of fame player, one *of* the best, but they are just part of a different standard and a member of the dubious club called *"the best never to have won a championship."*

Even looking at corporate athletes and executives, the most successful companies created legacies that the companies still excelled after they exited. Jim Collins in *Good to Great* labeled these leaders "Level V leaders". Those CEOs created an environment of capacity, not dependency.

The point is that the best of all-time does something different. The best makes others around them better!

...

It is a scary notion that we eventually give away the mindset that we possess.

This is frightening, because if we only have negativity, hate, fear, doubt, financial insecurity, stress, indecision, and pain in our lives, and these occupy our thoughts, then those are what we give away. We give our emotions away in our relationships with others, how we view difficulties, how we parent, and how we treat those closest to us.

We either give away from a mindset of abundance or one of scarcity.

If we have a mindset of scarcity, then we operate as if success is limited, fleeting, and self-centered. It is much like driving around a parking lot looking for a parking space. There are actually TONS of open spaces if we just park and walk up to the building. However, the scarcity mindset means that we feel there aren't enough parking spaces and we have to wait and drive around, looking for that one perfect spot closest to the entrance.

The scarcity mindset means, living like we are on vacation but needing to drop our towel off at the pool super early in the morning, to get the best lounge chairs.

Scarcity is functioning through life with the powerful emotions of guilt, anxiety, anger, shame, and fear. These overarching feelings can dominate our reality and cause slow downward spirals in our relationships.

Unfortunately, the reasons we possess a scarcity mindset is that there was a time when we lost, were cheated, were treated unfairly, have been hurt and we learned simply that we can't trust anyone. Since we can't trust anyone, *"if it is to be, then it is totally up to me"* attitude permeates our self. . We operate from the stance that *"I'll trust you when I get the security I'm seeking."* It actually makes sense, but the only issue is that we are the ones who are suffering. We are not experiencing joy and success in our lives because our mind is focused only on ourselves from a stance of scarcity.

...

The same announcement is made on all flights. In case of a loss in cabin pressure, oxygen masks will drop and *be sure to secure your own oxygen mask before assisting others.* They announce this because we aren't any good to others if we are not good to ourselves.

We must be deliberate in our own attitude on life and operate with a mindset of abundance. If we are not careful about our own outlook, then we'll face the possibility of constantly operating from scarcity. Then, we give away what we possess.

True success can only stem from a mindset of abundance. The abundance mindset is knowing that there are tons of parking spaces or pool deck chairs. When we are able to become other-person focused, an amazing transformation occurs. We start to get out of our own head and become of use to others.

The beauty about becoming a better *you* is that we do not have to do that ALONE.

DR. ROB BELL

FAITH

"God can move mountains, so bring a shovel." — Anonymous

An old man is in a busy food court at a mall. He is carrying around his food tray, but it is so crowded that he simply cannot find a seat. He looks up to the sky and starts to pray, "God, please help me find a seat!"

As he looks back down, he sees an open seat directly in front of him. He looks back to God and says, "Never mind God, I found one."

...

God is an experience. We may have been told about religion, God, and His almighty power. But only until we experienced God with certainty, were we truly able to understand the phenomenon of the spirit. After we experience this awakening and do not intellectually dismiss it, but acknowledge it, our lives change. This experience is different for everyone. Some of us may have to experience it daily.

God is everything or God is nothing.

It is our choice.

The alternative is that God is sometimes everything and sometimes nothing. If that is our belief, then it is a belief out of convenience. It is an *on-demand* God. We decide when and if God is good and we allow God to find us that seat in the crowded food court.

If we accept that God is nothing, then we are admitting to ourselves that we are, in fact, God. The belief is that "If it is to be, then it is up to me." Along our life, we learned that we needed to take care of our own needs. We were hurt, lied to, or taken advantage of, so we couldn't trust others. Oftentimes, this belief in ourselves actually served us well, because we were the ones who achieved success and recognition. However, only after a closer look can we see that any success was fleeting and didn't grant us any peace, but just more expectations.

The belief that God is nothing has everything to do with power and who doesn't crave power? Often, we get this power and control in our lives through our own performance. We are in control, we have the power, we are in charge, and we control every situation.

But, in order to keep power, we need to behave and act in certain ways. These ways have to do with controlling not ourselves, but others through praise, compliments, rewards, acknowledgements, love, or through manipulation, deceit, lying, guilt, shame, punishment, etc.

If God is nothing, then we can't trust God on this issue or that event. Not trusting God means that we remain in charge and this is the standpoint where we develop and cultivate a mindset of scarcity. I need to get mine.

When God is nothing and we play God, acting as if we are in charge, we become selfish and self-seeking. We begin to cultivate a mindset of, "If only the people around me did what I wanted, then everything would work out fine."

Playing God assumes much image management, but it is exhausting to maintain a certain image, impossible to control others or achieve certain performance results. When we struggle, we become fearful, stressed, and/or angry. We lose perspective, develop tunnel vision and lose sight of the bigger picture. It is a vicious cycle that repeats itself and forces us deeper into selfishness and self-centeredness. We lose control or realize that we are feeble gods with insecurities, doubt, resentments, or indecision.

If we are willing to accept that God is everything, then we are allowing ourselves to be transformed. This belief means allowing God to do for us what we could not do for ourselves. It aligns with the premise that no one gets there alone.

That God is everything means we are willing to rely on a power greater than ourselves. It doesn't mean we won't have the same difficulties and hardships and emotions like fear and anger. It is just that now we have a solution.

Willingness is key. This isn't a section that you have to believe in God. This is a section of just being willing. Be willing to accept new ideas, not out of coercion, but out of choice. Are we willing to accept the possibility of how God views us?

...

If God is everything- can we trust God in every situation, success, heartache, difficulty, hurt, suffering, grief, tragedy, mishap, or misstep? Can we trust God to meet our own needs?

It is difficult, because it means that we must give up control to a power greater than ourselves. But, in order to get control we must give up control. It requires letting go - make no mistake; it is difficult. It is allowing God to do for us what we could not do for ourselves.

There is a Bible verse, Matthew 10:39 which states, *"Whoever finds their life will lose it, and whoever loses their life for my sake will find it."*

Many critiques and writings about this passage have to do with the afterlife and having eternal life. They write about losing their life on earth, so they will have eternal life. Perhaps so, but I also think this verse has more to do with life here, on earth. The verse means more about doing away with our own interests to allow God to work through us and live by the spirit. It means that not only will God see us through the difficulties, but also will see us through the successes.

But, who wants to give God the power? We have the freewill and can make our own choices, even though our way does not always work in our relationships, often leading to anxiety and fear. We are unclear about how to allow God to do for us what we could not do for ourselves.

In Matthew 18:2, Jesus says that we must *"become as little children."*

As a child, there may have been times when our parents would strap us in our car seat or we would hop into the backseat. It was usually a short trip but we just got in without questioning the route our parents were taking. There may have also been an experience when learning to swim and our mom or dad was in the pool with arms wide open telling us to jump in. They would catch us. This is child-like faith.

But as we progressed in life, whenever we got in the car, we began to critique the driver and the route they were taking. We also no longer needed Mom or Dad to catch us in the pool. Our child-like faith became more about control, self-will, and power, rather than giving up control.

The childlike faith goes beyond how we approach people or things. It rests largely on how we respond to events and wrong doings to us. There was a time when my young son and I were play wrestling and he accidentally scratched my face. I reacted poorly and was pretty upset at the situation. I raised my voice and sent him to his room. He got scared. I was disappointed and felt remorse about the way I treated him and the situation. I wish I had been more controlled. After a while I went to his room and apologized. He was playing and I told him I was sorry, he forgave me, and went throughout his day. I doubt he ever thought of it again. This is the child-like faith.

In adult life, would we be so quick to forgive and move on? I have held onto resentments from people who dissed me for YEARS! The ability of children to forgive their parents is truly remarkable and an example of child-like faith. Remember the saying; *To err is human, but to forgive is divine.*

Think for an instant if we were able to forgive every unkind event or person that happened to us. How would it affect our current relationships with others?

It is only when we start to move away from our own selfishness and performance that we actually move toward becoming other-focused and become transformed. In return, we learn that we need and want less and less, but become more and more about helping others and being grateful for what we do have.

Let us face it; we are all selfish. Some of us less than others, but to a degree, we are interested in the fundamental questions, "Will my needs be met?" and/or "Will things work out the way I want them to work out?"

DR. ROB BELL

OUR IDENTITY

"Quit trying to stop messing up, and instead, focus on who you are in Christ. — Bart Millard

"Who are you?" is a simple question. We all answer it in different ways.

No one gets there alone means that even though we are supposed to get better, we do not get better alone. It is not possible to successfully move along this journey by ourselves. Yes, we will take certain steps, but it ultimately becomes about what God is doing for us, what we could not do for ourselves.

It starts with our identity. Once we define our spirituality, our spirituality defines us. It isn't about how we see God, but how God sees us. Looking at ourselves through our own eyes either leaves us feeling prideful or shameful. We examine our own performance and success, and our identity becomes more and more about our performance. It is a vicious cycle, which we may measure up or not.

However, do we know how God looks at us?

The *church* and religion have more to do with theology than faith. It has more to do with our head, than our heart. In Christianity, no one gets to heaven alone. But, it goes way beyond the afterlife. At some point, the church became a museum for the good instead of a hospital for the broken. It became about doing all we could, through our own strength and winning the favor of God. The belief is that if we just do enough good, it will outweigh our bad and as long as we just don't mess up too bad, God won't punish us.

An interesting thing is that the spiritual life is so simple that we stumble into it, but so difficult that we cannot live it. Christians trying to lead Christian lives lead it complexly, difficultly and simply not the way God wants. It is just like saying, "Christ is enough, but make sure you do this and that as well so God notices you."

If our identity is rooted in Christ, then through that belief, our identity has transformed. It is written that you are holy, righteous, redeemed, forgiven, blameless, faultless, justified, accepted, sanctified, a new creation, a saint, victorious, and free from condemnation. Our new nature and our identity is one with Christ.

Check out the promises of how God views us:
http://leavener.com/my-identity-in-jesus-christ.html

Of course, we will still mess up, make mistakes, and blow it. But our identity is not one of a sinful nature, but of a spiritual nature that never will change. God looks at us always through the lens of love.

The significance of NO ONE gets there ALONE is that we were never intended to do this journey on our own strength. God wants us to trust him and lean on His power, not our own. Thus we allow God to do for us what we could not do for ourselves.

Why is this important?

Our identity drives our actions and our actions confirm our beliefs. So if we can't accept Grace for something that we didn't do, it's difficult to give grace to someone else.

...

There are four types of prayer:

God, "thank you."
God, "help me."
God, "grant me or give me."
Finally God, "use me."

We have all used the first or second or third type of prayer, but it is the fourth prayer of USE ME that invites God's will into our lives. Watch what occurs when we focus our prayers on the fourth type, "God Use Me!" It is not a focus on what we can DO for God, or what God can DO for us, but who does God wants us to BE? How does God want us to use our individual and group strengths to be of service to others?

Be patient, be kind, be generous, be patient, be persistent, be confident, or be other person-focused?

...

No one gets there alone is about allowing God and others to help us as well. God uses other people to help us along the journey. In my own life, my race would not have finished if not for the moment of others. Recovery would not have happened if not for God.

Now, God cannot brush your teeth. As simple as it sounds, it's also true. Who is ultimately responsible for cleaning our teeth? As hard as we may pray for God to help, and his answer, we get to take action. We don't have to take action, but we get to. There are certain steps for YOU to create a better US. We need to step in if and when we want to become a better version of ourselves. God will be with us on our journey.

DR. ROB BELL

STEP #1- MENTAL TOUGHNESS

"If we literally did all the things we were capable of, we would literally astound ourselves." — Thomas Edison

My challenge was to complete a ½ ironman in less than 2 weeks. It became obvious that I couldn't achieve this on my own and I needed help from coaches as well as fellow competitors. All I could do was prepare and focus on building my mental toughness. Mental toughness alone will not achieve your goal for you, but not having mental toughness will lose it for you.

Most likely, in your own case, your *½ Ironman* is a different challenge altogether. Maybe it is running a marathon, improving your business, making a specific income, writing a book, hiking the Appalachian Trail, losing 20 pounds, finishing your Masters degree, or becoming a better owner of your business. Whatever your goal is going to be, building mental toughness will be key.

What is interesting is that we do not need to be mentally tough in order to be comfortable in today's society. We are already comfortable in our lives, so there is not always an immediate need to push ourselves.

However, we don't thrive in mediocrity; we survive.

Mental Toughness simply means being in the moment and it is the way that the Hinge connects in our lives. All success hinges upon these moments and people. If we are open, willing, and confident enough to take the shot, then our hinge can connect. If we do not want the shot or the ball in our hands, it simply won't connect.

Mental toughness, grit, or resilience is two-fold:

The first part of mental toughness is how we deal and cope with adversity and setbacks. We are all going to face times of hardship, adversity, and struggle. These are inevitable. It is a matter of when, not if. For everyone, these struggles are different.

The second part of mental toughness is how well we perform under pressure. There will be *have to* pressure moments. It may be a competition, race, or part of your career. You may face pressure in relationships or financial decisions. Basically, if there is an aspect of performance in your life, then you will encounter pressure.

The way we become mentally tough is to challenge our talent and ourselves.

BURN THE SHIPS

"When we are not all-in, we are just in the way." — Anonymous

In 1519, the Spanish explorer, Cortês arrived at the Yucatan peninsula. He landed his 11 ships with approximately 600 soldiers and about 100 sailors. They landed on a quest to conquer the Aztec empire, even though many of them were armed with only a sword and shield and never faced any real battle.

After landing, Cortês ordered his men to *"burn the ships."* He did this because there were a few men who were rumored to be conspiring to steal a ship and sail back to Spain.

Cortês knew the only way they were going to conquer was if they had no other choice but to conquer. They were either going to win or die. Cortês needed everyone committed to the goal without reservation or chance of retreat. He allowed no easy out, no exit strategy. He instead forced a commitment strategy.

...

My own burn the ships moment for a ½ Ironman that took place in less than two weeks, was indeed signing up. It is a lot harder to de-commit to something than it is to just not sign up. Too often, people will wait instead of immediately signing up for the event. It is the hesitation that fosters doubt and indecision. I burned the ships once I registered and paid my fee.

DR. ROB BELL

TURN YOUR EXCUSES INTO YOUR REASONS

"Your reason 'why' must make you cry. If it doesn't, then it's probably not your 'why'." — Dr. Rob Bell

As athletes, we cry. At the end of a season, athletes cry because the defeat was so painful, or they cry because of the joy of winning. They realized how much they have sacrificed and all of the effort it took.

If your passion is not deep enough to create tears, then frankly, it won't be enough to push through the difficult times. It must get to the point that you simply have to follow your passion, because life without it isn't much of a life. Maybe your reason is your family. Being a role model for them, providing for them, or dedicating your effort to them.

Your goal could simply be a need to prove something to yourself. Perhaps there has been an illness you or a loved one has experienced. Maybe your reason *why* is to prove people wrong. You may have had someone in the past tell you, "You're not good enough" or "that's a dumb idea."

Maybe you have gotten into a good physical shape in life and finally want to do something greater with it. Possibly there is been a life or business event that has temporarily crushed your spirit. Maybe you have not been in control of your own life and have been told what to do and how to do it for too long. Perhaps you have witnessed your own immortality, and it scared you a bit to realize that you haven't quite lived.

What is your reason "why?"

If your why doesn't scare you a little bit, then it is simply not challenging enough.

...

All of us have head trash that consists of limiting beliefs that keep us from a better us. We hold onto old ideas like they actually help us, and we do this because it is more comfortable than exploring our true possibilities and developing new patterns of thinking. It is difficult and uncomfortable to combat the old ideas that *we can't do something.* It is far easier and less taxing mentally to simply hold onto limiting beliefs.

An old idea could be "there is only one winner, and everyone else is a loser." This is a belief from a source of scarcity *(there is only one winner, so it's me vs. everyone)* rather than abundance *(I am confident I will reach my goals. Who can help me and how can I help others?)*

If we look for excuses not to do something, we will find them; however, if we search for reasons *why* to do something, we can find those as well. These excuses and limiting beliefs always involve people, places, or things. We grasp onto the times that we failed and were embarrassed and allow those moments or people to define our identity. We focus on our deficiencies rather than our strengths.

Most of the negativity and false identity is our perception of not being good enough to do something, which allows us, out of fear of failure, to create excuses for not being good enough.

It is a vicious negative cycle.

So, we play it safe and avoid taking the necessary risks for success. The reality about life is that we don't get credit for being safe! The only way to make our hinge connect is to take a chance, go for it, and just do it. Making our hinge connect requires that we challenge our old ideals we thought have kept us safe and take chances.

Each of us has excuses for not doing something, and the tough part is to be able to identify these excuses and use them to our advantage. We need to be able to use our limiting excuse and turn it into our empowering reason; our *why*.

We will have an excuse or a reason. The excuses exist for a reason; they are there to see who really wants it; who really will turn them to reasons to succeed.

Here are four common excuses, and my excuses for NOT doing a ½ ironman. However, there are also four reasons why as well, mine included.

Excuse #1: Time

We are either wasting time or investing time. It is the most precious resource!

Time is the number one excuse for not starting. Discipline is the number one excuse for not continuing.

Yes, time is the biggest limiting factor, but it also is an excuse. We all have the same number of hours. If we don't create the time for ourselves, then we simply do not want it bad enough.

We either make time, or we make an excuse.

Can we examine our actual time commitment? Are we hiding behind our kids schedule, our spouses', weekend drop-offs, work, or is it that we are just too tired? Do we waste time on netflix ® binges or making sure we watch the big game?

John Grisham would write in the early morning before starting his day job as an attorney in the courtroom. It took him four years to write his first best seller, *A Time to Kill.*

A friend of mine preparing for a race would get his long run in on the way to and from both of his kids' weekend soccer games.

It is about making time and getting creative with a lifestyle.

...

In my life, the time for not doing a ½ Ironman in less than two weeks was an excuse as well. I am a business owner, husband, father of two, golfer, and I travel a lot with my athletes and teams, and six months to a year of training is ideal. I hadn't previously signed up for longer races before because training for a ½ Ironman for six months wasn't appealing. I didn't want it bad enough.

Now, time was a major factor to prepare because I only had two weeks to train. It could have been a good excuse.

Reason #1: Time

Time in my case became an advantage!

If time was an excuse for not doing the race, I realized that I could devote less than 2 weeks to prepare for a ½ Ironman. My focus and life could accommodate this challenge. My first excuse turned into my first reason why.

...

Excuse #2: Fear

Remember as a kid when coach would tell us that if the baseball hit us, it wouldn't hurt? LIE! It hurts, and my broken nose can attest to that fact.

Well, I am not going to lie here either because attempting to achieve your goal will hurt as well. But, that is actually what makes it great. If it were easy, then everyone would do it.

If we don't *burn the ships* and commit to achieving a goal, then we will fail. Boom; problem solved! However, it also ensures that there is no way we will become who we want to be.

We then create a habit of not committing, or starting something, but never finishing.

...

My second excuse for not doing a ½ Ironman was fear. It was an unknown if I could finish the race or not get injured. But I was also scared by the commitment. I have accomplished marathons, half-marathons, Masters swimming, and the random road 5k or 10k. I have also trained with elite athletes and I have seen those people who simply kill the workouts and crush those types of races. I have also worked with professional athletes. The mind-set, the dedication, and the attention to detail are paramount. It takes a lot of sacrifice both individually and from their family. Having been a part of that culture, I know full well what it takes.

They are all-in!

These professionals are what the pig is to breakfast, while I was more like what the chicken was to breakfast. See, the chicken is invested in breakfast by supplying the eggs, but the pig is fully committed by providing the ham or bacon.

Reason #2: Commitment

While I realized the sacrifice and dedication necessary for greatness, my real goal was important; finish. I didn't need to be the pig, heck; at least the chicken still contributes to breakfast. I know the intricacies about what it takes to compete. I could do this. All I have to do is commit and *just keep moving.*

Part of the fear exists because we allow an "out." When we *burn the ships*, we make the commitment.

...

Excuse #3: Expectations

Tiger Woods used to say, "*I expect to win the tournament.*" Expectations are not confidence, but we confuse the two. Expectations and confidence are just cousins. We can have confidence in the things we can control, but we hold no control over how things actually work out.

Expectations are out of our control and involve other people's opinions of ourselves. Expectations of ourselves turn into tomorrow's resentments. Continuing to have the highest of expectations means we will struggle when we have to mentally trouble-shoot and reboot.

We basically only control our effort, our attitude, our confidence, and how well we let go of mistakes and refocus.

...

While I haven't been willing to commit the vast amount of time to training for a ½ ironman, I also suffer from a disease called "don't suck."

This attitude of *don't suck* is actually a cousin to perfectionism. I don't have to be perfect at things, but I find it unacceptable not to be *good* at everything. It is the reason why I play chess, ping-pong, golf, poker, run, swim, ski, write books, and can play almost any sport.

The obsession drove me to accomplish some okay athletic activities (*back in the day*), like running a sub 20:00 5k, breaking 1:00 in the 100 Freestyle, bench pressing 300 lbs, completing a marathon in 3:20, making a hole-in-one, and completing a tough mudder.

However, the *don't suck* disease is also the reason why I have never been the best at any one of these skills. My attention and passion get drawn toward other endeavors. You can't be the best at one thing, if you are trying to be the best at everything.

That is insanity. That is the disease. It was my deep- rooted excuse.

Reason #3: Past Performance

How do we know that we can do something? We have done *it* before. These experiences no matter how small must build confidence, not expectations. There is only one expectation, just keep moving.

My past experiences of having raced and competed before served as reasons why I could finish a ½ Ironman despite less than two weeks of training.

...

Excuse #4: Age

Every Thanksgiving, as a family, we run in a local 5k and I not only got smoked in my workouts leading up to the race, but I was also passed in the 5k race by a guy who was having knee surgery immediately after the race. This was a guy I went to the gym with and so I knew about his injury.

That sucked. Was I really getting that old?

Also, my body has started to break down on me. I have always had back issues since college and my near death experience of falling off a cliff. Now, my knee pain had progressively gotten worse and it hurt walking up stairs sometimes.

My age was an excuse for not signing up.

Reason #4: Age

We have never been older than today and we will never be any younger than today. None of us is getting any younger.

Before the movie, *The Bucket List*, was released, I wrote down 100 things I wanted to do before I die. As a former college professor, I would have all of my students perform this goal as well.

Complete a full Ironman was on the list. This was close.

Since nothing is guaranteed in life and tomorrow certainly isn't, I asked myself, "If not now, when?" "If not you, then who?"

My age now became my reason, "If not now, then when?"

STEP #2- GROW YOUR HUMAN TAPROOT

"If you want to change the fruits, you have to change the roots."
— Harv Eker

We are often all about *taking the first step*. Step one is usually focused on making the commitment. But, the real change takes place on the second and third steps, creating a taproot.

...

The dandelion is an interesting flower. If flowers possessed mental toughness, the dandelion would top the list. We spend billions of dollars every year as homeowners in the United States trying to rid the dandelion, but it keeps coming back.

It sprouts very quickly in most types of soil, growing in many climates, with little or lots of rainfall. Young children generally revere it, but at the same time, most homeowners hate it, because they believe it is just an annoying weed. Even though it does not need the approval of its owner to grow successfully, the Russian dandelion is now being purposely cultivated for its production of actual rubber.

It is a very hardy plant. Mental toughness is akin to the hardiness factor in plants, which is a plant's ability to survive in adverse growing conditions. The measurement of any plant's hardiness includes its ability to withstand *drought, wind, cold, and heat.* The process of gardeners developing strains of hardy plants and shrubs involves the process of "hardening" them to the elements. Ironically, the hardiest types of plants *(i.e., dandelions)* are usually the most undesirable to the typical homeowners.

The common trait among all hardy plants, however, is the taproot.

The taproot looks similar to a carrot or turnip and grows vertically down as opposed to branching off horizontally. It distributes water where needed and it makes the plant very difficult to displace, because it will continue to re-sprout.

Thus, developing toughness begins with developing a human taproot.

A human taproot is a perfect metaphor of mental strength. The analogy of a taproot is effective because it is unseen. Honestly, when we look at a tree or plant, we only focus on the branches, leaves, and perhaps the fruit. Unless you are a botanist, you will pay little attention to what you can't see, namely the taproot. Heck, we only pay attention to the roots when we trip over them.

Life is the same way; we can only notice one's outside appearance. The outward appearance of how they want us to view them. We can't see them when they are alone.

Coaches often label the human taproot as *the intangibles.* These unseen qualities are often immeasurable, yet the intangibles and the strength of the human taproot determine the success of each athlete.

Just as the strength of the taproot is what ultimately determines the longevity of the plant, the real key lies in the unseen, the intangibles, and one's resiliency. When you try to bury roots, they just grow!

If the roots are not strong, then the plant and person will eventually submit to the adverse conditions and they will quit.

In order to build the human taproot, we need a *why*. If you find your why, you can come up with any *how*.

Start training yourself instead of testing yourself.

TRAINING OURSELVES OR TESTING OURSELVES

"If I judged every day by whether I win or lose, yesterday would be considered a 'bad day'"
— Chrissie Wellington, 4x Ironman World Champion

There is a difference between training ourselves for something as opposed to testing ourselves. This mental shift makes a huge impact on our mental toughness.

We test the microphone. Actors and weddings have dress rehearsals. Bands do a sound check. However, imagine if a band did a sound check before the event and only if the sound check went well, then they would do the actual event. However, that is often what we do. We don't burn the ships.

Teachers in school don't give a test and then prepare you for it later. That is not how it works. That is what life does. Life first gives you the test and then the learning comes afterwards. Testing ourselves prevents us from full commitment. For instance, testing the waters, putting out feelers, or having irons on the fire are all non-committal.

A test is required to see how good you are, so it involves performance standards and an overall judgment mentality from others of *"how do I measure up?"* When we test ourselves, we are in constant evaluation mode. If a teacher gave you an important test on the first day you signed up, you probably wouldn't even sign up. The evaluation, judgment, comparison mindset prevents us from signing-up for an event, or causes us to shy away from an opportunity. We don't think that we are ready, so we either do not sign-up for an event, or shy away from an opportunity.

Testing ourselves blocks us from full preparation as well. Tests add undue stress especially in the presence of others. There is a reason why bands don't do a sound check if front of the entire crowd. If our superiors or others are evaluating us, then we quickly turn into show material. We have parts of our game to improve, but instead we are put in competition mode and thus we revert to neglecting our weaknesses and just focusing on our strengths and results.

Tests are needed and do provide benefit, but we utilize them on ourselves too often. We use every meeting, speech, practice, etc. as a way to measure ourselves and gauge our readiness.

Sadly, testing ourselves is flawed thinking. When we test ourselves, we are operating under the mentality of, "Am I good enough right now?" or "If today was the event, would I be ready?" The flawed thinking is simply fact based; our performance isn't here yet.

There may be some bad practices, and bad days, but if we are in the testing mindset, then these bad days can erode our confidence and cause undue worry about whether we will be prepared or if we should continue. Testing ourselves also does not allow us to freely work on our weaknesses.

However, when we are training ourselves instead of testing ourselves, our mindset entirely changes. When we train, we no longer evaluate if we are ready, but approach it more as if "what are the weaknesses I need to work on?" Yes, we will still think about our performance and compare ourselves, but now, there is a better context and a backdrop. Instead of testing ourselves for the event, we are now training ourselves for the event.

We operate much better in training mode as opposed to testing mode.

First, recognize the flawed thinking and when we actually need to be ready. A poor session or day may happen, so what can we learn from the session? Remind yourself that we are training. We also operate better in training our mindset by staying in the moment and not thinking too far ahead about if we will be ready. Jodie Wetuski had an awesome quote after a bad day, *"Just remind yourself that it is an investment."*

Someone asked me if I was ready for a keynote presentation that I was giving in a few days. I said, "I'll be ready then." I wasn't speaking at that exact moment, so I didn't need to be ready. No need to test myself, I was still training. I went home and practiced some more.

PROTECT THE DREAM

"Don't set sail using someone else's star." — African proverb

A great scene in the movie *Pursuit of Happiness* is when Will Smith's son is shooting hoops. Will Smith basically tells him to not get his hopes up playing basketball, but then apologizes and tells him instead, that if he has a dream, he has to protect it. To paraphrase, if people can't do something, they want to tell you that you can't do it.

If you want it, go get it, period! It is a motivating scene.

Almost every person who has been ultra successful had the adversity and blessing of actually having someone tell him or her that they *can't* do something! Odd, but the successful ones have that, *I'll show you* attitude.

That type of motivation is one reason why 33% of all millionaires in the United States alone are foreign born. Despite being financially disadvantaged for the first decade of life in the United States, by the 24th year, the immigrants have surpassed their native neighbor. Think about the drive and confidence it takes someone to relocate and move to the United States. That same mental toughness propelled them to success. [12]

Going for the dream meant going against the grain and battling naysayers. Almost 1/3 of all billionaires didn't finish or even attend college. Did you know that almost 40% of self-made millionaires have dyslexia? [13]

If these people listened to everyone else or allowed these obstacles to define them, then their path would have been different. People telling them that they can't do something only solidified their belief and confidence in order to persevere and overcome.

Here is the strategy of Protect the Dream.

Imagine if Martin Luther King Jr. said, "I have a mission statement" instead of " I have a dream."

Jerred Moon of endofthreefitness.com is a national coach and a huge mental toughness advocate. He wrote the book *Garage Gym Athlete*. An extremely good read! He once ran a marathon on a track (26.2 miles) without any training. He completed a Murph workout once a week for an entire year, which is run one mile, complete 100 pull-ups, 200 push-ups, and 300 squats, then run one more mile, for time. [14]

His technique for Protect the Dream forces us all to actually protect it.

You are going to do the opposite of the movie. So, instead of keeping your goal to yourself, you are going to share your goal with others.

He writes:

Write out ten people. Take 10 3x5 cards and write your goal on the cards. Then mail them to those people. Or take the technology advanced way and craft a text message.

Share with those who will support you. Share with those who care. Allow them in on your vision and dream, and you will be surprised that many can benefit from your ideas.

Are you willing to share it with others, and in turn, it will force you to protect it?

But, if you will continue to protect the dream by continually sharing it with others until you get a specific response. You are in search of the naysayer, the person who will tell you something like "that's not a good idea" or "don't you know how competitive that market is?"

The type of people you share your dream with goes a long way to determine if you will achieve it. Find the naysayer.

...

I initially texted 10 people on May 8th.

Complete the 1/2 Ironman on May 21st.

I added many more people to the list, dozens more actually, letting them know what I was going to accomplish. I also called some various friends to let them know what I was going to do and get their thoughts on it. My goal was to find that individual who thought it was a dumb idea and that I shouldn't do it.

Most people however were encouraging, but I finally found the one person who said, *"You shouldn't do it."* I actually admire this person so much because she is not only a great person, but also a successful triathlete.

Boom!

I saved the voicemail and used it as motivation. **Protect the Dream!**

My take is that the risk of attempting your goal and not being able to finish far outweighs the risk we take by not even signing up or trying. Not knowing if you could have completed your goal would be the real risk.

DR. ROB BELL

1% RULE

"Even slow walkers arrive." — African Proverb

John Hayes from Carnegie Mellon University sought out to discover how long it took musical composers to develop their masterpieces. He examined all of the classic master pieces between 1685 and 1900 and identified roughly 500 of the classics, (those which were played the most across the world.) [15]

Of those 500 classics, seventy-six different people had composed these masterpieces. He then examined how long each person had been composing before publishing his or her masterpiece. The results revealed that each masterpiece was only written after year ten (10) of composing.

The best example of composing was the prodigy Mozart, even though, recognized a genius at a young age, wrote music for ten years every day before becoming a true master.

In literature, it took J.R.R. Tolkien and Margaret Mitchell ten years to write their masterpieces of *Lord of the Rings* and *Gone With The Wind* respectively.

Robert Howard at The University of South Wales researched eight grandmasters of chess and discovered that each player reached their highest ranking only after an average of fourteen thousand hours of practice.

...

We basically can only get 1% better every day. We either get better or get worse just that 1% every day.

James Altucher is huge on this type of progress, not perfection technique for building any habit. If he writes 1000 words every day for one year, he will have amassed enough content for about 6 books. He stresses that we can't create habits in one day, but 1% improvement will create habits. No matter what the habit we are working on.

The interesting and stark reality of being an athlete, competing, and practicing is that there is a negative side that happens all too often as well.

In order to win, we first have to understand what loses. What loses is when we start to quit and go through the motions.

SADLY, ALL ATHLETES QUIT!

"First we create habits then our habits create us." — John Dryden

At the 1964 Olympics in Tokyo, Billy Mills would make history with his iconic sprint to win the gold medal for the U.S.A. in the 10,000 meters. He was so unknown that a Japanese reporter asked him after his win, *"Who are you?"* He is still the last American male to win the Gold medal in the 10,000 meters.

However, he was actually going to quit during the race.

Before the last lap, Billy Mills knew he had third place locked up, so he was going to pull up and let the battle be decided by the other two top runners, Ron Clarke and Mohammed Gammoudi. He knew it was *safe* to pull up, but as he looked into the stands in Tokyo with thousands of Japanese faces, he locked eyes with his wife who was crying... He couldn't give up.

Billy Mills pulled off the greatest upset in all of sports history. He ended up winning the Gold Medal, finishing almost a minute faster than his previous best time. He was also the last American to win the Gold medal at the Olympics in the 10,000 Meters.

It may be surprising to hear, but all athletes quit.

Quitting takes place when athletes (you and I) *go through the motions* or when we easily convince ourselves that "it doesn't matter" or "this isn't that important."

The hinge can't connect that way.

Professional athletes go through the motions when they are not in situations where they can win. For instance, a golfer on the PGA Tour will quit when the best finish that he could muster would be 40th place. It is an early tee-time, no T.V. coverage, and certainly no commentary or after the round interview. The money between 40th and 50th place also becomes insignificant.

So, golfers will still hit the shots, but not with as much focus and determination. They will *go through the motions*.

In our own lives, we go through the motions as well. When we are not in situations for a good performance or a win, we quit.

We go through the motions when we say, "Missing this workout doesn't matter" or if we say to ourselves before a sales call, "This call isn't that important." We quit when we are supposed to do a five-mile run and only do three or when we say this extra piece of cake or one more beer won't hurt.

Now, in reality, you may be 100% right! Missing one workout, eating an extra piece of cake, having another beer, or not making an extra sales call won't physically make a difference. However, here is the scary part. Quitting matters mentally.

It matters mentally because once we allow that mindset to slowly creep in about something not mattering and allowing ourselves that *out*, then it becomes an option for us. We are automatically wired, like water in a stream, to find the path of least resistance, so if we give ourselves an *out* then we take it.

We then slowly start to create negative habits. Every time we quit, it becomes easier for us later on.

Quitting then becomes a habit.

Rome was not built in a day is a popular cliché. However, Rome was not destroyed in a day either. It took years for the empire to collapse. Habits are the same way.

...

It is a lot easier to lie in bed, than it is to get out of bed. It is a whole lot easier to not do something or not push oneself, than it is to put forth our best effort. However, if we have not created positive habits when we need to really dig deep and push through, then our mental toughness may not be there.

Now, none of us is going to quit if we have a chance to win or if there is something on the line. If there is that carrot at the end of reaching a bonus, or a certain time, or trip, we will usually try our best.

It takes incredible amount of discipline to always give our best effort in everything we do. It is tough and sometimes painful to do our best when we are not in situations where we can win. I certainly haven't always done my best; anger and frustration got in the way. I have gone through the motions in more areas of my life than I care to admit. It takes discipline to never give up.

However, being an athlete is about progress, not perfection. Are we willing to do our best in one small area in our life, and create one habit in one area where we always give our best?

If we want to perform our best when it matters the most, every decision, practice, relationship is the most important one. At that point, we are creating the habit of grit, resiliency, and mental toughness.

It sounds simple and it is. But it is not easy.

Way too often, we give up or quit before we get that breakthrough, meet that person, or see our vision all the way through. We quit when all we need to do is just keep moving.

NO DEALS

"Complaining is the first small sign of giving up." — Anonymous

A friend of mine admitted that he could just *show up* and win races on the track. He was skilled enough to compete at almost every amateur level in the 5000 meters.

However, he didn't compete at his full potential because he made deals with himself.

During a race or competition, he used to say to himself, *"Keep up with [that guy] UNTIL this point and then let him go."* He admitted he wasn't as tough as he needed to be. His entire game changed once he refused to make deals with himself. Instead, during a race or practice, he would set goals. He would just say, *"Catch that guy"* or *"stay with this guy."*

To avoid the disastrous act of going through the motions and quitting, we need to stop making deals:

With our children, *"Honey, IF you pick up your toys, THEN you can get a snack."*

With God, *"Lord, if you get me through this, I will never..."*

With ourselves, *"If you [do this] then you can [do this]."*

Make deals with salesman at car dealerships, but not with ourselves. Deals do not build mental toughness.

When we make deals, we are actually beginning to quit. Deals mean that our motivation and focus have changed.

We are doing something to gain an immediate result, not long-term success. Deals undercut the habits we are trying to create. We feel a reward is needed for our efforts, such as *if you go to the gym three times this week, then you can eat all you want this weekend.* Making deals gives us an *out* a reason not to push further when it gets *really* tough...

Your goal however means having a plan of action without a fallback. It is stating, "I will do this" instead of "do this, so I can." It means keeping the focus on the immediate task at hand instead of rewarding yourself for what you already did.

No matter what happens, what obstacles you face, or adversity you encounter, don't make deals.

STEP #3- JUST KEEP MOVING

"Mental toughness means doing the things that you don't want to do."
— Dick Dullaghan

We perform like we train!

Many people ask me how I write all of my books. I simply tell them to call me at 5:30am and I will tell them. The answer is quite simple and I answer consistently with "I write." When I write one of my books on mental toughness, I write every single day for one hour. From 5:30 am-6:30 am or 6-7 am. No more, and certainly no less.

One of my favorite coaches at University of Notre Dame, Adam Schaechterle said, *"You don't need to be crazy about your preparation, you just need to be consistent."*

Consistency is key!

This book was no exception. Everything else in life becomes secondary during that time of day. I write for one hour; no email, and no distractions. This is challenging because I have many other entities vying for my attention, but writing for an hour everyday takes discipline.

Remember, we first create habits, then our habits create us.

Whatever we want to get better at, we must consistently do. Don't mistake action for achievement. If we want to get better at swimming, then swim, if we want to get better at public speaking, speak. If we want to improve our sales, get a coach. Period.

Training for your goal must take priority during specific times over everything else. I am not saying to neglect family or health, but to ensure that your focus is like being an athlete. When you are at practice, be at practice.

Strategy is more important than technique. Strategy involves a plan for the overall goal, whereas technique is the thing you do in a specific way.

Strategy is the *what*; technique is the *how*. Technique is important, but strategy is more important.

Every book on motivation offers the same goal, which is to improve and get better. The strategies and techniques are what vary.

The strategy for significance is echoed many times. *Just Keep Moving*.

Jason Minnick is a boxing coach and I once asked him how he knows if a fighter is mentally tough. He answered, "He gets beaten in the ring, but he still comes back the next day."

If we never give up, and if we just keep moving, then we will be successful.

Remember the person who gave up? Neither does anyone else.

JUST KEEP MOVING

"An inch is a cinch, a yard is hard, a mile is a trial." — Anonymous

Do you know how to finish a marathon?

JUST one step at a time. JUST a half-mile at a time. Then JUST one mile at a time.

Just keep moving becomes the goal. The more often you push yourself even if only a little bit, the more you are building mental toughness. You perform like you train.

The game of life and success is actually one of attrition. IF you NEVER give up, you will be successful. If you stay in the game long enough, you will make it; sometimes quickly, sometimes slowly. Remember, even slow walkers arrive.

Reaching your goals is more about tenacity and less about talent. It is about making the dedication and commitment to never give up and stay in the game.

When we start thinking about finishing our goal or success, it actually distracts us from the moment. For example, thinking about the ten miles you still have left to finish the marathon is when pain starts to set in the legs. It is natural for us to think, *"If it's this hard right now, how will I even finish?"* *"If I can't even make one sale, how will I reach my million dollar mark?"*

The picture gets way too big, and we start to stress out and then our approach changes because we are too focused on the outcome as opposed to our next target. That is why we need to JUST make it to a certain point.

We *just keep moving* by focusing on just making it to certain targets.

Set an intermediate goal for the next hour or two hours on what you want to accomplish. How many {blank} do you want to finish? What is your target? JUST focus on this project. JUST complete five {blank} in the next hour. Just talk with ten people in the next two hours. Just help out this one person.

Our goal is to stay in the moment and not focus on anything else. Address one problem at a time, and focus just on that goal. Short-term targets while we compete allow us to stay in the moment and focus our energy on the task at hand.

...

The reason why I signed up for a ½ ironman with less than 2 weeks of training boiled down to one simple variable. Could I keep moving?

No matter what happened in the race, no matter how bad it hurt, would I quit or would I just keep moving? I was able to answer this question, and knew if all I had to do was just keep moving, then I would finish.

The technique that I used during the actual ½ Ironman was to *just keep moving.* As this book is all about, I set short-term goals. I couldn't think about finishing the race with 7 miles left on the run and legs were in pain. It relied on "just." Just make it to the fire hydrant. Just make it to the bend in the road or just make it to the tree.

JUST KEEP MOVING.

...

These three action steps are ways to ensure that we will just keep moving. Our preparation matches our commitment.

Write Out The Training Plan.

There was once a lunch reception for a golf event, with a buffet line. Normally in buffet lines, there are two lines, one of each side of the table moving in the same direction. Well, this line was interesting because of the flow of the guests getting their food.

Yes, there were two lines, but the organizer of the set-up, put one set of plates at one end and another set of plates at the far end. Picture it for a second because people were meeting each other in the middle. The layout may have made sense looking at it, but it just did not work.

Our training and preparation is the same way. Writing down your training plan means putting your plan into action. Write out the training plan for the next two weeks and everything you need.

What doesn't get scheduled doesn't get done. We need to see our plan, how we will prepare, and what adjustments to make.

DO NOT SKIP THIS STEP. There are too many variables that are inherent with life, but having a written plan is not one of them. Life does get in the way, but if you have a plan, then you can adjust the plan.

Writing out the plan for the week allows you to see what the time and work look like, and anticipate any issues that you may have during that week.

I didn't even own a bike for my ½ Ironman training or race and no clue on how to best prepare, so I had to write it all out. For example, I had to do two a day workouts because there was such little time to prepare. I had to fit in two workouts a day around my schedule with teams and athletes. This required detailed planning on overcoming the potential obstacles.

Develop Your Daily Routine.

The first hour of the day sets the rudder for the rest.

A good routine saves time which leads to focus, which leads to being in the moment. Besides, you already have a routine. First, we create habits then our habits create us. Is your routine effective and productive or do you mistake action for achievement?

William Penn once said, "Time is what we want most, but what we use worst."

All successful people get up early. Maybe it's 3:30, 4:30, 5:30, or 6:30. If time is your excuse, make it your reason and just start rising 30 minutes earlier. You can do that, for the next two weeks, get up 30 minutes earlier.

However you organize your routine in the morning, make it a routine. Do you meditate, write out the daily goals, pray, exercise?

Start your routine on your schedule; you are the one in charge to develop your routine.

One of the parts of our routine is making a commitment to help others. It can be as simple as writing out the five people who we will reach out to today.

Start With The Hardest.

One of the PGA Tour players that I worked with taught me tons about mental toughness.

Before Scott Stallings won his first PGA Tour victory, we were at an event and we made a little wager that he had to complete a putting drill. This wager took place on the putting green and there was one very difficult putt. I figured he would save the toughest putt for last.

He pointed at the Rasputin of all holes and said, "I'm starting with that one!"

Tracy Thorsell attended the Naval Academy. She graduated with a degree in electrical engineering and speaks five languages. She took Chinese in high school because it was the toughest language to master.

Too often, we start with and only want the easy tasks. The idea is to create momentum in our day. However, we are actually just spending energy.

Get uncomfortable and build our mental toughness by starting with the hardest task. We will get confidence and momentum from accomplishing the most difficult first.

DR. ROB BELL

JUST ONE MORE

"If there's shouting after you, keep going. Don't ever stop. Keep going. If you want a taste of freedom, keep going." — Harriet Tubman

Columbo was an award winning TV detective series in the 70's. Columbo was the detective who would interview the possible culprit and finally be able to catch them in a lie through his unique style of questioning.

His technique included just one more. After *finishing* the interview with his suspect and turning to leave, he would get to the door, stop, and ask "just one more thing." The next line from Columbo packed one hell of a punch and got the suspect to realize they were caught.

Before the Super Bowl, 49ers QB Steve Young memorized all 300 plays with his quarterback coach Mike Shanahan. The night before the game after going through every play, Coach Shanahan told Steve Young, *"Let's do it just one more time."* After he completed it again, the coach told him *"Okay, now you're ready."*

The good ones practice until they get it right, the great ones practice until they can't get it wrong.

The way to build mental toughness is to approach our task with the attitude of *just one more.* It is when we are most tired, spent, and mentally or physically exhausted that we need to push ourselves. It is basically only during these instances that we can get exponentially better.

Billy Mills won the 10,000 Meters for Olympic Gold by sprinting past the two leaders in the last 100 meters. He finished every single practice by sprinting 100 meters and imagining himself blowing by the leaders to win the Gold Medal.

In whatever task we have, the goal when we are *finished* is to do **just one more.** Read just one more page, write just one more paragraph, do just one more push-up, push out just one more rep, rehearse one more time through, make just one more sales call, practice just one more shot on goal, finish just one more lap, read just one more page.

The way we improve our mental toughness is through pushing ourselves and the strategy for pushing ourselves is to just do one more.

It can even be as small as writing **just one more** sentence or just five more minutes, as long as you keep moving.

CHAMPIONS ADJUST

"It is not the strongest of the species that survives, nor the most intelligent, but the one most responsive to change."
— Charles Darwin

In the fall of 2008, a 47-year-old businessman, divorced father of four went to his crack dealer. He was on a fourteen-day binge and was so bad off that his dealer actually refused to sell him any more until he got some sleep. It was this man's low point.

After one final party binge about a year later, Michael Lindell quit alcohol and drugs. A success story in itself, but more impressive is that he grew a business empire from a drawing he sketched on his kitchen table. [16]

One early morning after a night of pitiful sleep, he drew a sketch of a pillow with all sizes of foam that could be adjusted however a person would desire. He told his daughter "I'm going to create the world's best pillow." That evening MyPillow® was created.

The journey for Lindell was not smooth, as his business since 2011 oscillated from extreme growth and successful infomercials to hemorrhaging money. At one point, he owed $30,000 to a fabric manufacturer with only a few days to pay or MyPillow would be forced to shut down. It was only after a chance meeting with an individual that he was able to get a meeting with investors and get the $30,000 loan with no collateral. He paid the manufacturer with just hours to spare.

MyPillow has become one of the top five-telebrand products and has sold more than 26 million pillows with a workforce of over 1,500 people. Michael Lindell's dream is to become a $1 billion dollar company.

It is not about the setback; it is about the comeback!

A boat is off course 99% of the time. The way that a sailboat finds its destination is by tacking. A series of zigzagging maneuvers by a sailboat and adjusting the sail back and forth to use the wind. Adjusting is how sailboats reach their final destination.

That is how champions adJUST. They just keep moving, making minor changes and course corrections along the journey.

One of the amazing things is that once Michael Lindell, now a Christian, shed his demons, he remained devoted to his own style and vision. His own infomercials and personality became a huge part of MyPillow's appeal.

In all areas of life, champions adjust. They find a way.

Mental Toughness isn't needed when things are going great. It is needed most when bad outcomes are happening, we are stressed and things are going wrong. How do we respond and adjust?

PREPARE FOR THE UNPREDICTABLE

"Prepare for the unknown by studying how others in the past have coped with the unforeseeable and the unpredictable."
— George S. Patton

Gwen Jorgensen won the 2016 Olympic Gold Medal in the triathlon. However, it was the London games in 2012 that taught her the biggest lesson. She was one of the medal contenders and was in the lead group on the bike.

However, at mile 13, she had an issue and fell off her bike. What happened next was that she experienced a shock to her system. She felt she had a mechanical problem and tried to get it fixed, but during those pressure moments, she was admittedly hysterical, her hands were shaking, and needed to calm down instead. The moments of panic took its toll and caused her to finish in 38th place.

Gwen later realized that she allowed a mechanical issue to bother her so much that it wrecked her race. Her mess became her message though, as she improved mentally and became the first USA female to win an Olympic Gold medal in triathlon.

...

Rich Allen, president of ProThree, a sports marketing and sales company, has been a multiple podium finisher and triathlon winner.

Early in his career, he would win and have podium finishes only when everything went well. If bad stuff occurred during a race, he would often overreact and not be able to adjust.

One of the techniques he developed to adjust was through distraction control. Distraction control became his ability to prepare for the unpredictable. His technique was to list out everything in the race that could go wrong and have a strategy for his response to that event.

A few examples of things that could go wrong: His bike chain could come off, he could get kicked in the face and his goggles may come off, his legs may cramp up during the run or he could get a blister, he could get an upset stomach, or the tire could go flat (wink, wink). If any of these or other situations happened, Rich Allen developed a strategy for how to adjust and overcome.

...

What are some of the possible things that could go wrong in the next two weeks or in the next two hours that would prevent you from just keep moving?

Write out the list: Death of a loved one, cancer, accidents, serious illness, and natural disasters are examples of tragedies.

However, you will probably see that most of the things that can derail us are just inconveniences: computer crashes, flat tire, the car wouldn't start, someone close needs something, kids get sick, call from school, spouse leaves town for work, poor weather, etc.

These inconveniences are distractions, but they are also opportunities and ways for us to remain committed to our vision, to find a way, and make adjustments.

STEP #4- PRAISE THE TAILWIND & CHEER THE HEADWIND!

"I run to see who has the most guts." — Steve Prefontaine

The most important days are the ones with natural adversity.

On one of my long training runs for the ½ Ironman, I was ready at 6:00am on a Saturday and the weather was plain crappy. It was 45 degrees, raining, and the wind was blowing 15-20 MPH. It was a day where you initially wanted to take the training indoor or modify the run, or just not do it at all.

However, these are the instances where mental toughness is won or lost. If we allow the conditions of our environment to dictate our mood and actions, then we are not building mental toughness.

My 10-mile running route consisted of an out and back run, 5 miles out, which is good because I just have to make it all the way out. Once you are out 5 miles, then you are forced to make it back, or stay out there.

On the five miles out, there was a 10-15 mph tailwind at my back the entire way. That is a significant amount of assistance. It felt so good because it helped me move much faster; I recognized it and praised it. I felt like I was flying!

After I made the turn to come back at mile 5, I then faced the headwind. I was at least able to prepare for it, but it was cold and fierce. The drops of rain stung coming in sideways to hit my face.

Wind is the most powerful element because of the impact it creates on all the other elements, fire, rain, snow, etc.

Oddly enough, too often we don't even recognize the tailwind. If the wind is ever so slight, it is tough to even notice the direction. Golfers and sailors success depends on being able to decipher the direction of the breeze.

Unfortunately, it is only after we stop experiencing the tailwind that we realize how much help there really was at our backs.

There is no tailwind in life without a headwind.

The headwind that day is what made me better. It forced me to push through and work harder. The tailwind was there to assist me, but the headwind was there to improve me.

In life, we will have both, but we improve by going through the adversity.

If we are going to praise the tailwind, we must also cheer the headwind. We can't have it both ways and I don't see too many people cursing the tailwind.

TRAIN THE PAIN OR EXPERIENCE THE PAIN

"Discipline weighs a pound, but regret weighs a ton." — Jim Rohn

There are two types of pain, the pain of discipline or the pain of regret. This is true in competition and in life. It just depends which pain you choose.

When my daughter was young and still in a stroller, I entered a 5k race. My mileage and tempo were no longer where it needed to be to set personal bests, but I figured I could still win at least the stroller division.

At mile two of the 3.1-mile race, a mother pushing her daughter passed my stroller and as bad as I wanted, I just couldn't keep up. I had no response to her surge and she took off...It was bad. I finished almost a minute behind her.

Now, I could share as many reasons as I wanted—*not training enough, or having the time, or not making running a priority*— all reasons, but they are just well thought out excuses. I experienced the pain of regret.

PAIN...

Pain is unavoidable, but we have a choice. Which type of pain do we want and when do we want it?

Are you going to train the pain or just experience the pain?

Training the pain takes discipline. Getting up early, pushing oneself, applying just one more technique, experiencing setbacks, and getting better. The pain of discipline is all about— being all in. If we face the pain, welcome the discomfort and cheer on the headwind, it is the pain of discipline.

Experiencing the pain means avoidance. If we only experience the pain, it means we haven't been willing to change, to push ourselves, to reach out, to help others or just do one more. Pain of this type turns into the pain of regret. We didn't do all of the little things and we experience the disappointment.

Pain is unavoidable. It hurts. Can we find meaning in our pain?

One of the biggest goal killers is pain. When pain strikes, it takes sheer will to push through. It is what separates corporate athletes from good to becoming champions. If one cannot train the pain, then they simply won't make it to becoming champions.

If we can't train the pain by just doing one more or just keep moving, then we will remain where we are, just experiencing the pain.

Pain tells lies.

One of the biggest lies that pain tries to convince us is that it is permanent. Think about it. When we experience pain, it feels like it is permanent; it hurts, and it does not feel like we will hold on. So, even though pain tells lies, there is some truth in it.

However, the lie does not outweigh the truth.

Here is the proof, during the ½ ironman, the run hurt at mile 8, but it did NOT hurt at mile 13. Those that aren't mentally tough often become distracted and start thinking too much about the pain. They think things like *"if it hurts this bad now, how will I feel later on?"* The only truth is that it hurts. In life, when facing pain, we need to rediscover our rhythm, endure, and be able to find our second wind.

If we do not train the pain of discipline, then we will experience the pain of regret.

Pain can also be a gift. If we are disciplined, pain forces us to stay in the moment to focus on this day, and this hour.

Whatever we focus on, we feel!

CONFIDENCE IS KING--FOCUS IS QUEEN

"It's NOT about motivation, it's about belief." — Anonymous

Confidence affects all of the other mental skills. Trust and believing in our coaches, our team, and ourselves is crucial to success. In chess, when the king dies, the game is over, similar to confidence. Not having or losing confidence is how the game is lost.

It is not how the game is won, however. We can't move our king around the board trying to win. The game is won through our queen, our focus. How and what we focus on. The queen is the piece that wins the game.

Our focus determines our level of confidence. If we focus on others by encouraging, or motivating them, our own confidence rises.

Confidence is King.

Confidence is the most important part of mental toughness. A funny thing about confidence it that there is a nosy neighbor with confidence named doubt. Wherever doubt lives, it does so, rent-free. Doubt is a squatter!

Doubt always wants to hang out with confidence, but they simply don't get along well. However, that doesn't keep doubt from following confidence around wherever confidence goes.

It is best to keep doubt as a neighbor rather than a roommate.

Everyone has doubts, even the best. This is normal, so just know that it is okay. What is more important than the doubt is that you determine how long you want to hang around with doubt. Do not allow the negative thoughts to stay around right beside your confidence. Doubt is a squatter in your house, so kick him out!

Here are two important facts about confidence: You owe it to yourself to be confident, and you can't afford to lose confidence for very long.

Many of the athletes I have worked with did an incredible job of preparing only to undercut themselves by not believing in themselves and not being confident at the moment of execution. They let their focus get distracted during the most important moments.

All of your preparation and ability can go for naught if you begin to think and act as if doubt is the real owner of the home, not confidence. If building and acting as if you are confident is important to you, then utilize the next strategy.

NOTHING BOTHERS ME!

"We can't predict the future, we can only prepare for the unpredictable."
— Anonymous

It is common for the major setbacks in life to bother and affect us. However, have you ever noticed when we get stressed that *everything* seems to bother us, like the person next to us in traffic, our own family, or forgetting our headphones?

These inconveniences become the first thing to annoy us when we lose our confidence.

When we allow little things to bother us, we believe that things will NOT work out. When things start to bother us, there is an indicator light that we need to work on ourselves.

There is a secret about the best performers: **The best simply let nothing bother them.**

When we are confident, little things don't bother us at all.

When we don't let anything bother us, we are agreeing to the belief that, *"I don't need everything to go my way in order to be successful."*

Those that get the most out of their potential believe in their process so much that they refuse to let setbacks affect their mindset or their mission. They are able to adjust from the mistakes and the setbacks.

It is amazing to see, but they manage to always keep their poise and focus. It is like they knew bad things would happen; yet they still kept their head while others were losing theirs. Nothing bothers them! It is the major impact of confidence and the true test of one's level of belief and mental toughness.

It is natural to get stressed, especially leading up to important events, but we must maintain a high level of confidence during these times. We get confident by implementing this strategy of *nothing bothers me.*

When we do encounter these setbacks and simply aren't feeling confident, we need to turn our thoughts towards someone else and get out of our own head.

CHALLENGE YOUR TALENT

"There is no traffic jam on the extra mile." — Zig Ziglar

This book was originally written on how everyone can crush a ½ Ironman in less than two weeks. It was changed however when I got the flat tire in the race. It became apparent in that moment that I would not have finished without others.

NO ONE gets there ALONE.

Life is a voicemail

One speaking event at my alma mater, Shepherd University, I made sure to invite my professor, Dr. Joe Merz. He was a hinge person in my life. If not for him, then Sport Psychology and the passion I live out everyday would not have happened.

I received a voicemail from him after the event.

The voicemail was about a minute long and went in-depth about and what an amazing job I did and how proud and impressed he was.

It felt good. I saved it. It is still on my phone today.

That same week though, I probably left a dozen voicemail and text messages to various people. I could not begin to tell you what I said or wrote. I forget emails that I write and linkedin messages as well.

We can listen to our voicemail messages right now on our phones. But, we have no idea of the influence the messages we left other people wield.

Life is the same way.

We remember the most impactful people in our lives. But, we often have no idea of the impact we made on someone else. We can't know. We are planting trees that we will never see. We are leaving messages that we will never hear.

On a much simpler level, perhaps we remember the person who waved to us today or held the door. But, we don't know the effect of our own kind gesture today.

We are literally and figuratively leaving voicemails all the time for people and it makes a difference, good or bad.

Every transaction we have with someone has the potential to be transformative. We can't know who or what will be the hinge. People will remember how we made them feel even for an instant and it has the potential to connect them to someone else.

So are we intentional about our messages? Are we leaving the jersey better than how we found it?

We give to people from what we possess ourselves. All of us have fired off an angry email or perhaps left a not-so-friendly voicemail. If we are filled with resentment, contempt, hatred, or lack of confidence, then that is the message of our transactions. It usually affects those closest to us as well.

However, if we can be deliberate about leaving messages that are encouraging, positive, filled with confidence and hope, then a miracle occurs.

We actually start to leave ourselves a message.

If we act and behave in ways that are focused on others, then we act our way into right thinking and our own mood and outlook changes.

...

If we want to KEEP our mental toughness, we HAVE to give it away.

If we help others to just keep moving, then we will keep moving. If we encourage others to not give up, then we persevere as well. If we share with someone else the importance of confidence, then we can't help but help ourselves with being more confident. When we communicate with someone else not to let a situation bother him or her, then we help ourselves by not allowing our own junk to bother us. Even if we are going through a tough period in life, if we do not isolate, but connect with others, then a better *us* starts to make a better you.

If we help enough people reach their goals; then we will reach ours.

Mental Toughness is not a secondary goal or aspiration, meaning if things are going well, then I will be tough. It has to be the sole focus. Before any endeavor, we need to be intentional about becoming other-person focused. As we develop our routine, are we considering who we want to be and who we can connect with? Or perhaps it is a matter of writing out in the morning five people who we need to re-connect with.

I'm in life for the miracles and there are around us everyday. The miracle for us is that we can be transformed. Allowing God to help us focus on others and to use our strengths. To give away what we want to possess in ourselves because as Ralph Waldo Emerson wrote, "*no man can sincerely try to help another without helping himself.*"

Will you be able to stop your own race to help others?

DR. ROB BELL

REFERENCES

1. Darley, J. M., & Batson, C. D. (1973). "From Jerusalem to Jericho": A study of situational and dispositional variables in helping behavior. *Journal of Personality and Social Psychology, 27*(1), 100-108.

2. Kerr, James (2013). *Legacy: What the all blacks can teach us about the business of life.* Constable.

3. Borah, Debajit & Gogoi, Dhrubajyoti & N. S. Yadav, R. (2014). Jadav Molai Payeng – the 'Forest Man of India'. *Current science.* 106. 499.

4. Fitzgerald, Matt (2012). *The Iron War.* VeloPress

5. *Sergio Aguero and Gabriel Jesus have a 'top relationship', insists Manchester City manager Pep Guardiola despite competition between the strikers* (September, 11, 2017). Dailymail.co.uk

6. Ibáñez, S. J., Sampaio, J., Feu, S., Lorenzo, A., Gómez, M. A., & Ortega, E. (2008). Basketball game-related statistics that discriminate between teams' season-long success. *European journal of sport science, 8*(6), 369-372.

7. Deci, E. L., & Ryan, R. M. (1985). *Intrinsic motivation and self-determination in human behavior.* New York, NY: Plenum.

8. Alcoholics Anonymous. (2001). *Alcoholics Anonymous,* 4th Edition. New York: A.A. World Services.

9. 'Don't Buy This Racket': Patagonia To Give Away All Retail Revenues On Black Friday (November 21, 2016). *Forbes.*

10. Ferrazzi, Keith, & Raz, Tahl., (2005) *Never eat alone and other secrets to success: one relationship at a time* New York : Currency Doubleday

11. Gottman, J. M., & Silver, N. (2012). *What makes love last?: How to build trust and avoid betrayal.* New York, N.Y.: Simon & Schuster.

12. Correia, M (June 13, 2013). 1 in 3 U.S Millionaires Foreign-Born or First-Gen Americans. *Bank Investment Consultant.*

13. Gill, Charlotte. (n.d.). *Dyslexia 'can be route to riches'.* Daily Mail.

14. Moon, J. (2016). *Garage Gym Athlete.* Createspace.

15. Hayes, John. (2015). *The complete problem solver.* Routledge.

16. Dean, Josh., (Jan 11, 2017). *The Preposterous Success Story of America's Pillow King.* Bloomberg

DID YOU LIKE THIS?

"There is no traffic jam on the extra mile." — Zig Ziglar

Thank you so much for reading **NO ONE Gets There ALONE.** I hope you enjoyed it! Hey, if you did, I could use your help! Please go here on Amazon and **leave a quick review.**

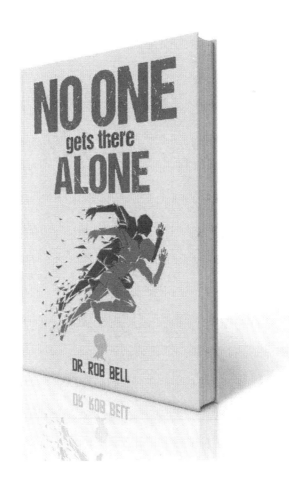

MORE BOOKS BY DR. ROB BELL

Mental Toughness Training for Golf

The Hinge: The Importance of Mental Toughness

NO FEAR: A Simple Guide to Mental Toughness

Don't "Should" on Your Kids: Build Their Mental Toughness

50 Ways to Win: Pro Football's Hinge Moments

-

Dr. Rob Bell is a Sport Psychology coach working with athletes, coaches, and teams on Mental Toughness. He is the owner of DRB & Associates in Indianapolis. He has worked with champions on the PGA Tour, USTA National Champion, and Olympic medalists. Speaking and coaching clients have included **University of Notre Dame, Indy Eleven Professional Soccer, Marriott, and Walgreens.**

The Love Dare Bible Study

MICHAEL CATT

ALEX KENDRICK

STEPHEN KENDRICK

As developed with Matt Tullos

B&H Publishing Group
Nashville, Tennessee

Published by LifeWay Press®. © 2015 Sherwood Baptist Church

ISBN 978-1-4300-3222-9 • Item 005644084

Dewey Decimal Classification: 220.07
Subject Headings: BIBLE--STUDY / LOVE / MARRIAGE

To order additional copies of this resource: write LifeWay Church Resources Customer Service;
One LifeWay Plaza; Nashville, TN 37234-0113; fax 615.251.5933; phone toll free 800.458.2772;
email orderentry@lifeway.com; order online at www.lifeway.com; or visit the LifeWay Christian Store
serving you.

Printed in the United States of America

Adult Ministry Publishing; LifeWay Church Resources;
One LifeWay Plaza; Nashville, TN 37234-0152

Contents

About the Authors

Alex Kendrick and **Stephen Kendrick** cowrote and produced the movies Courageous, Fireproof, and *Facing the Giants* and are authors of the New York Times best sellers *The Love Dare* and *The Resolution for Men.* They recently coauthored *The Love Dare for Parents Bible Study.*

Michael Catt has served Sherwood Baptist Church, Albany, Georgia, as senior pastor since 1989. He is the author of *Fireproof Your Life* and *Courageous Living* (B&H Publishing Group), among other books.

Matt Tullos, developer of this study with the Kendrick brothers, has been interpreting the truth of the gospel for 25-plus years, through preaching, teaching, writing, and drama. Matt currently serves through the Louisiana Baptist Convention.

About This Study

Each week *The Love Dare Bible Study* will challenge you to think differently—to learn, stretch, and grow individually and as a couple as you dare to live a life of selfless, sacrificial love. Tools for this journey include FIREPROOF teaching clips, *The Love Dare Bible Study* member book, *The Love Dare* journal, and Bibles.

Components of Each Session

IGNITE. This section includes lighthearted, engaging questions to warm up the group and prepare everyone for meaningful discussion and Bible study. Between sessions, doing approximately five dares in *The Love Dare* journal is a huge part of the experience. Beginning with session 2, the group will review insights or questions from that work.

GEAR UP. This interactive Bible study is the heart of each group session. The group will discover relational truths by watching a clip from FIREPROOF and engaging in Scripture search and application. As you allow the Holy Spirit to convict you, plus engage in open discussion, you will find your personal walk and your marriage growing stronger.

FIREFIGHTING. This section continues the Bible study with an emphasis on integrating truth into your life, thus transforming your marriage.

FIREPROOF NOW. This section focuses on further application, prayer, and opportunities to make commitments to God and to your spouse.

Perhaps you are hesitant to share about your marriage in a group. As the experience progresses and you develop friendships, your comfort level will improve. Make sure your spouse is comfortable with how you share; don't turn Bible study into group therapy. Confidentiality and trust are essential to this experience.

Ideally, couples participate together. This study is not just for newlyweds or couples whose marriage is floundering; every marriage needs a little fireproofing. You may find yourself being able to mentor other couples whose marriages need support and encouragement.

Group Covenant

Discussing group values is vital as this study gets underway. It is vital that participants covenant together, agreeing to live out important principles. Once these values are agreed upon, your group will be on your way to experiencing Christian community.

Priority: While we are in this course of study, we will give the group meetings and commitments to our marriages high priority.

Participation: Everyone is encouraged to participate. No one person dominates.

Respect: Everyone is given the right to his or her opinion, and all questions are encouraged and respected. Spouses respect each other in how they share within the group.

Confidentiality: Anything said in the meeting is never repeated outside the meeting.

Life Change: Throughout the next eight weeks, we will assess our own life-change goals and encourage one another in our individual pursuit of becoming more like Christ.

Care and Support: Permission is given to call upon each other at any time, especially in times of crisis. The group will provide care for every member.

Accountability: We agree to let the members of the group hold us accountable to the commitments we make in whatever loving ways we decide upon.

I agree to all of the above _____

Date: _____

Leading Your Heart

SESSION 1

This study is about love—what it is and
what it is not (1 Corinthians 13). This
experience is about daring to live a life
filled with loving relationships.

Your journey begins with the person who
is closest to you: your spouse.

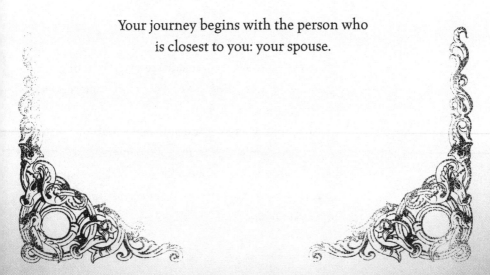

OPENING THOUGHTS AND CONVERSATION STARTERS

You have joined others who are on the same personal journey. Introduce yourself to your fellow travelers.

"Now these three remain: faith, hope, and love. But the greatest of these is love."

1 CORINTHIANS 13:13

1. The FIREPROOF movie is a major part of our time together. If a movie were to be made about your life, what genre would it be? Why?

❑ Thriller   ❑ Action/Adventure

❑ Drama   ❑ Romantic Comedy

❑ Tragedy   ❑ Love Story

❑ Horror

Who would play you? Who would play your spouse? (No bad casting allowed!)

Humorous episodes … dramatic scenes … thrilling mysteries still unfolding—we're all in different "acts" and "scenes" in our marriages.

No matter where you are or where you think you or your spouse should be, you have been invited into a life-changing process—that of exploring and demonstrating genuine love, even when your desire is missing and your motives are mixed.

8

Moment-by-moment, it seems, our culture bombards us with different messages about love.

2. **In general, what does society say to us about love? About following our hearts?**

   What phrases, titles, or situations (from songs, movies, TV shows) promote following your heart?

   When you think about the state of your own heart, highlight words that come to mind.

   cold   cynical   open   joyful   weary
   angry   exhilarated   other: _____

   Describe a time you followed your heart and regretted it later.

> "If love is just this overwhelming emotion that we can do absolutely nothing about, then no marriage is safe."
>
> VODDIE BAUCHAM

Following our hearts would be good if our hearts were always loving, in tune with God and desirous of the right thing. Since as humans we are self-centered, prideful, and often deceived, to follow our hearts will not always lead us to do the right thing.

Every area of life, including marriage, is impacted by the direction of your heart.

Gear Up

Engaging in Relevant Scripture Study

3. **From the clip, what does Caleb Holt seem to
   believe it means to be "in love"?**

4. **Why do you think Lieutenant Michael
   Simmons said, "When most people promise,
   'for better or for worse,' they really only mean,
   'for the better'?"**

Michael reminded Caleb: "That ring on your finger means
you made a lifetime covenant."

5. **Think back to your wedding day and the
   exchange of rings and vows. Were you committing to love your spouse unconditionally for a
   lifetime? How's it going?**

Following our hearts often means chasing after whatever
feels right at the moment. Our feelings can be deceptive,
leading us down the wrong path. Proverbs 16:25 cautions:
"There is a way that seems right to a man, but in the end it is
the way of death" (NASB).

*"Your heart will always be
where your treasure is."*

MATTHEW 6:21, CEV

Your heart follows your investments because your
investments are those things in which you pour your time,
money, and energy. It makes sense that they will draw your
heart because such treasures reflect your priorities.

6. If last week was typical for you, use it to evaluate areas in which you invested significant time, energy, or money. Try to recall actual percentages of time spent.

Job or retirement activities

Hobby (specify)

Spouse

Children

Church

Friends

Status/Wealth

How does your actual use of time, energy, and money match your stated priorities?

"Don't store up treasures on earth! ... Instead, store up your treasures in heaven, where moths and rust cannot destroy them, and thieves cannot break in and steal them."

MATTHEW 6:19-20, CEV

"If you are not in love with your spouse today, it may be because you stopped investing in your spouse yesterday."

THE LOVE DARE,
"LEADING YOUR HEART,"
PAGE 212

According to James 3:14-15 (margin) how might an angry or bitter heart take an individual (and a marriage) in the wrong direction?

"But if you have bitter jealousy and selfish ambition in your heart, do not be arrogant and so lie against the truth. This wisdom is not that which comes down from above."

JAMES 3:14-15, NASB

MOVIE MOMENTS

Watch **Fireproof**

clip 2, "Lead Your Heart."

Debrief using

activities 7 and 8.

7. Based on Michael's advice to Caleb, what had Michael learned about the heart?

"For one horrible year," Michael shared, "I got married for the wrong reasons, ... and then got divorced for the wrong reasons. ... I thought I was just following my heart. ... You've got to lead your heart."

Leading your heart means
- Taking full responsibility for your heart's condition and direction.
- Realizing that you have control over where your heart is.
- Asking God for the power to guard or protect your heart by taking it off the wrong things and setting it on the right things.

**ADDITIONAL
LEADING YOUR
HEART SCRIPTURES**

1 Kings 8:61

Proverbs 23:17,19,26

John 14:27-28

Philippians 2:3

2 Timothy 2:22

James 4:8; 5:8

8. In the preceding list, identify the bulleted action(s) you will try. Pray about this statement: *If you choose to lead your heart to invest in your spouse, then your spouse is more likely to become your treasure.*

Love is a decision, not just a feeling. It is selfless, sacrificial, and transformational. And when love is truly demonstrated as intended, your relationship will change for the better.

Firefighting

COMPELLING COUPLES TO TRANSFORM THEIR MARRIAGES

Setting your heart on the right things should be a consistent commitment, not just a random attempt.

"Search me, God, and know my heart; test me and know my anxious thoughts. See if there is any offensive way in me, and lead me in the way everlasting."

PSALM 139:23-24, NIV

9. **If you were to put your heart under the same microscope as David did in Psalm 139—asking God to search you and know your heart—what would you discover?**

"Above all else, guard your heart, for everything you do flows from it."

PROVERBS 4:23, NIV

10. **How do the proverbs in the margin recommend that we guide our heart?**

"My heart is set on keeping your decrees to the very end."

PSALM 119:112, NIV

11. **What do you think the psalmist David meant in Psalm 119:112 when he determined to set his heart on God's decrees "to the very end"?**

"Listen, my son, and be wise, and direct your heart in the way."

PROVERBS 23:19, NASB

David was absolutely resolute, completely focused in the right direction, fully committed to God's ways for all his life.

Fireproof Now

Committing Through Reflection and Prayer

"Since, then, you have been raised with Christ, set your hearts on things above."

COLOSSIANS 3:1, NIV

Fireproofing your marriage takes a resolute commitment. Don't wait until doing the right thing feels right. Don't wait until you feel in love with your spouse to set your heart and invest in your relationship. Instead, start pouring into your marriage now. Reset the very coordinates of your marriage and invest in those areas in which your heart should focus.

A Prayer for a Transformed Heart

"[Love] bears all things, believes all things, hopes all things, endures all things. Love never fails."

1 CORINTHIANS 13:7-8, NASB

Lord Jesus, Master of our hearts,
We are desperate to see You reign in our marriages
with power and majesty.
We see the need to grow up emotionally
and become more intentional.
Lord, teach us to guard and lead our hearts
according to Your will.
This week give us the power to change old habits
and break free from old ways as we redirect
the coordinates of our hearts to You and one another.
Master of our lives, we ask for Your help and courage! Amen.

LIVING THE LOVE DARE THIS WEEK

As you begin *The Love Dare* readings this week, read:

Introduction and Days 1-5
Appendix 4 (give particular attention)

The Power of Influence

If you are not leading your heart, then someone or something else is. The people you listen to and the influences you allow into your life impact your destiny as a couple.

Ignite

Opening Thoughts and Conversation Starters

1. Enjoy letting your group get a glimpse of the story of your life and marriage.

   How did you meet your mate?

   What's one crazy thing you have done as a couple?

   Is there a couple whose marriage you admire?

"Therefore, submit to God. But resist the Devil, and he will flee from you."

James 4:7

Your Love Dares in Action

Days 1-5 in *The Love Dare* challenged you to live in kindness and patience with each other.

2. What was the most significant result of your Love Dare experience last week?

   How challenging was it "to demonstrate patience and to say nothing negative to your spouse at all"?

If the past week challenged you, realize that you have an enemy who detests your choosing to participate in this journey of demonstrating genuine love. You also have a God whose power is greater and who will honor your commitment to your marriage.

Love requires thoughtfulness on both sides—the kind that builds bridges through the constructive combination of patience, kindness, and selflessness. Love teaches us how to meet in the middle, to respect and appreciate how our spouse uniquely thinks.

Would you be surprised to discover that the success of your marriage is directly related to the influences around you? Look together at both the positive and negative influences on life and love.

3. **It is hard to grow a rose in a house fire! How does the metaphor of an out-of-control fire reflect the state of many marriages today?**

"A woman is like a rose. If you treat her right, she'll bloom. If you don't, she'll wilt."
MICHAEL IN FIREPROOF

How does our culture make it difficult to succeed in marriage?

Which of these influences do you think poses the greatest threat to marriages today?

_____ Media/Internet
_____ Relationships   _____ Money/debt
_____ Work   _____ Schedules
_____ Recreation   _____ Other:

Which ones also have potential for positive impact on relationships?

17

Gear Up

MOVIE MOMENTS

Watch **FIREPROOF**
clip 3, "He Said, She
Said/Phone Call."
Debrief using activity 4.

ENGAGING IN RELEVANT SCRIPTURE STUDY

As we look together at Caleb and Catherine's marriage, ask and answer for yourself, *Who or what is whispering in my ear?*

4. **What influences do you observe from Catherine's conversation with her friends? From Caleb's phone call to his father? In the folowing movie description, highlight positive influences and record negative influences for each spouse.**

Caleb and Catherine are pulling away from each other. Once Catherine was bolstered by her mother's counsel; now that support is gone. Harsh words, anger, and disrespect characterize her treatment of Caleb. The pressure of friends pulls Catherine away from Caleb and pushes her to consider divorce. Gavin represents all that seems to be lacking in Caleb.

Caleb's father and mother encourage and pray for him. Buying the boat is a higher priority to Caleb than to his wife. In a high-pressure job, Caleb finds a true friend in Michael. Michael's words and marriage are testimony to a redemptive, godly marriage. Caleb's anger, along with his Internet addiction, intensifies.

The Love Dare is part of what helped Caleb realize his need for God—and understand the only way he can love his wife unconditionally.

Well-meaning friends, in an attempt to look out for what is best for us, can become strong negative influences. Even some of Jesus' friends, seemingly out of love for Him, tried to talk Him out of going to the cross!

Are your closest friends champions for or enemies of your marriage? Choose your friends carefully.

> "Not everyone has the material to be a good friend. … In fact, anyone who undermines your marriage does not deserve the right to whisper in your ear."
>
> THE LOVE DARE, DAY 23

5. **What lies about marriage has the friend in this email bought into?**

Hey Dan
Thought I'd send you this email because I know you are going through some pretty difficult stuff. I know you're committed to marriage but if you are that unhappy, maybe you should just go ahead and divorce. I know you're concerned about your kids, but remember kids go through the divorces of parents and turn out fine.

Plus, if you really want to help them, you are going to have to find your joy, and it certainly seems like there's no joy in your marriage. Just some friendly advice …

> "[The Devil] is a liar and the father of liars."
>
> JOHN 8:44

6. **According to Proverbs 20:8, "A king sitting on a throne to judge sifts out all evil with his eyes." How does this proverb encourage a wise spouse to respond to negative influences in marriage?**

This proverb contrasts wisdom with foolishness. A wise spouse is able to recognize influences that could harm his or her marriage and quickly diverts attention from them ("sift out all evil with his eyes"). While some influences are easy to spot, others are much more challenging to recognize.

MORE ON POWER OF INFLUENCE

Proverbs 1:10-15

Proverbs 27:12

Ecclesiastes 4:9-10

Matthew 5:29

1 Corinthians 12:2

Acts 9:31

7. Look at your situation. As spouses, list the positive and negative influences on your marriage.

	Positive Influences	*Negative Influences*
Husband		
Wife		

FOR HELP, CONSIDER THESE VERSES

Titus 2:2-3

Proverbs 31:10-31

In the "He Said/She Said" clip, Caleb told Michael, "Our marriage has been fine until this year." Do you believe this to be true? Why or why not?

Caleb and Catherine's marriage had been eroding for some time, even though they were not aware of it. Genesis 3:1-6 reminds us how Satan uses subtlety and cunning to turn a spark of influence into an outright blaze!

Satan still whispers in our ears, "It won't hurt you"; "Did God really say that? He didn't mean it" and "No one will ever know." The enemy uses his knowledge of God and Scripture to plant doubts and to entice us in wrong directions.

8. What subtle sparks of negative influence did you note in activity 7? Do any have potential to become a roaring fire? Identify the risk on Today's Danger Level.

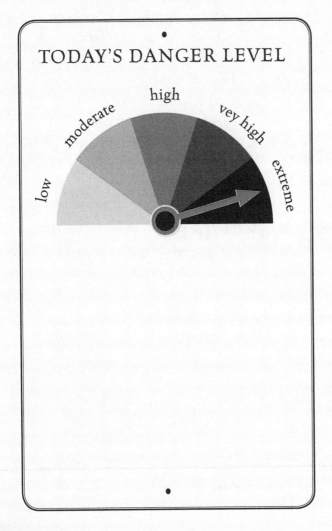

TODAY'S DANGER LEVEL

low   moderate   high   vey high   extreme

YOUR FIRE ESCAPE

"No temptation has overtaken you except what is common to humanity. God is faithful and He will not allow you to be tempted beyond what you are able, but with the temptation He will also provide a way of escape so that you are able to bear it."

1 CORINTHIANS 10:13

Firefighting

COMPELLING COUPLES TO TRANSFORM THEIR MARRIAGES

Recognizing the sparks that threaten to burn down our marriages is one thing. Extinguishing the blaze is something entirely different. It is critical that we pursue godly advice, healthy friendships, and experienced mentors to benefit from the wisdom they have gained through their own successes and failures.

Proverbs 13:20 tells us, "The one who walks with the wise will become wise, but a companion of fools will suffer harm." Who is qualified to speak into *your* marriage? How do you filter *your* friends?

"You must guard yourself against the wrong influencers. Everyone has an opinion and some people will encourage you to act selfishly and leave your mate in order to pursue your own happiness. Be careful about listening to advice from people who don't have a good marriage themselves."

THE LOVE DARE, DAY 35

Couple Questions:

• **Which couples do we know who bring a strong, positive mentoring influence to our marriage?**

• **How might we connect with them?**

Gaining wise counsel is like having a detailed road map and a personal guide on a long, challenging journey. It can mean the difference between continual success or marital failure.

Fireproofing your marriage is about embracing the power of influence by resisting negative hazards and inviting positive influences to speak truth into your life and marriage. This is one way you choose to lead your heart. When you do, you safeguard your covenant relationship and your marriage becomes a positive influence to others.

Fireproof Now

COMMITTING THROUGH REFLECTION AND PRAYER

9. If you were to express a personal commitment based on the word *love*, what might it look like? Note an action that reflects your heart's desire.

Lord, as I ask for godly influence to fireproof my marriage, I choose to …

__ *L*ove *my spouse by* …
choosing to listen to godly wisdom and the Word of God.

__ *O*bey *God by* …
making wise choices about friends, mentors, and companions in the workplace, in recreation, at church, and in other settings.

__ *V*alue *my marriage by* …
believing that God will honor my choice to stay within the covenant of marriage and by spending time and effort to make my marriage one that influences others in a positive way.

__ *E*xpress *these truths by* …
continuing in this Love Dare journey and valuing this time of renewal and challenge.

A Prayer for Godly Influence

Father God,
I pray that Your voice will be so prominent an influence
that my mind, will, and emotions will desire to relentlessly
pursue a God-honoring marriage.

I confess that my heart is easily influenced by lesser voices.
So give me an unfailing desire for Your ways, not mine.
Help me to seek Your truth, not a false, deceptive counterfeit.

Bring people into my life who will guide me
into a deeper love for You and my spouse. Amen.

LIVING THE LOVE DARE THIS WEEK

As you take a look at the next five love dares, continue
to take action! Encourage others in your group;
initiate conversations and emails during the week;
and pray for yourself, your spouse, and other couples.
Most of all, join God in His work to strengthen
marriages and see what happens. Live the dare!

This week in *The Love Dare* read and do:
Days 6-10

Honoring and Cherishing Your Spouse

SESSION 3

Learning to rein in negative thoughts and
focus instead on your spouse's positive
attributes will help you honor your
marriage in your heart.

As you place your marriage under the
shade of God's unconditional love,
His love will become your kind of love.

The footprints of the past often show up in the present. Even after many years, most of us vividly recall moments of rejection and fear as well as times of joy and honor.

1. Who was your greatest hero growing up?

Do you recall ever honoring or dishonoring someone in your heart?

> "Nobody can acquire honor by doing what is wrong."
>
> THOMAS JEFFERSON

YOUR LOVE DARES IN ACTION

The apostle Paul described love as "the most excellent way" (1 Cor. 12:31, NIV). We honor our mates with our unconditional love. As a couple, read these descriptors of love.

Love accepts the pain of the relationship.
Love listens to her anger.

Love smiles when she sees him.
Love is him looking deeply into her eyes in return.

Love shares intimacy through contact, both verbal and physical.
Love doesn't brag about the weight loss in front of the mate who needs to lose some weight too.

Love doesn't parade her talent in front of his inability.

Love doesn't remember all his past exploits and victories
  to make her feel lucky that he even sticks around.

Love doesn't complain about his wife.
Love doesn't rejoice in seductive images on TV.

Love believes in her husband and wants the best
  for him.
Love never gives up.

2. **How did you do with the Love Dare lists you created this week? (Days 6 and 7)**

   Can you think of a time you received the blessing of your spouse when you didn't deserve it?

   Share with the group a positive attribute of your spouse that you could write on your Appreciation Room walls? (Day 7)

Honor can be defined as holding someone in high esteem, viewing someone or something as rare or special. In contrast, opposites include strong words like *shame, despise, caring little for something,* and *disrespect.*

Gear Up

ENGAGING IN RELEVANT SCRIPTURE STUDY

3. **Highlight words in 1 Peter 3:7-8 (NIV) that describe a marriage of honor: "Husbands, in the same way be considerate as you live with your wives, and treat them with respect as the weaker partner and as heirs with you of the gracious gift of life, so that nothing will hinder your prayers. Finally, all of you, be like-minded, be sympathetic, love one another, be compassionate and humble."**

What is one result of a husband not being considerate of his wife?

Your spouse is as much a part of you as your hand, your eyes, or your ears. Honor (or the lack of it) becomes apparent in our conversations with one another—and with God. Our words, reactions, facial expressions, and tone of voice all shout a clear message to our spouses. They either say "You are priceless to me!" or "You are worthless to me!" In "The Big Fight" clip, watch for the message being communicated.

4. What do you think caused Caleb to explode?

MOVIE MOMENTS
Watch FIREPROOF
clip 4, "The Big Fight."
Debrief using
activity 4.

Everything in this scene screams "You're worthless to me!" What principles of honor do you think were destroyed?

As Caleb recovered at home from his heroic rescue, he reassured his mom that he really was OK—and let his dad know he will not give up on his marriage. In the latter conversation Caleb observed: "The newspaper called twice wanting an interview. It seems I'm a hero to everybody but my wife."

MOVIE MOMENTS
Watch FIREPROOF
clip 5, "A Hero to
Everyone." Debrief
using activities 5–7.

5. Do you know someone who went through a similar time of disappointment in marriage?

Why do you think it is so easy to lose the respect of our spouses?

6. Rate the honor in these statements (high or low). Rewrite one statement to reflect respect and honor.

_____ "She used to love to call me. Now it seems the only time she calls is when she wants something."

_____ "My husband is so selfish! He thinks clean socks just fly from the hamper to the washer and dryer, and then back to the dresser."

_____ "Making love ... It has turned into a duty. How can I enjoy intimacy with someone who drives me crazy?"

_____ "She's a total ditz when it comes to finances. She barely knows how to write a check, much less balance a checkbook."

Ephesians 4:25-27, 29 (margin) describes how foul language (corrupting talk, ESV; unwholesome talk, NIV) can become a habit, gradually eroding relationships.

7. What should come out of our mouths instead? Why? (Also see Eph. 4:15, right margin.)

What do you think is meant by verse 27, "Don't give the Devil an opportunity"?

Are there times you are more vulnerable to saying hurtful words to your spouse?

"*Since you put away lying, Speak the truth, each one to his neighbor, because we are members of one another. Be angry and do not sin. Don't let the sun go down on your anger, and don't give the Devil an opportunity. No foul language (emphasis added) should come from your mouth, but only what is good for the building up of someone in need, so that it gives grace to those who hear.*"

EPHESIANS 4:25-27,29

Jesus is the perfect example of viewing people as priceless and of great value—valuable enough to die for. He related to each person through a lens of honor and respect.

"But speaking the truth in love, let us grow in every way into Him who is the head—Christ."
EPHESIANS 4:15

8. **Depending on the lens through which you are looking and interacting, you are telling your spouse he/she is either priceless or worthless. Mark the column that indicates what you most frequently are communicating to your spouse in these areas.**

What I tell my spouse ...	You Are Priceless!	You Are Worthless!
By my words		
By how I treat his/her body		
By how I meet needs		
By how I make requests		
By my behavior in conflict		
By keeping my commitments		

The Bible tells husbands to love their wives in the same way Christ loved the church (Eph. 5:25). When you love and honor your spouse, you are honoring and respecting Christ. The opposite is also the case.

Firefighting

COMPELLING COUPLES TO TRANSFORM THEIR MARRIAGES

WORDS/ACTIONS TO AVOID IN CONFLICT:

- "Always"
- "Never"
- "You" statements
- Name-calling
- Demands
- Threats

"Let marriage be held in honor (esteemed worthy, precious, of great price, and especially dear) in all things. And thus let the marriage bed be undefiled (kept undishonored); for God will judge and punish the unchaste [all guilty of sexual vice] and adulterous."

HEBREWS 13:4,
THE AMPLIFIED BIBLE

CONFLICT IS INEVITABLE

When you tied the knot as bride and groom, you joined not only your hopes and dreams but also your hurts, fears, imperfections, and emotional baggage. From the moment you unpacked from your honeymoon, you began the real process of unpacking another person.

"Pretty soon your mate started to slip off your lofty pedestal, and you off of theirs. The forced closeness of marriage began stripping away your public façades, exposing your private problems and secret habits. Welcome to fallen humanity" (*The Love Dare*, Day 13).

9. **How do you handle conflict in your marriage? Identify all the ones that apply.**

___ Escapism	___ Loving acceptance
___ Denial	___ Sarcasm
___ Brutal honesty	___ Substance abuse
___ Angry attacks	___ Long talks
___ Surrender	___ Humble apology

Using Hebrews 13:4 as a guide (margin), what are some practical ways you might esteem or highly value your marriage?

Fireproof Now

COMMITTING THROUGH REFLECTION AND PRAYER

HONOR RISKS TO MEET NEEDS

King David experienced the honor of his closest companions during battle: " 'Oh, that someone would get me a drink
of water from the well near the gate of Bethlehem!" So the
three mighty warriors broke through the Philistine lines,
drew water from the well near the gate of Bethlehem and
carried it back to David" (2 Sam. 23:15-16, NIV).

David didn't ask anyone to act but the mighty men
observed and listened. With great valor and honor, at the
risk of their lives, they acted to fulfill the need.

**10. What do you think that kind of honor would
feel and look like in your marriage?**

In session 2 you were introduced to the LOVE acrostic as
one means of expressing your personal commitments. In
our closing time together, complete "Love my spouse by ... "
with your own actions.

Lord, as I ask for godly influence to fireproof my marriage, I choose to …

__ *L*ove my spouse by …

__ *O*bey God by …
lavishing honor upon my mate even when it seems difficult or irrational.

__ *V*alue my marriage by …
allowing nothing to move this covenant I've made to my spouse and to God.

__ *E*xpress these truths by …
seeking real peace and contentment, knowing true pleasure follows the one I honor.

A Prayer for a Servant Heart

Heavenly Father, I choose to make my expression of love to my mate in a way that leads to greater intimacy with You. I am powerless to do this in my own strength. I need You! Teach me, Jesus, to revel in the life of a servant. Amen.

LIVING THE LOVE DARE THIS WEEK
This week in *The Love Dare* read and do:

Days 11-15

Living with Understanding

We enjoy discovering as much
as we can about the things we really
care about. You are challenged to earn a
lifelong doctoral degree in the study of
your spouse—a wonderfully complex
creation of God.

OPENING THOUGHTS AND CONVERSATION STARTERS

> "The difference between the right word and the almost right word is the difference between lightning and the lightning bug."
>
> MARK TWAIN

1. Share a humorous story of miscommunication in your marriage. What false assumptions did you have?

Do you or your spouse have code words that mean something to you but not to anyone else?

YOUR LOVE DARES IN ACTION

Last week you were invited to read and do the love dares for days 11-15.

2. What are you learning about love?

About communication?

> "*Agape* love is 'in sickness and health' love, 'for richer or poorer' love, 'for better or worse' love."
>
> THE LOVE DARE, DAY 10

Phileo and *eros* describe the kind of love that is responsive in nature and that fluctuates based on feelings or circumstances. *Agape* love is selfless and unconditional. You are being challenged to "Agape Love" your spouse.

The Bible tells us, "In this is love, not that we loved God, but that He loved us and sent His Son to be the propitiation for our sins" (1 John 4:10, NASB). God doesn't love us because we are lovable but because He is so loving. Unconditional love is God's kind of love.

A METAPHOR THAT'S TOO REAL

Some days life seems like a jigsaw puzzle. We try to put it all together but all we see are seemingly unconnected pieces.

3. **A talk show host once had a segment called "Things that make you go *Hmm* …" What one thing about your spouse makes you go "*Hmm* … "?**

What do you think leads to misunderstandings in marriage?

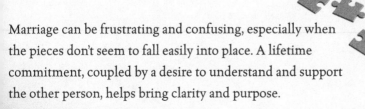

Marriage can be frustrating and confusing, especially when the pieces don't seem to fall easily into place. A lifetime commitment, coupled by a desire to understand and support the other person, helps bring clarity and purpose.

Gear Up

ENGAGING IN RELEVANT SCRIPTURE STUDY

MOVIE MOMENTS

Watch FIREPROOF
clip 6, "Study Your
Spouse." Debrief using
activity 4.

The Holy Spirit worked in Caleb's life through *The Love Dare*. Watch the FIREPROOF clip for insights that began to impact Caleb's relationship with Catherine. Then think about your answers to these questions: *Do I know my spouse's greatest hopes and dreams? Do I fully understand how he or she prefers to give and receive love? Do I know my spouse's greatest fears and why they are a struggle?*

4. **Based on what you know about your spouse's likes and dislikes, what degree do you hold in your marriage?**

    ___ **A master's degree**
    ___ **A doctorate**
    ___ **A GED**
    ___ **I'm in remedial studies.**

Don't you enjoy discovering new things about your hobbies, passions, and interests? Of course you do! Make the same highly valued practice a part of your discovery of the most important person in your life.

A Portrait of Compassion

The first chapter of Mark (1:40-45) presents us with the picture of Jesus encountering a leper. In the first century a leper was an outcast of outcasts, a reject who not only suffered a horrible skin disease but also debilitating loneliness. Yet, in this setting, when "a leper came to Jesus" (NASB), the Lord showed compassion to him.

In the original language, the word *compassion* doesn't mean to feel sorry for a person. It doesn't mean pity, as some would imagine. Even the word *empathy* falls short. The word *compassion* means to actually get in the middle of the mess. Jesus was moved to take on the burden of the leper.

Jesus doesn't just want to connect physically or emotionally with us. He desires to be in the middle of our wreck.

DIG DEEPER

2 Kings 13:23

Nehemiah 9:27

Psalm 103:13

Isaiah 54:8

5. **Can you recall a time you seemed to physically feel your spouse's pain?**

In any marriage, there is no passion without compassion.

"A wise man will hear and increase in learning, And a man of understanding will acquire wise counsel."

PROVERBS 1:5, NASB

A person's heart is a guarded vault of priceless treasure. People tend to open their hearts only to those with whom they feel emotionally safe and completely trust. Is the heart of your spouse an open door to you or a closed wall?

6. **Why do you think it is so hard for some people to ask for help from their mates? Highlight attitudes that might contribute to this barrier.**

_____ **When I ask for something, I feel less independent.**

_____ **My spouse should be more perceptive and know what I need without my having to ask.**

_____ **I've tried to ask for things but always seem to be disappointed so I've stopped asking.**

_____ **I'm afraid she will hold it over my head if I ask for something.**

Is there anything you need from your spouse that you have not yet verbalized?

GOD WANTS MORE FROM US

"But God demonstrates his own love for us in this: While we were still sinners, Christ died for us."
Romans 5:8, NIV

The world's system proclaims that if someone wrongs you, then payback is coming hard and heavy. Our sinful nature causes us to retaliate. Yet God wants more from us!

"'An eye for an eye' religion? Not with Me," Jesus said many times in words and in action. Jesus' example of mercy and grace is foundational to living with understanding.

Firefighting

COMPELLING COUPLES TO TRANSFORM THEIR MARRIAGES

LEARN, LEARN, LEARN

The salt-and-pepper analogy in FIREPROOF is a great reminder of the uniquenesses of men and women—differences God has ordained since creation.

7. **Which perceived differences between men and women have you experienced personally? For one example, read "The Lost Wallet."**

The Lost Wallet

She was frustrated that I had lost my wallet. Again.

She's so organized and rarely loses anything. I must have walked around the block five times. *Why does she make me this crazy? Why can't I handle this?*

As I walked, I kept hearing, *You lose everything! Why can't you grow up and take responsibility for things! You are still a dumb scatterbrained, ADD kid. You'll never change!*

I began to realize it wasn't my wife's voice that was ringing in my ear; it was my dad's. Years of his constant frustration with me came back with a vengeance. Then I realized that this incident (the lost wallet) was really about that (a wounded child).

8. **What harmful baggage have you carried into your marriage that needs to be cast out? Does your spouse understand its impact on you?**

FOR FURTHER READING

- *The Five Love Languages*, Gary Chapman
- *The DNA of Relationships*, Gary Smalley
- *Captivating*, Stasi Eldredge and John Eldredge
- *Wild at Heart*, John Eldredge
- *For Men Only* and *For Women Only*, Shaunti Feldhahn
- *The Secret to the Marriage You Want*, Les and Leslie Parrott
- *The Family God Uses*, Tom and Kim Blackaby

"Wise men store up knowl-edge, [b]ut with the mouth of the foolish, ruin is at hand."

PROVERBS 10:14, NASB

PRACTICE LISTENING FIRST

"My dearly loved brothers, understand this: Everyone must be quick to hear, slow to speak, and slow to anger."
James 1:19

9. Practice by turning to your spouse and asking, "What is one thing that causes you concern in our lives?"

LISTENING TIPS
Your spouse wants to know you are listening. Sometimes that means to *not*
• give advice.
• try to "fix it."
• defend your view.
• even apologize until your spouse knows you have fully heard.

At the appropriate time, repeat what you have heard.

How difficult was it to listen without responding or trying to "fix it"?

INTENTIONALLY SHOW RESPECT

"Husbands, in the same way be considerate as you live with your wives, and treat them with respect as the weaker partner and as heirs with you of the gracious gift of life, so that nothing will hinder your prayers."
1 Peter 3:7, NIV

10. How can you show respect for your spouse's …

Time?

Needs?

Body?

Emotions?

Fireproof Now

COMMITTING THROUGH REFLECTION AND PRAYER

Prayerfully express your "Obey God by ..." action in such a way that you show compassion toward your spouse.

> Lord, as I ask for godly influence to fireproof my marriage, I choose to ...

__ *L*ove my spouse by ...
listening, really listening to what my helpmate is saying without immediately defending my own actions or judging.

__ *O*bey God by ...

"God, who knows secrets about us, loves us at a depth we cannot begin to fathom (Eph. 3:19). How much more should we—as imperfect people— reach out to our spouse in grace, accepting them for who they are and assuring them that their secrets are safe with us?"
THE LOVE DARE, DAY 17

__ *V*alue my marriage by ...
discovering new ways to love my spouse so that I show complete devotion to my mate.

__ *E*xpress these truths by ...
ordering my life to facilitate closeness in communication, physical touch, gifts, recreation, and intimacy and affection.

A Prayer for Understanding

Lord Jesus, my Designer and King,
I pray for divine insight and inspiration in my life.
Give me the discernment I need to bless my family and spouse.
Teach us both to live by faith, having the ability to navigate
through difficult issues and hard times.

Give us communication that isn't just surface talk. Help us
to spend our words wisely and listen with a heart of compassion.

You brought us together. You claimed us.
And we claim each other for the glory of Your Kingdom. Amen.

LIVING THE LOVE DARE THIS WEEK

This week in your *The Love Dare* readings, you will
be challenged further to become a true scholar of
your mate's needs, desires, and passions.

This week in *The Love Dare* read and do:
Days 16–20

Unconditional Love

SESSION 5

You cannot give what you do not have.
You must have the love of Christ before you
can truly give unconditional love
to anyone else.

We are to have a relationship with our spouse
that relentlessly, stubbornly,
sacrificially loves.

OPENING THOUGHTS AND CONVERSATION STARTERS

1. **When you entered the room today, someone gave you a gift. How did you feel? What did you do to deserve this gift?**

   Can you recall another time when someone gave you a no-strings-attached gift?

YOUR LOVE DARES IN ACTION

This past week you were invited to read and do the love dares for days 16–20.

2. **Day 16 challenged you to pray for your spouse's heart. As you feel comfortable, share one of the ways you are praying for your mate.**

   How does praying for your spouse change your view of your marriage?

Did you find time for a special dinner together (Day 18)? If so, share briefly.

Every couple experiences moments in marriage when love seems to fade. Life can beat us up at times, whether through a disappointing year or the death of someone we hold dear. In the midst of storms, couples may find themselves either pulling together or pulling away from each other.

We can lead our hearts to choose love. Yet, at the same time, the kind of love we need—love that is able to withstand every kind of pressure—is beyond our reach. We need someone who can give us that kind of love.

God is your source for unconditional love. As you walk with Him, He can give you a love for your spouse that you could never produce on your own. He wants to love your spouse through you.

The Bible clearly tells us, "God is love. When we take up permanent residence in a life of love, we live in God and God lives in us" (1 John 4:17, The Message). Allow those words to absorb you, to go down deep within you—much deeper than Sunday songs and bumper-sticker slogans.

God is love, and His love is unconditional. He's not a cosmic commando ready to fire spiritual missiles at you every time you mess up. God is not the enemy. He loves you. He is for you. And if you have never reached out to Him, know He has been reaching out to you your entire life.

3. **When have you felt the complete and total love of God?**

"Beloved, let us love one another, for love is from God; and everyone who loves is born of God and knows God. The one who does not love does not know God, for God is love. By this the love of God was manifested in us, that God has sent His only begotten Son into the world so that we might live through Him."

1 JOHN 4:7-9, NASB

In difficult times, do you and your spouse tend to cling to each other or claw at each other?

Gear Up

ENGAGING IN RELEVANT SCRIPTURE STUDY

MOVIE MOMENTS
Watch FIREPROOF
clip 7, "Trust Him with
Your Life." Debrief
using activity 4.

"I've bent over backwards
for (Catherine). I've tried
to demonstrate that I
still care about this
relationship. … I've
taken her insults and
sarcasm. But last night
was it. I did everything
I could to demonstrate
that I care about her, to
show value for her and
she spat in my face! How
am I supposed to show
love to somebody over
and over and over who
constantly rejects me?"

CALEB TO HIS FATHER
IN FIREPROOF

4. In this scene, where is Caleb coming from regarding his view of God and salvation?

Why do you think Catherine is so unresponsive to Caleb's attempts to complete *The Love Dare*?

How does the cross change our perspective about love?

"God demonstrates his own love for us in this: While we were still sinners, Christ died for us (Rom. 5:8, NIV). This is how we know what love is. Jesus Christ came to "seek and to save" *you* and *me* (Luke 19:10).

Jesus places a high commodity on love! His command (and example) to *Love one another* is a command that is above and beyond any commandment before or since.

Jesus tossed the old self-preserving, me-first mindset and calls us to be the most passionate, curiously peculiar lovers that the world has ever known. He taught: "Love your enemies. Help and give without expecting a return" (Luke 6:35, The Message).

His is the kind of love that makes a practice and a lifestyle of unconditional love. Such love goes deeper than appeasing, compromising, and tolerating. It runs beyond treaties, borders, and time limits. This love is a powerful, courageous love. It is putting skin and bones on this life called *Christianity*. Unconditional love endures. It hopes. It believes.

In other words, don't just practice this radical mission of unconditional love on the good days when the car works, the garbage has been taken out, and the kids are sweet and admirable. Don't just camp out in the wilderness of love. Build your home there.

"I give you a new command: Love one another. Just as I have loved you, you must also love one another. "

JOHN 13:34

"[Love] always protects, always trusts, always hopes, always perseveres. Love never fails."

1 CORINTHIANS 13:7-8, NIV

5. **Everyone has been touched by the pain and tragedy of divorce. In situations you know about, what was the major cause?**

___ Addictions	___ Abuse	___ Infidelity
___ Finances	___ Illness	___ Anger
___ Lies	___ Boredom	___ Other

Does unconditional love give up when things get tough? How does love respond, instead, to help heal these issues?

ATTRIBUTES OF UNCONDITIONAL LOVE

Unconditional love is steady and relentless.

6. In Revelation 2:2-4 (margin), Jesus speaks to the church at Ephesus about love. What is He saying about the relationship of His bride (the church) to Himself?

"I know your works, your labor, and your endurance, and that you cannot tolerate evil. You have tested those who call themselves apostles and are not, and you have found them to be liars. You also possess endurance and have tolerated many things because of My name, and have not grown weary. But I have this against you: you have abandoned the love you had at first."

REVELATION 2:2-4

Unconditional love is binding and unifying.

Read Romans 8:38-39 (margin).

Unconditional love goes above and beyond reasonable expectations.

"For I am persuaded that not even death or life, angels or rulers, things present or things to come, hostile powers, height or depth, or any other created thing will have the power to separate us from the love of God that is in Christ Jesus our Lord!"

ROMANS 8:38-39

Unconditional love is a rare commodity these days. People love when they receive love. They love when they are treated as lovely.

However, unconditional love isn't bartered love, traded on the open market. It is the kindness of the Samaritan who ministers to a beaten man whose nature is to despise him. Love is a woman at the end of her desperate rope, breaking and pouring her life savings to honor the life of her friend. Love is offering dying mercy to a criminal in his final hour—the last person to whom you would want to extend kindness and hope and grace.

7. **Read the parable of the lost son in your Bible (Luke 15:11-32). Who are the main characters?**

   Who personifies conditional love? Who personifies unconditional love?

8. **How can you best communicate unconditional love to your spouse?**

   When he or she fails?

   When he or she seems unlovable?

   When you feel like giving up?

Remember your vows! When you married, did you vow to love your spouse when you felt like it; or in sickness and in health, for richer and for poorer, for better or for worse?

FIREPROOF

The Love Dare Bible Study

COMPELLING COUPLES TO TRANSFORM THEIR MARRIAGES

> "Wives, submit to your own
> husbands as to the Lord,
> ²³for the husband is the
> head of the wife as Christ
> is the head of the church.
> He is the Savior of the body.
> Now as the church submits
> to Christ, so wives are to
> submit to their husbands in
> everything. Husbands, love
> your wives, just as Christ
> loved the church and gave
> Himself for her."
>
> EPHESIANS 5:22-25

BRINGING UNCONDITIONAL LOVE HOME

A godly marriage is a metaphor of unconditional love.

9. Read Ephesians 5:22-25 (margin).

Who sacrifices in this passage?

Who serves in this passage?

Are the roles different? How?

What is more sacrificial—the wife who is called by God to respect the leadership of her imperfect husband or the husband who is called to love his imperfect wife so much he would die for her? Both require you to die to self and to put another person's needs above your wants.

> "Just as the Father has loved
> Me, I have also loved you;
> abide in My love. If you
> keep My commandments,
> you will abide in My love;
> just as I have kept My
> Father's commandments
> and abide in His love."
>
> JOHN 15:9-10, NASB

This type of love is impossible apart from a close relationship with Jesus Christ. When we walk with Him on a daily basis, His Holy Spirit pours out unconditional love in our hearts (Rom. 5:1-5; Gal. 5:22-23). Then we can love our spouse and others with that love. Jesus modeled the servanthood required for a marriage to work, in Philippians 2:5-11, As you look over this passage, you will see Him consistently put the needs of others above His own rights.

Fireproof Now

COMMITTING THROUGH REFLECTION AND PRAYER

As you make your personal commitments to your spouse and your marriage, do so in light of Philippians 2. Continue filling out your own LOVE acrostic, this time looking at the letter V and "Value my marriage by ..." What better way to value your marriage than by committing to a lifestyle of unconditional love. Record your commitment(s).

"He humbled himself by becoming obedient to death—even death on a cross!"

PHILIPPIANS 2:8, NIV

Lord, as I ask for godly influence to fireproof my marriage, I choose to ...

__ *L*ove my spouse by ...
being accepting and open, trusting God to renew my mate into the person He has called.

__ *O*bey God by ...
accepting the role of a servant toward my beloved and practicing the art of agape love.

__ *V*alue my marriage by ...

__ *E*xpress these truths by ...
offering love as an act of worship to God and covenant to my mate.

A Prayer for Selfless Love

Lord Jesus, Son of God,
How rich is Your mercy toward me!
How amazing Your grace! In times when
I turn my back on You, You relentlessly reach out
to me. So much love, Lord Jesus.
It is hard to take it all in.

You loved me unconditionally when You broke the bread
and offered the cup of forgiveness.
Thank You, Jesus, Son of God.

Give me the courage to follow You into a selfless
love affair with my spouse. From this day forward, love my mate
through me. Amen.

LIVING THE LOVE DARE THIS WEEK

This week you will be challenged to go deeper into
a more intimate spiritual relationship with Christ
and in your partnership with your spouse. You will
be challenged to get out of your comfort zone spiritually. Take the leap! It's worth it!

**Continue your journey this week by reading
and doing:**
Days 21–25

Walking in Forgiveness

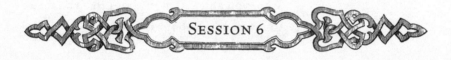

Complete forgiveness means holding
nothing between you and your spouse and
deciding, "I will make a daily commitment
to practice forgiveness as a lifestyle."

1. Take a few minutes to share the most unusual or funny accident you have ever had.

   What was damaged?

   Were you able to laugh about it at the time? Can you laugh about it now?

   Did you have to apologize to anyone?

Accidents happen and we sometimes have to apologize for unintentional actions or outcomes. It's easy to become defensive about our actions when life seems to fall apart. You may have heard (or even said!) such things as "I apologize even though I wasn't at fault." "Look, if you want an apology, here goes: Sorry!"

YOUR LOVE DARES IN ACTION

You were challenged last week to ask God to reveal areas in which you struggle to do the right thing.

2. What did God show you?

   How did you wrestle with those areas of struggle last week?

What did you discover about expectations you place on yourself? On your spouse? On God?

Great marriages don't happen because couples stop sinning and failing one another; that's impossible. Great marriages happen because couples learn to never stop apologizing and forgiving one another. When couples don't forgive and mercy runs out, things like this begin to happen:

> How long do I live like this? I can't seem to do anything right. I walk on eggshells afraid that I'll mess up. And when I feel like that, I'm not able to share anything real with her. Even intimacy seems forced and cold.
>
> Where did I go wrong? Lord, can you really give us a new start because it doesn't seem possible. We're so broken now. Some days it seems like we're just in this thing for the kids. (Anonymous)

3. **Why do you think it is so hard for some couples to get back to a place of romance and health in their marriages?**

Couples can reconcile even after being devastated by affairs, addictions, or "irreconcilable differences." However, there is one universal factor that is required for any marriage turn-around: COMPLETE FORGIVENESS.

Gear Up

ENGAGING IN RELEVANT SCRIPTURE STUDY

MOVIE MOMENTS
Watch FIREPROOF
clip 8, "Take All the
Time You Need."
Debrief using activity 4.

"Catherine, I'm sorry. ...
I have been so selfish.
For the last seven years
I've trampled on you
with my words and my
actions. I have loved
other things when I
should have loved you.
In the last few weeks
God has given me a
love for you that I've
never had before. I have

4. **How has Caleb's attitude changed since he began *The Love Dare*?**

What's the difference between forced apologies and the attitude Caleb expresses in this scene?

Circle the adjectives that best describe Caleb's attitude in this scene.

Showy	Insincere	Remorseful
Scared	Peaceful	Sarcastic
Flexible	Angry	Vindictive

When it comes to apologizing, do you consider yourself strong or weak? Why?

5. How does unforgiveness affect you:

Physically?

Emotionally?

Spiritually?

Sexually?

In your relationship with your friends?

In your relationship with your kids?

> asked Him to forgive me and I am hoping and praying that somehow you would be able to forgive me too. I do not want to live the rest of my life without you."
>
> CALEB TO CATHERINE, IN FIREPROOF

THE IMPACT OF UNFORGIVENESS

Unforgiveness causes bitterness and poisons every area of our lives. Physically it raises our stress level, hardens our facial features, and lowers our resistance to disease. Emotionally it makes us perpetually angry, irritable, and drained. It also is damaging spiritually.

When Jesus commands us to forgive from our heart, He is teaching us to live the way God lives while also protecting us from the poison of bitterness.

In Jesus' vivid parable of forgiveness (Matt. 18), did you notice the denominations of money mentioned? The servant owed the king 10,000 talents, a debt he would not be able to pay in 1,000 lifetimes.

In the same passage an acquaintance of the servant owed his peer 100 denarii, practically one-third of a man's yearly earnings.

> "Whenever you stand praying, if you have anything against anyone, forgive him, so that your Father in heaven will also forgive you your wrongdoing. But if you don't forgive, neither will your Father in heaven forgive your wrongdoing."
>
> MARK 11:25-26

6. What "100-denarii" debts do we owe in our marriages?

1 Denarius= 1 day's wage
1 Talent= 10 years' wage

What "10,000-talent" debts do we owe God?

"You will again have compassion on us; you will tread our sins underfoot and hurl all our iniquities into the depths of the sea."

MICAH 7:19, NIV

God doesn't skimp when it comes to forgiveness! The word *forgive* can be translated "pardon." According to Psalm 103:12, "As far as the east is from the west, so far has He removed our transgressions from us." God plunges our sins into the very depths of the sea.

FALLACIES OF UNFORGIVENESS

7. **Read these statements of forgiveness and discuss as a group or as couples why they simply are not true.**

   "When I say I'm sorry, you should forget about the problem that I created."

   "You shouldn't forgive until he has first apologized and fixed his problems."

   "Since she was 'more' wrong than I was, I don't have to apologize for my 'smaller' part."

   What other statements could you add?

8. Highlight the results of unforgiveness you have observed or experienced personally.

Pain   Isolation   Hate

Anger   Irritability   Bitterness

Sickness   Rebellion   Spiritual Dryness

WHAT DOES IT MEAN TO TRULY FORGIVE SOMEONE?

Forgiveness begins when you choose to treat another person the same way you want God to treat you. It's when you extend the same undeserved mercy God extended to you through the sacrifice of His Son. Forgiveness happens when you let God be the Judge of another and release all your anger and vengeance over to Him. It means that you set the offender free from the debt owed and let him or her out of the prison of anger you have kept in your heart.

Consider making this statement a habit in your life and marriage: "I will forgive others the same way that I want God to forgive me!"

"Be kind and compassionate to one another, forgiving one another, just as God also forgave you in Christ."

EPHESIANS 4:32

Know this, my beloved brothers: let every person be quick to hear, slow to speak, slow to anger; for the anger of man does not produce the righteousness of God.

JAMES 1:19-20, ESV

Firefighting

LEADING YOUR HEART TO FORGIVE

We can begin to start putting His pattern of love and forgiveness into practice in our relationships and attitudes.

"Christ has redeemed us from the curse of the law by becoming a curse for us, because it is written: 'Everyone who is hung on a tree is cursed.' The purpose was that the blessing of Abraham would come to the Gentiles by Christ Jesus, so that we could receive the promised Spirit through faith."

GALATIANS 3:13-14

9. Indicate one action you will attempt to put into practice in some area of your life next week.

___ Ask God to show you *why* you do what you do (**Ps. 139:23**).

___ Confess so healing can begin (**Jas. 5:16**).

___ Extend mercy and forgiveness to anyone who has hurt you (**Mark 11:25**). Say, "I forgive." We often carry guilt even after someone is deceased. We still need to forgive.

___ Receive forgiveness by accepting God's forgiveness and forgiving yourself (**1 John 1:9-10**).

___ Celebrate forgiveness with thankfulness and worship (**Pss. 30; 32**).

___ Make a commitment to never stop forgiving others (**Ps. 19**).

"[He] is able to do far more abundantly beyond all that we ask or think, according to the power that works within us."

EPHESIANS 3:20, NASB

The act of forgiveness begins and ends with complete surrender to Christ! As Galatians 3:13-14 and Ephesians 3:20 show (margin), when you surrender yourself to Christ, His power works through you. Yet, even at your very best, you are not able to live up to God's standards.

But with Him we can be freed and can forgive. That is how you love your spouse unconditionally.

COMMITTING THROUGH REFLECTION AND PRAYER

One way to express your commitment to walk in forgiveness is to let your spouse off the hook and accept him/her unconditionally—the same way Christ accepts you. It's time for you to write your own commitment for "Express these truths …"

Lord, as I ask for godly influence to fireproof my marriage, I choose to…

___ *L*ove my spouse by…
never allowing the sun to go down on my anger.

___ *O*bey God by …
following Christ's example of forgiveness in my marriage. I choose not to hold onto the past. I choose to forgive.

___ *V*alue my marriage by …
listening to my spouse and feeling the pain of my sin when I miss the mark. I will not defend my position but will seek to understand and take responsibility for my actions.

___ *E*xpress these truths by …

A Prayer for Forgiveness

*Father, The greatest miracle of my life is the wideness
of Your forgiveness. I am amazed by Your love for me.*

*I admit that there are times when I have wounded
and times when I have been wounded. I pray that
the grace, love, and forgiveness that flowed down
on me will also flow freely in my marriage.*

*Teach me how to forgive as I have been forgiven.
I pray that You will help me be the first
to initiate reconciliation in my home. Amen.*

LIVING THE LOVE DARE THIS WEEK

This week take the dare to express your love in a tangible
way to your spouse. Begin praying for inspiration and
creativity. Go all out as you live the dare!

This week in *The Love Dare* read and do:
Days 26–30

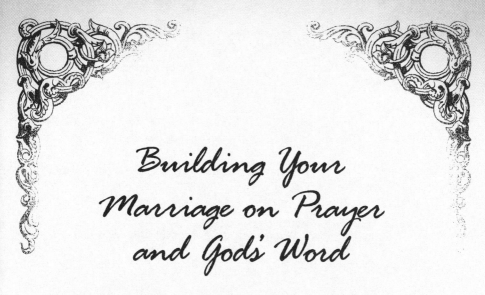

Building Your Marriage on Prayer and God's Word

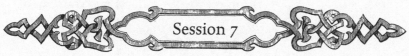

Session 7

Marriage is God's beautiful, priceless gift.
By remaining teachable, you learn to do
the one thing that is most important
in marriage—to love (1 Cor. 13:3).

Placing all aspects of your marriage
under the authority of God's Word
and prayer is the greatest decision
for ultimate marriage success.

Ignite

OPENING THOUGHTS AND CONVERSATION STARTERS

1. What were some favorite meals growing up?

What recipe disaster do you recall?

Do any recipes for disaster exist in life?

YOUR LOVE DARES IN ACTION

This past week, in days 26-30 of *The Love Dare*, you were able to spend some time talking together about past issues.

2. What types of issues did you face? Can you share any that you are facing together?

___ Financial   ___ Children
___ Communication   ___ In-laws
___ Trust   ___ Sexual
___ Behavior

What difference did it make when you gave attention to any unrealistic expectations you had been holding about your spouse? (Day 27)

Gear Up

ENGAGING IN RELEVANT SCRIPTURE STUDY

Ken:	Are you sure we can do this?
Ann:	Doug and Jane do it regularly. She says it's the best thing that's ever happened to their marriage.
Ken:	Really? That's what she says?
Ann:	You have to notice the improvement.
Ken:	So, they just walk in and say whatever's on their minds?
Ann:	Absolutely.
Ken:	What's he going to think?
Ann:	He already knows, I think.
Ken:	I feel inadequate and a little embarrassed. So, what are you going to say?
Ann:	I'm not sure. I don't know where to start either.
Ken:	Do we need to study a little more first?
Ann:	Ken, you know we need it. Let's just start.
Ken:	You're right. OK.
Ann:	Let's go.
Ken and Ann:	"Lord, we're here."

3. Why is it so hard for some couples to pray?

Prayer sets our directional course and power—the light on the runway; the communication with the control tower. Yet many people, like Ken and Ann in our dialogue, don't know what prayer is or how to begin, much less tap its vast resources. Prayer is direct communication with God.

MOVIE MOMENTS
Watch FIREPROOF clip 9, "Praying at the Cross." Debrief using activity 4.

4. In this clip, why do you think Caleb is so desperately pouring out his heart to God?

What happens when we begin to pray for our spouse this way?

Describe a time when you prayed for a breakthrough in your marriage.

Getting Started

1. Pray for yourself.
2. Pray for your spouse.
3. Pray together.
4. Pray with your family.

Prayer works. It's a spiritual phenomenon created by an unlimited, powerful God. And it yields amazing results.

Do you feel like giving up on your marriage? Jesus said to pray instead of quitting (Luke 18:1). Are you stressed out and worried? Prayer can bring peace to your storms (Phil. 4:6-7) Do you need a major breakthrough? Prayer can make the difference (Acts 12:1-17).

STRONG BUILDINGS

The Sermon on the Mount gives us a practical guide on which to build our marriages and homes.

> 5. Read Matthew 7:24-27. What principles from these verses apply to marriage relationships?

Failing to build on the right foundations is both foolish and dangerous. According to 1 Samuel 12:23: "I vow that I will not sin against the LORD by ceasing to pray for you. I will teach you the good and right way." Samuel pointed to prayererlessness as sin against God. We should pray *for* and *with* our spouses.

Samuel's call to prayer came to Israel on the heels of a terrible threat of war by a wicked kingdom. Saul called the men to war, but he was acting in self-confidence and he battled under the sole resource of his own strength. It was not enough and Samuel knew it.

We are called to cooperate with God in our personal battles. God wants us to join Him, but we often tell Him, "I'll fix it myself."

Prayer should be ...

Authentic

Strategic

Consistent

Biblical

Unlimited

Immediate

Passionate

What words would you
add as you encounter
God in prayer?

Prayer does not have to be complicated or sound pious with big religious words. It can be your simply sharing honestly with God about where you are and what you are feeling and needing. Don't try to impress anyone during prayer. Just be humble and honest before God.

MOLDING US FOR HIS PURPOSES

Building on the right foundation also means spending time in God's Word, the Bible. God's Word is how He reveals Himself to us.

One of the most impressive things about the Bible is the way it is linked together, with consistent themes, from beginning to end. Although written over a span of 1,600 years and composed by more than forty writers of various backgrounds, the Bible is sovereignly authored by God in one united voice.

The Bible is holy, inerrant, infallible, and completely authoritative (Prov. 30:5-6; John 17:17; Ps. 119:89). God continues to speak through truth to us today.

The Bible is profitable for teaching, reproving, correcting, and training in righteousness. These verses place a holy seal of approval on the Word of God for molding our lives and our marriages to Him.

> "All Scripture is inspired by God and is profitable
> for teaching, for rebuking, for correcting, for train-
> ing in righteousness, so that the man of God may be
> complete, equipped for every good work."
> *2 Timothy 3:16-17*

6. How has the Word of God ...
   • **corrected or rebuked you over the course
     of your marriage?**

- **trained** you to become a godly spouse?

- **equipped** you for every good work, including standing strong during a difficult season?

COUPLE TIME

7. **Share with each other three things you wish your spouse would begin to pray about for you.**

What dreams for the future do you have that will require prayer?

The Bible Is the Word of God.

If I ...
Believe its truth, I will be set free (John 8:32).
Hide it in my heart, I will be protected in times of temptation (Ps. 119:11).
Continue in it, I will become a true disciple (John 8:31).
Meditate on it, I will become successful (Josh. 1:8).
Keep it, I will be rewarded and my love perfected (Ps. 19:7-11; 1 John 2:5).

FROM "THE WORD OF GOD IN MY LIFE," APPENDIX IX, THE LOVE DARE

Husbands and wives bring their own cultural traditions and family habits into marriage. They have ideas about how their new home should operate. The most unifying practice is to filter all these traditions and ideas through the Word of God and let its voice bring direction for how they live as a couple and as a family.

Firefighting

COMPELLING COUPLES TO TRANSFORM THEIR MARRIAGES

TEST YOUR FAMILY INFLUENCES

Do this exercise separately and talk about your answers as a couple. Note the letter(s) that represent sources of strong influence on each area of your marriage and family life. For example, if your views on roles are based on what your parents believed, write the letter F.

C - Culture
F - Family Traditions
P - Personal Preferences
G - God's Word

Family values/priorities: _____

Family goals/directions: _____

Roles of husband and wife: _____

Our view of marriage: _____

How we work through conflict: _____

Child-rearing: _____

Financial decisions: _____

Our sexual relationship: _____

Fireproof Now

COMMITTING THROUGH REFLECTION AND PRAYER

As you express your commitments, be assured that prayer and God's Word are your power source to accomplish those commitments, not just to your spouse but to Him.

Lord, as I ask for godly influence to fireproof my marriage, I choose to …

___ *Love my spouse by …*

___ *Obey God by…*

___ *Value my marriage by…*

___ *Express these truths by …*

A Prayer for Pursuing God

Father God,
I am so often tempted to act rather than pray!
Forgive me for the busy, distracted life that I often live outside the
bounds of your Word and Your voice.
I choose today, to seek You first.

First before self-saving actions
First before urgent voices that pull me out of Your presence
First before the opinions of others
First before my hunger to be seen or admired.

I declare Your Word as faithful and true. You are my foundation,
my light, my direction, and my hope. Help us to quit making our
marriage about us. It's all about You. Amen.

LIVING THE LOVE DARE THIS WEEK

We challenge you to pray with your spouse tonight
before going to bed. Pray about the three items each
of you shared during this session. Then make this a
new habit in your marriage!

This week in *The Love Dare* read and do Days 31-35.
As we approach the end of an incredible journey,
remember that day 40 is just as important as day 1.

Establishing a Covenant Marriage

SESSION 8

Marriage is holy matrimony, a covenant
relationship in which God is glorified.
When your wedding vows are expressed
to Him as well as to one another,
your marriage honors God and
is a testimony to others.

Ignite

OPENING THOUGHTS AND CONVERSATION STARTERS

In marriage we learn a lot about each other through the daily activities of living.

1. **Share a few "unwritten rules" in your marriage. Is there a story behind any of them?**

   What is the most serious contract you have ever signed?

YOUR LOVE DARES IN ACTION

As you live out the principles in Days 31-35 of *The Love Dare*, you continue to lead your heart to forgive, honor, and unconditionally love your spouse.

2. **So far, which dare has had the greatest positive impact on you and your marriage? Share with your group.**

   What characteristics of Christlike behavior did you observe and affirm in your mate this week?

   How are you relying more on your spouse's input and concerns as together you face critical decisions?

Gear Up

ENGAGING IN RELEVANT SCRIPTURE STUDY

We live in a world of prenuptials, starter wives, and no-fault divorces. Marriage is viewed as a piece of paper, a contract. By definition, a *contract* is a means of setting legal accountability and limited liability; of making certain that first and foremost our own issues are addressed, and of ensuring that someone adheres to certain minimum requirements. A contract must be in writing because it is built around distrust and can be broken by mutual consent.

3. **What dangers do you see in applying a contract mentality to your marriage?**

Have you ever had to break a contract?

Throughout history, God has initiated loving, trusting, permanent relationships with His people. He makes verbal promises called *covenants* for our good—promises He has never broken and will never break. Our God is a covenant-making God.

In the margin note examples of biblical covenants. Have you ever noticed how a covenant is often marked by a symbol (circumcision, a rainbow, Passover cup and bread)?

COVENANTS

NOAH: God would never again destroy all humanity by flood.

ABRAHAM: An entire nation would come from his descendants.

MOSES: Israel would be God's special people.

DAVID: A ruler would sit on his throne forever, and the Messiah would come from his lineage.

NEW COVENANT: Jesus' blood provides forgiveness and eternal life to those who believe in Him and His saving work.

MOVIE MOMENTS

Watch FIREPROOF
clip 10, "Renewing Vows."
Debrief with
activity 5.

4. **What symbol do we normally associate with a marriage covenant? For what reason?**

5. **How do you think this renewal of wedding vows was different from the vows Caleb and Catherine exchanged to start their marriage?**

"[God] *no longer respects your offerings or receives them gladly from your hands. Yet you ask, 'For what reason?' Because the Lord has been a witness between you and the wife of your youth. You have acted treacherously against her, though she was your marriage partner and your wife by covenant.*"

MALACHI 2:13-14

Read Malachi 2:13-14 (margin). What do you think it means that God is "a witness" to our vows? What difference does that make?

Intentionally or not, even the act of writing our own vows is evidence to the fact that we have begun to define marriage in our own terms. For God to "witness" our vows (Mal. 2:14), means that the vows we make to our spouse, we are also making to God. We are creating a covenant between ourselves, God, and our spouse that is not to be broken—ever.

A Lifelong Covenant Marriage Means ...

Lifelong Companionship
The marriage relationship is a gift that offers rich, deep, and meaningful companionship for a lifetime (Gen. 2:22-24).

6. **How do you think this kind of companionship compares to simply enjoying time together?**

    What do Jesus' words in Matthew 19:6 (margin) indicate about the nature of the bond between husband and wife?

"Then the LORD God made the rib He had taken from the man into a woman and brought her to the man. And the man said: This one, at last, is bone of my bone, and flesh of my flesh; this one will be called 'woman,' for she was taken from man. This is why a man leaves his father and mother and bonds with his wife, and they become one flesh."

GENESIS 2:22-24

Lifelong Support
"Two are better than one, because they have a good return for their work: If one falls down, his friend can help him up. But pity the man who falls and has no one to help him up!"
Ecclesiastes 4:9-10, NIV

7. **How have you experienced or observed other couples experiencing the support of which Ecclesiastes 4:9-10 speaks?**

"So they are no longer two, but one flesh. What therefore God has joined together, let no man separate."
MATTHEW 19:6, NASB

What is God seeking in this verse?

"Has not the one God made them you? You belong to him in body and spirit. And what does the one God seek? Godly offspring. So be on your guard, and do not be unfaithful to the wife of your youth" (Mal. 2:15, NIV).

MARRIAGE
VOWS ARE …
Premeditated
Publicly spoken
Witnessed by others

Covenant marriage doesn't just provide support for each spouse, but also for children. God's plan for procreation is within the one-flesh, for-a-lifetime covenant of marriage.

How can husbands and wives support each other in:

Parenting   Spiritual Intimacy

Vocation   Finances

Health   Forgiveness

Habits/Addictions   Lifelong Strength

8. **Can you recall a time you were stumbling through difficult circumstances and your spouse was able to encourage you, "warm you," or even battle on your behalf, as Ecclesiastes 4:11-12 (margin) mentions?**

"Also, if two lie down together, they will keep warm. But how can one keep warm alone? Though one may be overpowered, two can defend themselves. A cord of three strands is not quickly broken.

ECCLESIASTES 4:11-12, NIV

Lifelong Accountability

"Therefore, I urge you, brothers, in view of God's mercy, to offer your bodies as living sacrifices, holy and pleasing to God—this is your spiritual act of worship. Do not conform any longer to the pattern of this world, but be transformed by the renewing of your mind. Then you will be able to test and approve what God's will is—his good, pleasing and perfect will."

Romans 12:1-2, NIV

MARRIAGE VOWS ARE …
Legally binding
Spiritually binding
Physically binding

9. **According to Paul's challenge in Romans 12, how do you think the big picture of following Jesus is enhanced by covenant marriage?**

"Make your own attitude that of Christ Jesus: who, being in the form of God, did not consider equality with God as something to be used for His own advantage. Instead He emptied Himself by assuming the form of a slave, taking on the likeness of men."

PHILIPPIANS 2:5-7, NIV

Can you recall a time when your spouse helped you maintain an attitude of servanthood, as described in Philippians 2:5-7 (margin)?

Firefighting

COMPELLING COUPLES TO TRANSFORM THEIR MARRIAGES

"Rejoice in the wife of your youth … Be exhilarated always with her love."

PROVERBS 5:18-19, NASB

John 10:10 tells us that while the thief comes to kill, steal, and destroy, Jesus comes so we might have life abundant.

10. Take a moment to list ways the thief (Satan) can kill, steal, and destroy the covenant of marriage.

"God … richly provides us with all things to enjoy."

1 TIMOTHY 6:17

What do you think abundant life might look like in a covenant marriage?

Marriage should be fun! Covenant marriage takes that joy to even deeper, more enriching dimensions. The relationship Caleb and Catherine discovered is characterized by both transformation and surrender.

"Make my joy complete by being like-minded, having the same love, being one in spirit and purpose."

PHILIPPIANS 2:2, NIV

Husbands: What would happen in your marriage if you devoted yourself to loving, honoring, and serving your wife in all things?

Wives: What would happen if you made it your mission to do everything possible to promote togetherness of heart with your husband? (*The Love Dare*, p. 147)

When couples live out their marriage this way, it is truly holy matrimony. Scripture teaches that covenant marriage is a clear picture of the relationship of God the Father to God the Son and of Christ to His bride, the church (1 Cor. 11:3; Eph. 5:22-25).

COMMITTING THROUGH REFLECTION AND PRAYER

11. **In what ways can you picture your marriage becoming a testimony to others?**

When your covenant vows are vertical, expressed to God as well as to your spouse, then your marriage becomes a testimony to the world of the glory of God.

Lord, as I ask for godly influence to fireproof my marriage and those of this group, I choose to …

___ *L*ove my spouse by …

___ *O*bey God by …

___ *V*alue my marriage by …

___ *E*xpress these truths by …

A Prayer for Covenant Marriage

Father God,
We are a group that wants to follow You
in authentic relationships and covenant.
We need You to sharpen our vision and restore
the brokenness we encounter deep within our spirits.

We need the unity that only You can bring.
We need to follow You with unswerving loyalty
so we are asking for Your strength and the
transformation that is offered in Your world.

Without You, how can we promise anything?
We are desperately dependent on You.

Give us passion and strength to fireproof our marriages
In the name of Jesus, Amen.

Catherine:
 "So what day are
  you on?"
Caleb:
 "43."
Catherine:
 "There are only 40."
Caleb:
 "Who says I have
  to stop?"

KEEPING THE LOVE DARE ALIVE

Prepare for a life-changing experience of the
reaffirmation of your vows to each other and to
God. Create or participate in an experience you
will treasure forever.

Who says you
have to stop?

Finish this group process by completing your
readings and love dares for Days 36-40.

Leading a Small Group

As a leader, you can never transform a life. You must lead your group into the power of redemptive community, trusting the Holy Spirit to do the work of transformation along the way.

Each meeting should feel like a conversation, not a classroom lecture. Be careful not to say something like, "Now we're going to answer the 'Gear Up' questions." Don't be afraid of silence. If you create an environment where you fill silence, group members will quickly learn they need not join in.

Every group has individuals who tend to dominate. This is unhealthy and frustrating for the group. Try to deal with this situation assertively yet politely, by saying something like, "Thanks, Scott, for your thoughts. Now let's hear from someone we haven't heard from yet."

Each session contains more material than you can use in an hour. Interactive activities are boldface and numbered; if you do not have time for all parts, use only the main question.

If you have the option, extend to 90 minutes. If only one hour is available, try to at least extend sessions 1 and 8 to allow special touches (refreshments, evaluation, and so forth).

For some intense issues raised by the FIREPROOF, you may want to consider making professional referrals.

Power Truths from The Love Dare

For Session 2 review

DAY 1 *Love is patient:* Patience helps give your spouse permission to be human.

DAY 2 *Love is kind:* The kind spouse smiles first, serves first, and forgives first.

DAY 3 *Love is not selfish:* Loving couples are bent on taking good care of the other flawed human with whom they share life.

DAY 4 *Love is thoughtful:* Thoughtlessness is a silent enemy to a loving relationship.

DAY 5 *Love is not rude:* Good manners say to your spouse, "I value you enough to exercise self-control around you."

For Session 3 review

DAY 6 *Love is not irritable:* Love is hard to offend and quick to forgive.

DAY 7 *Love believes the best:* Rein in negative thoughts and focus on positive attributes of your spouse.

DAY 8 *Love is not jealous:* Because love puts others first, it refuses to let jealousy in.

DAY 9 *Love makes good impressions:* A good greeting sets the stage for positive and healthy interaction.

DAY 10 *Love is unconditional:* Love is not determined by the person being loved but by the one choosing to love.

For Session 4 review

DAY 11 *Love cherishes:* Just as you treasure your eyes and hands, treasure your spouse as a priceless gift.

DAY 12 *Love lets the other win:* The moment one says, "I'm willing to go your way on this one," the argument is over.

DAY 13 *Love fights fair:* Establish healthy rules of engagement.

DAY 14 *Love takes delight:* Accept this person, quirks and all.

DAY 15 *Love is honorable:* When people marry, each becomes "holy" to the other.

For Session 5 review

DAY 16 *Love intercedes:* Rather than scolding or nagging, try interceding for your mate in your prayer closet.

DAY 17 *Love promotes intimacy:* Reach out in grace and understanding, accepting your spouse and assuring him/her that any secrets are safe with you.

DAY 18 *Love seeks to understand:* Make your spouse your chosen field of study. Commit to really get to know him/her.

DAY 19 *Love is impossible:* *Agape* love is something only God can do. Yet He chooses to express His love through you.

DAY 20 *Love is Jesus Christ:* Jesus invalidated the idea that you are unloved. If you ever feel that way, look at the cross.

For Session 6 review

DAY 21 *Love is satisfied with God:* Stop expecting your spouse to fulfill you. Only God can as you depend on Him.

DAY 22 *Love is faithful:* Give undeserved love to your spouse because God gave undeserved love to you—repeatedly.

DAY 23 *Love always protects:* Protect your spouse's vulnerability by never speaking negatively about him/her in public.

DAY 24 *Love versus lust:* Like a warning light, lust alerts you to the fact you are not allowing God's love to fill you.

DAY 25 *Love forgives:* Great marriages are created by people who keep "no record of wrongs."

For Session 7 review

DAY 26 *Love is responsible:* Admit when you have failed and ask for forgiveness. .

DAY 27 *Love encourages:* Live by encouragement instead of expectations.

DAY 28 *Love makes sacrifices:* Love inspires you to say no to what you want and to say yes to what your spouse needs.

DAY 29 *Love's motivation:* When God is the reason for your love, your ability to love is guaranteed.

DAY 30 *Love brings unity:* Two distinct individuals are spiritually united into "one flesh" (Gen. 2:24; Mark 10:9, NIV).

For Session 8 review

DAY 31 *Love and marriage:* Leave. And cleave. And dare to walk as one.

DAY 32 *Love meets sexual needs:* You are the only person called and designated by God to meet your spouse's sexual needs.

DAY 33 *Love completes each other:* Joined together, you are greater than your parts.

DAY 34 *Love celebrates godliness:* Love rejoices in the things that please God.

DAY 35 *Love is accountable:* Spouses must pursue godly advice, healthy friendships, and experienced mentors.

DAY 36 *Love is God's Word:* When your home is founded on God's unchanging Word, it is ensured against destruction.

DAY 37 *Love agrees in prayer:* A man and woman who regularly pray together form an intense, powerful connection.

DAY 38 *Love fulfills dreams:* Sometimes love needs to be extravagant.

DAY 39 *Love endures:* When threatened or challenged, love keeps moving forward in faith.

DAY 40 *Love is a covenant:* Marriage as a covenant expresses, "I give myself to you and commit to this marriage for life."

The Love Dare Bible Study

Leader Guide

A Movie Synopsis

When he's battling blazes, Captain Caleb Holt adheres to the firefighter's adage to never leave your partner behind; at home, it's an altogether different story.

Caleb and his wife, Catherine, have been married for seven years; but lately arguments over career, housework, finances, and outside interests have driven them hopelessly apart. Just as Caleb and Catherine prepare to officially dissolve their marriage, Caleb's father, John, presents his son with a most unusual challenge: commit to a 40-day experiment called the Love Dare and take one last shot at saving his marriage.

Caleb agrees to take a chance on the Love Dare, despite being rejected by his skeptical, embittered wife. When Caleb asks his father how he can love someone who refuses to give him a fair chance, John explains that this is precisely the love that God shows for humankind.

With God's help, Caleb begins to understand what it means to truly love his wife. But is it too late to fireproof his marriage? Now the man who makes headlines for saving lives will fight to be a hero to the one person who matters most—his wife.

Small-Group Format

IGNITE (10 MIN.): Opening thoughts/conversation starters and, beginning with session 2, Love Dare review

GEAR UP (15-20 mIN.): Engaging in relevant Scripture study

FIREFIGHTING (15 MIN.): Helping couples transform their marriages

FIREPROOF NOW (10 MIN.): Committing through reflection and prayer

Get Started

Consider launching your study by watching FIREPROOF together in a home. Consider concluding with a covenant renewal ceremony. For small groups meeting in homes, this in an excellent marriage study; all you need is a TV/DVD system. You may want to use this study to start new groups.

Whatever your purpose, evaluate what is best for the busy couples you're trying to reach. To better reach people who are not church members, group couples according to the same age or life experiences. In a large-group setting, consider meeting around small tables with a facilitator to lead discussion. Men and women may want to process some activities separately.

Session 1

IGNITE: Enthusiastically welcome the group to *The Love Dare Bible Study* and distribute books. Introduce yourself and leaders. Use icebreakers to help couples get better acquainted. Keep **activity 1** lighthearted; emphasize of daring to think differently. Overview the Group Covenant, especially confidentiality.

As an option to *Describe a time you followed your heart and regretted it later*, give your own example. The group may not yet be ready to share at that level.

Hand out *The Love Dare* journals. Briefly discuss the format and how future sessions will have review time.

GEAR UP: Set up FIREPROOF if your group has not viewed it together. Movie Moments provide a way to examine biblical themes and issues and incorporate them into our relationships.

Clip 1 ("For Better or for Worse") reveals ways people think about love. The salt-and-pepper metaphor is powerful (Salt and pepper are always distinctive with unique purposes = God's plan from creation). Michael's gluing the shakers together introduces covenant marriage and the permanence of vows. Help couples examine their relationships by looking at what they treasure. Use Scriptures and **clip 2 ("Lead Your Heart")** to distinguish between following your heart and leading it.

FIREFIGHTING: At the appropriate time, ask a volunteer to read Psalm 139:23-24 aloud. Guide the group to personalize ways to guard their hearts and lead their hearts toward God.

FIREPROOF NOW: Each week a printed prayer captures potential commitments. As you conclude, pray for transformed hearts. Encourage spouses to pray for each other and the group.

Conclude: *As you start* The Love Dare *readings 1-5, discover what it means to practically live out leadership of your heart.* Highlight Appendix 4 and the Introduction.

Session 2

This session focuses on leading your heart by examining positive and negative influences. In advance, secure two roses and let one wilt (or microwave it.) Place both roses in a vase.

IGNITE: Welcome returnees and newcomers. Play "Hot Potato" and have the recipient answer a question.

Devote extra time to review, using "Power Truths from *The Love Dare*" (pp. 86-87). Share a story of encouragement.

GEAR UP: Showing the roses, say: *It's more than hard—it's impossible—to grow a rose in a house fire!* Continuing the firefighting motif, move to **activity 3**.

Use **clip 3 ("He Said, She Said/ Phone Call")** with **activity 4** to contrast cultural pressures with godly influences. Other movie themes are impact of words; respect; male-female differences.

Before **activity 8**, ask a volunteer to read Genesis 3:1-6 aloud. Spend time assessing how negative influences slowly erode a marriage. Remind the group that they lead their heart by replacing negative influences with godly ones.

FIREFIGHTING: Invite couples to discuss Couple Questions together.

FIREPROOF NOW: Introduce the LOVE acrostic as a way to express marriage commitments (**activity 9**). Explain: *You will build your own acrostic during this study.* Invite couples to gather and pray silently for godly influences as you direct them through this acrostic.

Love Dare Readings Challenge
Encourage: *Join God in His work to strengthen your marriage. Live the dare! Read and do days 6-10.*

Session 3

Place a sports award, plaque, or other recognition in a visible part of the room.

IGNITE:: Share a picture of yourself as a child or high-schooler. Be ready to indicate someone you admired as a child. Ask a couple to alternately read the modern love descriptors. Be affirming as you debrief with the "Power Truths."

GEAR UP: Be sensitive to the intense impact of **clip 4, "The Big Fight."** Be prepared to respond to thoughts and emotions. Enlist three volunteers to read a statement at the appropriate time, or prepare visuals. Ask volunteer 1 to read Honor defined: "Treating someone or something as rare or special"; follow with **activity 3**. Ask volunteer 2 to read "A man is about as big as the things that make him angry" (Churchill). Then watch clip 4 and do **activity 4**. Talk about how the rules of honor were totally destroyed in this scene.

Watch **clip 5**. Using Scripture and **activity 5-7**, discuss ways disappointment can creep into a relationship.

FIREFIGHTING: Suggest spouses use **activity 8** to evaluate their words and actions. Honor and respect play into how a couple handles conflict (**activities 9 and 10**). Before activity 10, call on volunteer 3 to read: "To say your mate should be "holy" to you doesn't mean he or she is perfect. … A person who has become holy to you has a place no one can rival in your heart." Help couples begin their LOVE acrostic.

FIREPROOF NOW: Remind couples: *If you are cherishing your spouse, you are honoring Christ!* Close with prayer.

Love Dare Readings Challenge
Remind: *The Love Dare is a book to be experienced. That is the way it works!*

Session 4

IGNITE: Enjoy couples sharing humorous missteps along the marital path. Review with **activity 2** and "Power Truths from *The Love Dare.*"

GEAR UP: Ask for ways couples have cleared up marital misunderstandings or false assumptions. Discuss **activities 4-6** in light of **clip 6** and Mark 1:40-45.

Option: Develop an Emotional Safety Meter. Have couples evaluate (1 not at all, 10 completely) the extent to which their spouse *Trusts Me Completely; Feels Emotionally Safe; Shares Feelings and Needs; Shares Secrets with Me; Knows I Will Not Humiliate or Reject Him/Her.*

FIREFIGHTING: **Activities 7-10** help couples learn about, listen to, and respect their spouses.

FIREPROOF NOW: Allow couples to continue their LOVE acrostics.

Love Dare Readings Challenge
Highlight Appendix 2, "20 Questions for Your Spouse."

Session 5

IGNITE: Without comment, hand everyone a small gift of the same value. To review, use questions in **activity 2** and the "Power Truths" chart.

GEAR UP: Set up Movie Moments **clip 7** and supporting activities: *Caleb has been doing The Love Dare for 20 days and he's about ready to toss the entire thing because Catherine is unresponsive.* Emphasize how this clip depicts the depth of God's unconditional love to us. Highlight ways the cross changes everything.. Watch for signs of conviction from anyone who is not a Christian, and be available to talk.

Allow couples quality time to unpack **activities 7 and 8**.

FIREFIGHTING: **Activity 9** can help couples see how each spouse sacrifices and serves out of unconditional love. Discuss contemporary examples.

FIREPROOF NOW: Allow couples to spend time on their LOVE acrostics as they discover ways to take unconditional love home. They can make new commitments or reaffirm earlier ones.

Conclude with worship and praise. Ask a few people to voice prayers, thanking God for the cross.

Love Dare Readings Challenge

Conclude: *Get out of your spiritual comfort zones next week with days 21-25! Watch what God will do!*

Session 6

As the group enters, play music about being sorry or apologizing.

IGNITE: To review, use questions in **activity 2** and "Power Truths from *The Love Dare*." Prompt brief sharing of issues couples have worked out together.

Discuss this statement: "Great marriages don't happen because couples completely stop sinning and failing one another. They happen because couples learn to never stop apologizing and forgiving one another."

GEAR UP: The apology scene, **clip 8**, sets up true sorrow and forgiveness in contrast to a forced apology. Exploring differences in Caleb from earlier scenes to this one should enable some couples to see their relationship in a new light. The contrast will be dramatic.

(Use the example of an X-ray of a broken bone: If something is broken, it must be set or will not heal properly.)

Emphasize being willing to ask and answer, What does it mean to truly forgive someone?

FIREFIGHTING: Allow spouses to assess practical ways, in **activity 9,** to lead their hearts to apply forgiveness.

FIREPROOF NOW: Suggest couples unpack the printed prayer for some new insights into forgiveness.

Love Dare Readings Challenge
Encourage the group to continuing praying for each other during the week. Dismiss: *This week, take the dare to express your love in a tangible way to your spouse!*

Session 7

IGNITE: Build on the fun as you transition to a heavy week of love dares. Goals are for couples to (1) begin praying for and with one another and (2) start building their marriage on God's Word.

To review, use questions in **activity 2** and "Power Truths from *The Love Dare.*" Affirm couples as they grapple with tough issues.

GEAR UP: Vary your teaching by asking an animated couple to present

the drama sketch to set up the focus on prayer. Don't assume everyone knows what prayer is or how to pray.

Clip 9 illustrates Caleb's heartfelt prayer of surrender to God, for Catherine to be saved, and for nothing he did to stand in the way. Help couples consider what can happen when they pray this way (**activity 4**).

You may want to give each couple a rock and a zip-lock bag of sand as they examine Matthew 7:24-27 (**activity 5**). Highlight: *Jesus contrasts two foundations for life: a secular view and a life based on God's truths.* Move into a look at the role of God's Word in marriage (**activity 6**).

FIREFIGHTING: Encourage couples to take the Test of Family Influences as spouses and to discuss their answers together. Debrief as a total group.

FIREPROOF NOW: Couples may want to write their LOVE acrostic commitment to each other based on what they hope to apply from this session. Announce plans for session 8.

Love Dare Readings Challenge
Draw attention to Appendices 1 and 3, *The Love Dare,* as additional content.

Session 8

Use Day 40 in your preparation. You may want to allow more time for this session. Gather items for Gear Up in advance.

IGNITE: Share rules developed over time in your marriage. If funny, share a story but stay on task. To review, use **activity 2** questions and "Power Truths from *The Love Dare.*" Allow a few to share their most meaningful dare.

GEAR UP: Bring a wedding photo and a legal document. Briefly talk about uniquenesses of a contract and a covenant, including biblical covenants.

Use **clip 10** and **activity 5** to examine the difference God makes in our marriages. Involve couples in examining the lifelong impact and benefits of a covenant marriage (**activities 6-9**).

FIREFIGHTING Use **activity 7, part 3**, and **activity 10** to help couples make day-to-day applications. *Option:* Invite couples to write Ten Commandments for their marriage, to build a hedge of protection. Like the biblical Ten Commandments, some statements should address their relationship with God and others, their relationship with each other.

FIREPROOF NOW: Ask individuals to develop their LOVE acrostic as a commitment and an action plan. Invite individuals, couples, or subgroups to share some commitments made. Ask the group to continue to pray for each other.

If planned, prepare your group for the incredible experience of reaffirmation to covenant marriage. Explain: *This event will not only be meaningful for you, but also for those who witness it.*

Love Dare Readings Challenge

Encourage: *Like Caleb, don't stop now, as some of the most enriching dares come after this session, in love dares 36-40. Celebrate the progress and continue your commitment.*

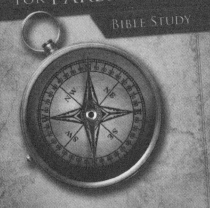

Newlyweds can travel anywhere in the world for their honeymoon.

But where should they go when it's over?

The LifeWay marriage site offers a variety of resources to help keep relationships going and growing. Discover books and Bible studies. Peruse magazine articles or respond to our new blog. And sign up for newsletters or a weekend event. Visit us today and see why our site is a favorite destination for married couples.

www.lifeway.com/marriage

LifeWay | Adults

Lottery

One of the Worst Threats to Our National Security

Tony Matula

authorHOUSE®

AuthorHouse™
1663 Liberty Drive
Bloomington, IN 47403
www.authorhouse.com
Phone: 1 (800) 839-8640

Published by AuthorHouse 07/24/2018

ISBN: 978-1-5462-0846-4 (sc)
ISBN: 978-1-5462-0844-0 (hc)
ISBN: 978-1-5462-0845-7 (e)

Library of Congress Control Number: 2017914220

Contents

From the Author

1957

This story begins to unfold on January 5th,

NOTE: Usama bin Mohammed laden Awad was born March 10th, 1957. Imagine that little bastard of a brat screaming already). In the Cold War period after World War II a United States foreign policy pronouncement by President Dwight D. Eisenhower, the Eisenhower Doctrine, promised military and/or economic aid to any Middle Eastern Country needing help in resisting Communist aggression. The doctrine was intended to check increased Soviet influence in the "Middle East". This influence resulted in the supply of arms to Egypt by Communist Countries. In addition, there was rising tension produced by recent Diplomatic bribes by Russia in the Middle East. The same year Russia had just completed the successful launching of "Sputnik", the first earth orbiting satellite. Beginning the space age.

It also resulted in strong Communist support of Arab States against an Israeli, French, British and American attack on Egypt in October 1956. Iraq, being one of those States.

Eisenhower proclaimed, with the approval of Congress, that he would use the armed forces to protect the independence of any Middle Eastern Country seeking American help. (All they had to do was to raise their hands.) America will now take the leading role in supplying military and or economic aid to those Middle Eastern Countries who want to thwart off Russian aggression and/or any Middle Eastern country that supports such aggression.

"LOTTERY" will take you to a chilling end that spans over 6 decades of Hatred-Revenge-Patriotism- *War & Love*-Murder-Suicide-Marriage Divorce-Illicit Affairs-Character Assassination-Money Laundering-Deceit-Fair Weather Friends-Lies and Truths, even among family & loved ones. And, what you are reading could become a reality and prove to be one of the biggest threats to The United States of America's National Security.

Eisenhower Doctrine signing "1957"

The Eisenhower Doctrine Read:

Authorize the United States to co-operate and assist any nations or group of nations in the general area of the Middle East in the development of economic strength dedicated to the maintenance of National Independence.

> *Authorize the executive to undertake in the same region*
> *programs of military assistance and co-operation with any*
> *nation or group of nations which desire such aid.*
> *Authorize such assistance and cooperation to include the*
> *employment of armed forces of the United States to secure and*
> *protect the territorial integrity and political independence*
> *of such Nations requesting such aid against overt armed aggression*
> *from any nation controlled by international Communist.*

The Eisenhower Doctrine, for the first time, drew lines between American Allies and American enemies in the Middle East, Below, the stark contrast of Iraq from ally in 1957 to enemy in 1958.

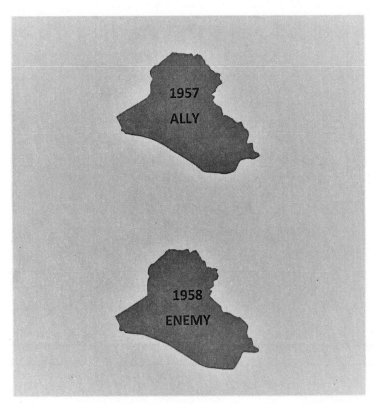

1957
ALLY

1958
ENEMY

Before and after the signing on the Eisenhower Doctrine.
"1957"/"1958"

As this Doctrine spreads thru the Middle East, which lies at the center of our earth, and, at it's very heart, (Iraq) the United States will become the EVIL EMPIRE and must be destroyed. Iraq, which is nestled between the 2 great rivers, Tigris and Euphrates, with shipping lanes going from the Persian Gulf to the Indian Ocean to Basra, is where the first codes of justice were laid down with in the walls of Babylon. Iraq will take a major role that will have you experience a mind blowing climatic event that will put you in a state of reality. Iraq is now, for the first time a legitimate enemy of the United States of America. Iraq is thrust into a non-ally relationship with the U.S.A., Russia begins to offer their support to Iraq. Iraq did not raise their hands. Iraq will be changing its colors and allegiance with the United States like everyone changes socks during the next 60 years. which you will travel thru up to the present date.

The news of the Eisenhower doctrine around areas of Iraq is read in some almost barbaric antiquated ways. No matter where the message went or how it was read, it always said the same thing, "The United States is an evil empire".

The reaction is swift, and as real soldiers do, put up their armor and their defense.

In this case, they smell blood, it's in their make-up. They are okay with cutting something off.

We take our selves into a middle class Iraqi farm house, and the lives of the renaissance of the characters and the roll they will play in achieving their goal of destruction of any size of The United States of America.

Our story begins.

We are in a 2-story farm house. The residents are somewhat well-to-do, the rugs alone take your breath away. The Patriarch Abdullah, addresses his progeny in the kitchen. You see and hear him yelling with rage at his youngest grandchildren, six-year-old Amirmoez and eight-year-old Darzi. *"You will move to the United States and your mission will be to live and take as many generations of our family necessary to destroy the United States of America and the evil vile of their ways".* As the elder's family, including his two sons, Aban, husband of Amira (She is the pretty one and has an ax to grind with America. Only to make herself look better).

And, is due to deliver a baby boy in the months to come. Their baby boy will be named Tawfeek. You hear and see her clapping and saying *"Yes, Yes, Yes"*! She will patronize for her own benefit and wants her husband to be the grand poo-pa. She will be seen over the next four decades in time taking control as she is by far the most "Western cultured' female in their family. And, Hakim, husband of Abida. (Abida is the name of both boys & girls) listen. They are hooting and hollering in joy and approval. Everyone except Gabir 58, The family Matriarch. She will not look at Abdullah, her back to him and facing the East. Toward Mecca. You can hear her soft voice in prayer. *"Oh, you who I believe, I see patience and perseverance. For you God. Are with those who patiently persevere."* Abdullah has gathered several extended family members and friends to hear his orders. As we begin to familiarize with this family, we see they have the money to pull this off and get a good start.

Abdullah throws out his last orders. "You must learn the English language". Instructing the wives to learn the language as well. But, convince every American they meet they only speak Arabic. To become flies in the enemy's ointment. The ointment intended to spoil the otherwise civilized way of life in America.

During this same period, Eisenhower's plate is full of other homeland distractions. And, Americans themselves are wrestling to keep that life of civilization secure. September 24th, the "Little Rock Nine" integrate Arkansas High School message. Eisenhower sends troops to quell the violent mobs and protect the students after Governor Orval Faubus defies Federal Orders by refusing to allow black Americans in the school.

The average American is ignorant to the tension and building of military aggression that has been blossoming at a rapid rate in the Middle East. On the flip side, America is transfixed on the Broadway debut of Lenard Bernstein West Side Story. Which it's production was one of the first to bring violence to the stage.

We take you back to Iraq and watch as the next few years go by and grasp the relentless effort by all to learn the new language. And, Amira delivers a healthy boy, Tawfeek.

This family are farmers. Living in the town of Hilla, which lies on the Euphrates, raising wheat, barley, sunflower and sugar beets. It is a very physical and healthy productive way of life both in Iraq and The United States. Amira and Abido are being 100% housewives while Amirmoes and Darzi attend school. The little one Tawfeek is home with mom. You can smell the coriander and cress, lentils and courgetti in the air as the wives prepare for their husbands and their attending school children to return home to their farmhouse.

There are three classes of Iraqis. City Man, No Man and peasant farmers, which comprise of nearly ¾ of Iraq's population Today, Hilla it is home to the University of Babylon.

Back on the farm, as the language sessions continue, the family recruits a tutor/translator named Zaid. He is in his young 20's and very good looking. And, just the right amount of personality. And that doesn't please Aban. Aban is insecure and fills the void with jealousy. It's in the air but everything remains functional. Zaid is a young scholar who loves the English language. We see the language lessons gruelingly move on. The elders become frustrated. Aban directs his frustration at Zaid. He yells in disgust and disbelief. "2, too, 2, two, 2, to" Then "farm f-a r-m, Pharmacy, p-h-a-r". That is when Zaid turns to the children and politely asks them to explain to the adults the structure of this very difficult language. That's when Darzi, who is now 9 years old looks at his father Hakim and says, without any hesitation," *T-O is a preposition which begins a prepositional phrase or an infinitive*".

"*T-O-O is an adverb excessively or also. T-W-O is a number*".

Darzi continues. The Romans translated Greek "PH" and pronounced closer to "f".

Zaid, becomes aware that the children are learning at a much faster pace than the elders.

(The children, still ignorant to why they are learning their new language).

Eventually Zaid has the young tutoring the Elders.

Queema, a minced meat, is being served for one of their weekly dinners dedicated to studying the English language. We will find them sitting around the floor, out in the back yard, the family room, anywhere they are most comfortable.

We watch as their lives become more and more obscure among their own people. In this case, Unclear-Uncertian-Unknown-Hazy-Vague-Concealed-Hidden-Vailed-Masked.

Kind of like, "The Fifth Column"

(Meaning of "The 5th Column" Traitor-One who betrays a country, Friend and/or Principle. Sellout for their own gain-Wendel-Any group of people who undermined a larger group from within in favor of the enemy, group or nation.)

1960

Late 1960 Aban & Hakim move to America themselves for a 1-month period. They begin their plan to transition themselves and their families into their new life.

After much diligent and painstaking paper work, Aban and Hakim finely have their work visa's and all other paper work complete. At present, The United States has strict restrictions on travel and immigration.

They travel to America. After landing at the Philadelphia International Airport, they meet with fellow Iraqi named Ajam in the Philadelphia, Pennsylvania area. "Ajam, an attorney who has been living in America for nearly a decade and has taken a (Pro Bono roll) in assisting Iraqi families thru the transition of moving to America. Ajam is obscure and unaware of their mission. Aban askes "How is the steel mill employment opportunities? We have decided to move our families to America, Ajam replies "The northeastern and western parts of Pennsylvania are ripe with employment opportunities. I have connections with people here in the northeast who are presently looking for hard workers. And, the work is hard. But it pays well and is secure. Good insurance and benefits with a good pension to boot."

Aban replies, "We are ready and eager. We will be here for nearly a month and our goal is to return home with secure employment and hopefully good housing." Ajam arranges for both Aban and Hakim to have a job interview in the Steelton, Pennsylvania area. They arrive at the steel mill and immediately impress the personal department. They both are willing to work any of the three full-time shifts and prove they have the strength and the ability to lift and learn. They are hired. Aban looks at his brother and exclaims, "We accomplished that goal in such short time, we must look for housing." With the help of Ajam and steel mill personnel they find a nice 4-bedroom row home in a small community in walking distance to the steel mill. Everyone they meet seemingly embrace the idea of having them as new neighbors including school officials at the local Catholic Parish. The Pastor, Father Michael, who has a reputation of being ahead of the times, sees this as an opportunity to help his parishioners to understand and blossom regarding the world's religious stage. Yes, Father Michael is without a doubt ahead of the times. "There is a place with in our community" Their trip has been a success beyond their own tortured minds could imagine.

They return home to an anxious and proud family.

Upon their return, there are some reservations and concerns among the ever so calculating Family. Especially amongst the elders. Adbyllin is at odds on how they will live.

The discussions and debates include, the western style of life, the women wearing veils, Catholic schooling, eating habits and their own religious worship and the next generations worshiping just to name a few. Aban, with the authority of a Matriarch in training, speaks to the concerns.

"Our wives and daughters will wear veil cover during devotion and piety. And that veiling will be of their own choice. They will honor their religious identity and self-expression. There will be no influence. We have a mission, Just That. Our children will keep their faith. Our decision is to be a member and participate with in unified setting. We will change nothing regarding our religious culture. Fasting etc. Our family will attend one of two Mosques. One local and a grand Mosque in Washington D, C,"

The Families begin their Exodus to America!

1961

After nearly 5 years of planning to leave Iraq, the children and their parents shuffle off to Philadelphia. Aban and Hakim will periodically return home to conduct business regarding their family and their mission.

The family leaves quietly. The Family arrives quietly.

They are squeaky clean do to the fact, when they arrived in the early 60's, the only profiling that was going on, was if you were black.

OPEC
September 10th thru September 14th
The Petroleum Exporting Countries are a permanent intergovernmental Organization.
Created By: Iran, Iraq, Kuwait, Saudi Arabia and Venezuela at the Bagdad Conference
U.S.A., Russia, Mexico and Canada are not members
As these non-members Nations increase their oil production over the next 40 years,
OPEC's influence will plunge

Which will inerasable cause political problems in
some OPEC Countries, Including IRAQ
Resulting in lower oil prices
Another thorn in their side caused by the U.S.A.

O.P.E.C. "1960"

1962

Movie-Lawrence of Arabia

Marilyn Monroe Dies

They settle in a community that is a Hard-working beer drinking steel mill community. They have found work in the steel mill with hopes to eventually return to farming. Aban will always believe he is in charge and wants to be the patriarch over here in the United States. Remember, he has only one son, which is to his advantage, and he is the eldest. Family squabbles take place because of the power to make final decisions arise repeatedly. It is less important to identify these squabbles as it is to remember there is Aban, who wants, and will become the next patriarch. It's just a preview.

There are little to no social ills in this tight knit community. (It's a good climate) Slovak-American, Catholic culture. Their children attend a small Catholic School two blocks from their home and one block to the Steel foundry. As traditional in the 60's and 70's, this community had 4 small grade schools with in a 30-mile radius. Saint Patrick's, Saint Mary's, Saint Joseph's and Saint Gertrude's where Aban's son Tawfeek and Hakim's sons Amirmoez and Darzi will attend. We witness thru the next generation a national trend. Catholic Diocese's began to consolidate and reduce the numbers of grade schools. While the families begin to settle in, they do everything humanly possible to become just another neighbor with no drama. Ironically, this small knit community is witnessing a drama of their own. Which in turn has over shadowed their place in the community. An illicit affair has engulfed the close-knit Catholic parish. We watch as this parish welcome their newest member, A newly born little girl named Beth is born September 12th, 1962 She is black. Mom and Dad are not. Even with that. There is not a negative eye or action from anyone. This parish and community stand tall when it comes to "Love thy neighbor" Yes, there will be taunting in grade school as there always will be. But not so much for both Aban and Hamik's children and their Iraqi heritage, but for Beth. We must remember, during these times the United States is embroiled in the Civil Rights movement. Focusing on race and woman's rights, and again, the only profiling was race. Not religion or culture. Civil Rights marches were at their peak and riots were at their worst. And, Martin Luther King was still alive.

1963

* <u>U.S. President John F. Kennedy is assassinated.</u>

President John F. Kennedy Dallas Texas "1963"

*<u>The Civil Rights March on Washington draws 200.000 supporters, blacks & whites.</u>

*<u>Martin Luther King delivers "I Have a Dream" Speech.</u>

*<u>Viewers tuned into NBC and witness Jack Ruby shoot Lee Harvey Oswald.</u>

*<u>The French Chef Julia Child Debuts</u>

*Academy Award goes to "Lawrence of Arabia".

While willfully and as misleading as it may be, and, not missing a step, Aban and Hakims families attend Communion parties, confirmations, etc.

At one event, Father Michael approaches Amira, Aban's wife, who is now 34 years old and Abido, Hakim's wife, who is now 32 years old, and graciously invites them to help with the making of the, fasnacht, which is a traditional feast before the Catholics Church observance of "40 days and nights of fasting." As he attempts to (with hand motions) describe the making of them, including strudel, nut rolls and Kibosh. The two women, (while understanding every word he says) express their somewhat limited understanding. Hakim translates and with a good white washing explains, "Amira and Abido do not speak English".

There will be festivals, carnivals and Christmas bazaars.

The men will frequent the locally owned corner bars as the children will frequent the mom and pop corner stores to buy penny candy, bread, milk, butter some eggs for the wives to make meals and the neighborhood playgrounds.

During their first Christmas bazaar, Amira and Abido wore veils. Father Michael directed two nuns wearing "High" nun habits join them at the table to work with them side by side. The message was clear, we are all children of God. As the three days of heating the un-pasteurized milk to its absolute correct temperature using their fingertips, they add the butter, yeast, sugar, flour, eggs and lemon zest. They let the dough raise, cut them, sugared them and then boxed the finished, fasnachts. Aban and Abida began to share their own tastes of Iraq with the same ingredients. Aban, who was everywhere, began intriguing and fascinating within the Catholic community with a religion of their own. There seems to be a mutual respect for each other's faith.

Aban and Hakims families will worship during "'Eid Al Fitr" the end of Ramadan on June 25th, the festival of fast breaking. They celebrate "Eid Al Adha" Feast of Sacrifice and "Mawlid al-Nabi" when the lunar cycle deems necessary at a Mosque located in the Harrisburg area. This Mosque was founded in 1888. The U.S.A. Chapter was established in 1952. That is also the year Abida falls in love with Norman Rockwell. She began her collection with the little one's at the doctors and the Barber shop.

Authors Note:
Don't be fooled by what everyone may perceive
as examples of their genuine gratification and or
loving it so much to be here in the US.
When it comes to getting the mission done,
this family will deliver an Oscar winning performance.
They don't forget January 5[th,] 1957-EVER

May 15th Patriarch Abdulla Dies.

Only Aban goes home to Iraq for a week. While there, he mourns the loss of his father. He speaks with comrades of the mission. And he emphasizes it's only been a few years. He reminds them and says, "Our mission has no deadline. Our patience has allowed us to fit in. The money is good. The work is hard. We have made a lot of progress in a short period of time." He considers the money that has been sent home to Iraq, and adds, "The money laundering is working", But the amounts must pick up a step. This visit was short.

November 22nd Gabir, the family matriarch dies. The family mourns her in the U.S. As in most customs, here in the US, the neighbors bring their condolences along with cakes, macaroni and cheese, breads, spreads, quiche, etc. The mood is solemn and the neighbors, under the assumption Amira and Abido do not speak English, make their point by placing their hands in a prayer position, they bow in condolence, they even held their hands. Losing your own has no boundaries.

1964

* Peyton Place debuts on ABC and is the first prime time soap opera.

*U.S. Surgeon General Luther Terry confirms that cigarette smoking causes cancer.

1964 will also mark the first visit back home to Iraq for both Aban and Hamik together.

They are given an update on the family money, which has been sent home on a regular basis. The money being laundered has been all but matched by Patriots living in Iraq, big dreams and a mission that has no deadline. News about fertilizer/manure is making headlines as one of the newest terroristic tool. There was no Ammonium Nitrate in 1964, which is a cheap substance routinely used decades later to be the explosions flint, creating the most powerful explosion. Currently the recipe is all natural and it has grabbed Aban's keen interest. Although this explosive is not widely used yet and/or not taken seriously, IT WORKS, and Aban knows it. Before returning to the United States, they spend two weeks experimenting with the mixtures on their farm in Iraq.

Upon their return, to their delight, the news that was capturing the country's and the world's attention was about to take place.

1965

The Seminal Immigration and Nationality Act of 1965 is signed into law by President Lyndon B. Johnson at the foot of the Statue of Liberty. Before 1965 many Arab immigrants that immigrated to the United States were members of the established elite in countries like Egypt, Syria and "Iraq". The 1965 immigration and Nationality Act reform allowed a new wave of Arab States to immigrate. These reforms opened doors and put on the fast track the opportunities needed for Aban and Hakeems families to obtain legal and permanent resident status in the United States. They took advantage of the opportunity and obtained legal permanent residency in the United States in the next few years. It also opened the doors to recruitment of future martyrs.

President Johnson signs Seminal
Immigration and Nationality Act
"1965"

1966

*The Sound of Music Premiers

*Feminist Group National Organization for Women(NOW) Formed.

*Medicare begins. Capturing the attention of Abido and more so Amir.

*The 1st Star Trek episode is broadcast.

*The Food and Drug Administration declares "THE PILL" safe for human use.

1967

*First Arab-Israeli (6 day) war.

*Snow White, the book is released.

*(August 23ʳᵈ) Iraqi airfields attacked. Iraqi troops enter Jordan. But do not engage in battle. "Diplomatic relations broken with U.S." These events are closely being watched by Aban and Hakim.

*Abido becomes pregnant and delivers Hakim his 3ʳᵈ baby boy May 25ᵗʰ· They name him Tony, a decision to be more welcomed in the western culture. His middle name is Abdulla.

This pregnancy was not in the plan.

These terrorists will experience the downfall of the steel industry and lose their job just like everyone else in their community and they fit right in. The difference lies in their next move, most proud men living within the community are suddenly broke and without income. Social ills become abundant. Before the exodus of the steel mills across the North Eastern United States, thousands of these men went to local bars in the morning after work. Now it's when they get out of bed. The social ills include vulnerability, irresponsibility, abuse, alcoholism, divorce and more. And no jobs to boot. This is when you'd think the family from Iraq would become part of those social ills that go along with what has taken such a terrible toll on these entire families. Not them. They have a mission with no deadline. They are patient.

1968

*Martin Luther King is assassinated

*Senator Robert Kennedy is shot and killed in L.A.

*60 Minutes debuts.

1969

<u>*U.S. war in Vietnam peaks.</u>

<u>*Woodstock happens.</u>

<u>*Sesame Street debuts</u>

The Resilience begins to show
(Turn the page)

1970

Aban, now 43 as is his wife Amira, Hakeem and son Tawfeek now 13 years old, Hakeem, now 40 as is his wife Abido, their sons Amirmoez, now 20, and brother Darzi 22 years old, pull up roots in a fashion that make it seem they were never there. "Mission obedience"

They begin their plan to move back to farm living and have themselves become ambiguous and obscure. It's a long process. Both Aban and Hamik are "Together" personally applying for farm hand positions. We don't have to remind you they are better ready because of their own antiquated equipment back home in Iraq. The kind you feed.

1971

Between their farming experience and will to work, they have no problem landing a job at the farm of their choice with generic housing for the brood and a small airport close by to boot. During this time, in the early 70's there were hundreds of small airports scattered around the U.S. Anywhere from one to two or as many as 15 to 25 planes calling it home.

The farm is owned by honest, Godfearing, old school values type of family. A father of three, his name is Jake, who is 30 years of age and is married to wife, Amelia who is 31.

They are proud parents of, son Mark who is one, daughter Anna who is two, and son John who is three years old. This is not an Amish family, but nestled in an Amish community. The Iraqi family fits right in. There are mostly neighboring farms that are owned and operated by Amish families who are also their friends. The farm produces corn, barley and have several hundred-live stocks. Cows, pigs and a small chicken production. Because of their "New" life on this picturesque farm, there is a heart to be broken. Tawfeek now 13 years old and Beth who is 8 have become inseparable during the past two years. He vows to stay in touch. He once told her their friendship defies gravity.

Aban decides to, while working full time on the farm, to land a part time job. YES! At the local St. Petersburg Airport. Another piece of the mission's puzzle. He is hired as maintenance. During this period, most of these airports had grass runways. This one is in bad shape. He's hired to maintain the runway while splitting his time between the farm and airport. After six months of leveling, weeding, seeding, watering and maintaining it, Aban turned the runway into his own dream runway. The owner takes notice. Aban waters in the middle of the night and puts in hundreds of unpaid hours. He gets the job done.

The airport owner is very impressed. And as a perk, Aban receives free flying lessons. One of the first employees he meets at the St. Petersburg Airport is Wendel Bowman. (Wendel is a 5th column) Wendel was blatantly clear from the get go. He is against the establishment, his bosses, local, State and Federal Government, his wife and his whole life in general. He feels he got the short end of the stick, people owe him and he is a bully. It's obvious this character is gullible, uneducated but pretty much what Aban needs to build a coalition between them. And we're not talking about watching football. Pretty much of what Aban needs to build, is a manipulating coalition to use this guy to help himself to become more a part of the airport from top to bottom. Wendel is just 21 years old, unhappily married with three children and one on the way. Wendel will become a force for their mission as the years go by. He is a piece of shit that will sell his soul and or Country for money, another piece of the mission's puzzle for decades to come. It's evident Wendall holds a grudge. He will never forget and always reminds everyone how he was taunted ever since grade school with everyone calling him Wendy. Even today you hear him say, "Wendy Bowman, Wendy Bowman, Wendy Bowman. I will never get over that".

Hakim, like his brother Aban, while working full time on the farm, also landed a part time job with one of the largest produce trucking companies in the state. Yes, another piece.

Tawfeek is now 14 years old and entering high School. He has been casually keeping in constant contact with Beth who is now nine years old with no one's knowledge.

The men, now both having two jobs, are out working more than they are home.

Tony Abdullah is now five and well behaved. He looks up to Tawfeek as a big brother.

Amira and Abido spend more time together, alone at home. They talk about the possibility of their final days here in the United States and whether they will still be alive if the mission is complete in their life time. Amira, the antagonist, rival adversary and opponent asks Abido, "Do you even want to be alive when the mission is complete?" Abido responds, "That's hard to answer. We've given as a country, but lose as a family." Amira scolds her, "Our family gains. Have you no honor for our martyrs?" Abido looks at Amira, straight in both eyes, turns around and walks out of the room. Later that day, we find them sitting across from each other in the kitchen holding hands and quietly weeping. A rare moment for Amira because she always considered those action as weak.

The families plan, in the event this mission does come to fruition in their life time, is for both Amira, Abido and the children to be back home safely in Iraq weeks before any of the first explosions. It is clear and expected, this mission has no deadline. The children to date have been kept naive to the mission. Although Tawfeek has seen red flags indicating there is something unknown. He is not ready to question anything. The children are told to wait and marry a woman of the Muslim faith. Once they return home. They will never return to the U.S.

We start to see Amira begin to take control. Even though it's not known if she will return home. She is hellbent to be the queen if she does. PERIOD! She is seen and heard deciding what responsibilities the woman have. And it's clear she is not the cook or maid! Abido, who has always been lower key and restrained, genuinely embraces the role of "Not being in charge"

1972

<u>*A 15-year treaty of friendship and cooperation is signed between Iraq and the Soviet Union. *A stark reminder of the Eisenhower Doctrine.</u>

<u>*The Supreme Court rules the death penalty is unconstitutional.</u>

<u>*Movie "The God Father"</u>

Early January will mark the second visit for both Aban and Hamik to return to Iraq together. While home is another update on the money accumulated for the mission including the amounts that have been sent home to Iraq and the matching funds by Iraqi loyalists. The men update them on the use of manure in explosions. They will always update on the family and their accomplishments.

Abans son Tawfeek is now 15. And still in love with Beth! Hakim's son Amirmoez is now 22 and Darzi is 24. Their new son Tony is only five years old.

Aban and Hakim intensify their manure exploding experiments on their farm in Iraq. They also meet three young future martyrs who will take part serving the mission and will be arriving in the United States within the next year. Their names are Asera, Malik and Rahim. All in their mid to late teens. While home in Iraq, they will all speak freely of the mission. Aban and Hamik fill them in. The three wear their country well and proudly offers their lives as homage.

Back in the United State, Tawfeek, now 15, is getting to know his cousins 21-year-old Amirmoes and 23-year-old Darzi. Darzi told Tawfeek about the few insults hurled their way because of their heritage in the grade school playground when they were younger and asked Tawfeek "Do you have many friends? Tawfeek said "I am friends with everyone. Especially Beth" who is now 10 years old. Then Tawfeek said, "I heard someone call Beth a nigger". Darzi asked Tawfeek, "what did you do?" Tawfeek said, "I told her I liked her. I didn't care if she was a nigger", Beth said, "Thank you. Do you know what that word nigger means"? I said, "kind of." Then Beth looked at me with a few tears rolling down her cheeks, looked me straight in my eyes and said, "It's ignorance my mother told me. It is just that. And, you must understand that; they don't know what their saying. That's what they hear at their dinner table. But the word "Nigger" does fly around at times." And it always' hurts". Darzi asked Tawfeek, "what did you say?" Tawfeek said, "nothing, I hugged her."

When the two men return to the United States they are accompanied by 18-year-old Shada for one of his sons to marry.

Aban & Hakim will embark on a major project creating small scale explosions on the farm's outskirts in Pennsylvania. Aban and Hakim both work on a farm that directly manufactures manure. To have an explosion is not difficult, but the process would be very uncommon and would raise red flags and be questioned. He has as much feces as he needs. They create these small explosions naturally by placing the feces in a manure pit. Up to 90% smaller than the farm operated ones. They will be small and hidden on the hundreds of farm acres. Then capping it air tight to prevent the odor to abscond. At present, to the best of his knowledge, it was the odor alone that built up the explosive result. As the years move on he will be educated about methane, which is the natural flint to a type of explosion.

1973

*Academy Award goes to "The God Father"

Aban and Hakim are discussing the news that OPEC has pledged to increase oil prices by 200% to all countries supporting Israel. Their promise is to decrease oil production by 5%. American consumers begin to find more fuel-efficient cars.

NOT MADE IN AMERICA

A strike by Iraq that hits America

Meanwhile, Aban, who has been completely ingulfed in the beginning of the Water Gate hearings seen walking around the house with hands in his pockets, head tilted back and repeats, "I am not a crook. I am President Richard Milhouse Nixon" No matter how many times he would act out that mockery, the family rolled on the floor laughing.

1974

*OPEC end the oil embargo during Yom Kipper war.

*Nixon resigns. President Ford grants full, free and absolute pardon to the ex-President.

1975

*The Algiers Accord, codified in Bagdad Treaty, fixes southern Iraqi-Iran Border along Thalweg of Shatt al Arab and formally ends Kurdish rebellion.

*"Saturday Night Live" debuts. George Carlin hosts.

*U.S. Supreme Court rules that the death penalty is "not" inherently cruel or unusual and is a constitutionally acceptable form of punishment.

*N.B.C. broadcasts "Gone with The Wind"

*Star War hits the theatres.

*Pope Paul VI dies at 88. Pope John Paul dies 34 days later at the age of 65.

*Sony introduces the first Walkman. This portable stereo really captured Tony's attention. It's seemed like no one ever saw Tony without a Walkman. Tony is eight years old.

*Norman Rockwell dies. Abido became addicted in collecting anything and everything Norman Rockwell.

1976

The first of three additional Doomsday Patriots Aban and Hakim met while in Iraq in 1972, Aasera 21, Malik 21, and Rahim 22 arrive and settle in Indiana. All of them get warehouse jobs; driving trucks, loading trucks and unloading trucks. (Learning the trucking ropes if you want to call it that). No wives, no children planned. They know they will die on Doomsday and beam with pride inside knowing their lives are secondary to the mission and their Country. They call themselves Martyrs. They will also obtain their pilots license in the coming years.

There is very little if no contact between any participants in Doomsday who reside in the United States. All contact is directly with a communication wheel located in Iraq. The wheel (Iraqi patriots) keep everyone in the loop. The rule being not to communicate or acknowledge the existence of fellow cohorts or comrades within the United States. The wheel always communicates directly from family member to family member to avoid any assumption of association by the United States Government. This wheel has been in operation prior to 1957.

1977

Tony is now 10. He is having a rough time at school. He has become detached from his family and seems to be in a world of insecurity. He seems to have gender bending body language, not expected or accepted by both Abans and Hakims families. Tawfeek is the only family member who reaches out and tries to comfort Tony and encourages him to have more confidence in himself.

1978

*Anwar al Sadat wins the 1978 Nobel Peace Prize for his contribution to the two frame agreements on Peace in the Middle East. And on Peace between Egypt and Israel. Signed at Camp David September 17, 1978.

A family with four boys to be part of mission in any capacity they are needed including a commitment to no marriage, children and the capacity of becoming a martyr for their country arrive and settle in the Boston, Massachusetts suburbs. Profiling Middle Easterners is on the rise and looks to continue. The signing of the Johnson Immigration Act works in their favor. They learn how to abuse Americas freedoms. They are Jamal three years old, Yusof four years old, Raheem five years old and Uda is six years old. They will be brain washed for the love of their Country and putting their country above their lives. (Martyrs) A new generation who may have to continue the mission.

Their parents, Mancha 26 and his wife 25 (Sabeen) will go home when Aban's Brood does. If the mission completion is to take in their life time. Remember, no deadline. The unsaid time is rumored to be between 2022 -2025

1979

*"Boat People" Start to flee Communist Regime in Vietnam and arrive on U.S. soil.

* (February 5th) 15 days after the departure of the Shaw of Iran, Ayatollah Ruhollah Khomeini takes control of Iraq.

*Soviet invasion of Afghanistan stirs world protests.

*(March 28th) Three Mile Island near Harrisburg Pa: One of two reactors lost its coolant which caused overheating and partial meltdown of its uranium core. 144,000 people were evacuated.

It was a time where you we witnessed people walking with a huge transistor radio smack against their ear hoping not for the worst. President Jimmy Carter visited and walked the grounds of Three Mile Island. There was a strange sense of silence, fear and more than a few concerned phone calls to and from Iraq.

Tawfeek now 22 years old, is still hellbent in love with Beth who is now 17. They have been seeing each other without anyone's knowledge ever since Tawfeek received his driver's license.

The last year or so they have become romantically involved and rendezvous when they can. Usually at one of their most popular pass times, the Drive-in movie. Beth becomes pregnant. This was defiantly not in the plan. Aban tells his son Tawfeek. "There is no discussion. There is no choice. Your baby's blood is family blood. And there is no exception. The only exception is that Beth is Black and beautiful, inside and out." Beth moves in with Tawfeek and family. They wed on July 30th. There will not be a traditional Iraqi wedding, just the immediate family held at the local Mosque. On October 12 their son, Ali Jared is born.

1980

* Iran/Iraq war ensues for 8 years

Tony Abdulla, son of Hakim is almost 14. Rumor has it he is gay. He is found hung in the barn. They called it suicide by hanging. Rumor has it he was left hanging for 5 minutes before he was taken down. Tawfeek is heartbroken. He and Beth both fear this was an "Honor Killing" The killing of a relative perceived to have brought dishonor on the family. Their son Ali Jared will never know Tony Abdulla.

ARA News 01/26/17 7:44 P.M. EST

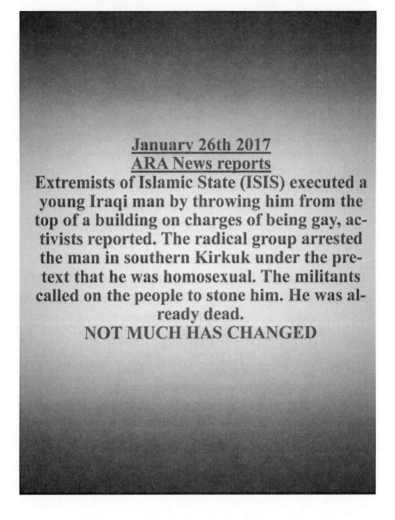

January 26th 2017
ARA News reports
Extremists of Islamic State (ISIS) executed a young Iraqi man by throwing him from the top of a building on charges of being gay, activists reported. The radical group arrested the man in southern Kirkuk under the pretext that he was homosexual. The militants called on the people to stone him. He was already dead.
NOT MUCH HAS CHANGED

The militants called on the people to stone him.

"The Quran Specifically prohibits the killing of innocent people"

This is the year Hakim and Aban decide to sit down and take inventory.

They discuss the roles of Aasera, now 27, Malik, 27, and Raham, 29, who reside in Indiana. The dependency of Jamal who is now 6, Yusof (6), Reheem (7) and Uda, who is 8 in the event the mission is not complete in their life time.

They discuss the updated information sent through the wheel regarding the Indiana Patriots and their working experiences and success in obtaining their pilot licenses.

They envision trucks and planes, creating an apocalypse. But they realize it is going to take a hell of a lot more money than they saved and sent back home to Iraq. They remain residual and confident because this mission has no deadline.

They agree sometime in the future it might be necessary to meet their fellow patriots face-to-face, including their own sons and having them make a choice as to what role they want to play in the "Mission" if any.

1981

Israel attacks an Iraqi nuclear research center at Tuwaythah near Bagdad.

August 13th, 1981. Now that inventory has been taken, Aban and Hakim and family's sit down to what is what they all have been waiting for and know has been earned. A peaceful meal with no mission talk. An evening with no out-side interference. A rare and priceless moment. The moment does not last long. Abido, who is always soft spoken and comfortable *not to be heard*, catches the entire family by shock." *I am ashamed of Iraq" She says. "We all know we are using chemical weapons against our neighbors" There is a short silence when Amira demands an apology for Abido being blasphemy. Abido quietly excuses herself from the table and leaves the room. The room remains quit and somber. They all know Abido is correct. They all know it is wrong. And, they all know it could be their baby's.*

1982

*Michael Jackson releases THRILLER

*Cats opens on Broadway.

In an Ironic twist. The year 1982 painted a different picture that was in stark contrast the consequences of the 1975 Eisenhower Doctrine's world will soon learn that the United States under the Regan Administration has been secretly providing highly classified military intelligence and the sale of American arms to Bagdad. While at the same time arming Iran. Aban and Hakim are not impressed with the support Iraq is receiving from The United States. They know Americas underlined agenda and why they have intervened. Both Aban and Hakim are very well-schooled on a regular basis on the current state of the Iran-Iraq war. In many cases sometimes more than The United States Government. The Iraqi wheels informational source is priceless intelligence. The bottom line, The United States has been arming both sides in its desire to see neither side dominate the vital resource of the oil rich regions. In the next coming years, Aban and Hakim will be proven right by the American Courts. And there will be no love lost. This family This family lives like its 1957 every day. There is no trust and there never will be. According to Aban, America does not give handouts with out a price. And that price is greed! This, resulting in fuel being added to their mission.

1983

*Terrorist explosion kills 237 Marines in Beirut.

*Crack cocaine is developed in the Bahamas. Soon appears in the U.S.

1984

The Cosby Show debuts

Ali Jared is now 5 years and well behaved.

Hakims son Darzi, who is now 38 years, has always been a huge fan of the Western Culture Heavy Metal bands. Metallica, Megadeath and slayer to name a few. Oblivious to what the future holds, his favorite Heavy Metal Band is ANTHRAX

(Turn the page)

1985

*Madonna launches her tour, "The Virgin Tour

Iraq begins to obtain much of its anthrax supply from the American type culture collection. Between 1985 and 1989, it obtained at least 21 strains of anthrax from ATCC and about 15 other class III pathogens, the exact bacteria that pose extreme risk to human health.

These occurrences are heard loud with in the cells of the Iraqi terrorist world including the wheel, in turn, Aban and Mallik. Also in 1985 Rihab Taha al Azawi (born November 12, 1957), an Iraqi microbiologist, who will later be dubbed Dr. Germ by the United Nations weapons inspectors, went to work for Iraqs germ warfare program. She later will become chief production officer of in al-Hakam., Iraqs top-secret biological-warfare facility at the time. Taha will become a household word in the world of terrorists and later marry British educated General Dr. Amir Mohammad Rashid al Ubaidi, the former Iraqi oil minister and director of Iraqi's Military Industrials Cooperation. She will then be known as Dr. Rihab Rashid Taha al Azawi.

April 9th, Amirmoes, now 35, son of Hamik gets married to Shada now 32. The bride's Mother, Father and her 2 sisters will travel from Iraq for the event. Shada's mother's name is Sanaa. Her father' name is Jamail. The elder sister's name is Shatha while her younger sisters name is Leyla. Leyla is 7 years old. Ali Jared and Leyla will take part in the wedding. Shada and her family will be staying at Aban's house because Shada is marrying Hakim's son. Their wedding will have all the tradition expected in your Iraqi wedding, which is an event, not celebrated quietly like Tawfeek and Beth's wedding. But with glory and distinction. This marriage even has the old-school tradition of being arranged by the parents.

At the local Mosque, there will be traditional drums to announce their engagement. Those gathered at the announcement are called, "The Assembly for the Queenly Bride". Their wedding will be held at the Grand Mosque in Washington D.C. The U.S.A Chapter was established in 1922 and is among the oldest American-Muslim organizations. Located a few blocks from the White House and nestled with surrounding Embassy's and is the first Mosque in the Nation's Capital. They both will wear white with garland around their necks. The groom's family will express their desire for the union. We will see them visit the bride's home. They arrive to see Aban is cutting the hair of more than several male family members. Everyone will be looking their best. They will take gold coins, mirror and candelabras. The reception is lavish as will be the meal. The party is called paghosah. Special soup called ash will be made by the bride's mother along with whiskey, beer and vodka.

Wendel Bowman gets rowdy at reception. Still a bully. And rumored to be abusive.

He and his wife sadly go thru an unseen divorce. Nobody comes near. Nobody cares.

(Just like Father McKenzie). His life has now become the St. Petersburg Airport.

1986

*Secret initiative to send arms to Iran is revealed.

*Ex-Navy analyst Jonathon Jay Pollard 31 found guilty as a spy in Israel.

1987

<u>*Iraqi Missiles kill 37 on U.S. Frigate Stark in Persian Gulf. Iraq President Hussein apologizes.</u>

Tawfeek and Beth's son Ali Jared will be turning g eight years old on October 12th. The little one's mother wants traditional Iraqi birthday party. Beth has always been known to be very respectful. His celebration will be attended by family and his school classmates. Although allowing of the western culture is prohibited by the Quran, and forbidden by Sharia law, the present Iraqi generations have been more and more embracing the idea of celebration. Aban and Amira, both 59. Give their grandson a small wooden knife in a velvet green box. Hakim and Abido, both 59. Give their nephew a "Talisman" A written prayer roll, with gold *lettering*. Its case is decorated with special stones. Malik tells Ali Jared, "This is to protect you against evil eye, bad spirits and disease. Also, on board is Shada 34, wife of Amirmoez. Amirmoez who is now 37 is not in attendance, he has been distancing himself from the family with no explanation. And Darzi 39. The celebration comes to an early end for Aban. Wendel Bowman is at it again. "Spousal abuse" He leaves to intervene.

1988

*Iraq is accused of using chemical weapons against the Kurdish town of Halabjah.

*U.S. Navy war ships down Iranian airliner in the Persian Gulf. Mistakes it for a jet fighter. 290 people are killed.

Amirmoez, son of Hakim. Dies of an apparent Cocaine overdose

1989

*Iraq Ayatollah Khomeini declares Author *Salmon Rushdies book 'The Satanic Verses" offensive and sentences him to death. His book is published in the U.S. "The Satanic Verses" sparked immediate controversy. Islamic Militants' put a price on the publisher's head

1990

*After the invasion, Rihab Taha's team was ordered to set up a program to weaponize their biological agents. By January 1991 a team of 100 scientists and support staff filled nearly 200 bombs and 16 missile war heads botulin toxin.

Eight years after America supplying Iraq with highly classified military intelligence and the sale of American made arms, there is a complete turnaround. America is now imposing sanctions on Iraq in retaliation for invading Kuwait. It was America who led the 34 Nations to an intensive bombing campaign against strategic Iraqi locations. Aban, as do his fellow Iraqi's, have been hoping that Iraq would gain a significant bargaining power as the Gatekeeper of the Middle East oil. In another ironic twist, Iraq has one of the worlds largest military force. In part, because of America suppling Iraq with American made weapons to fight against Iran. It's all about following the oil.

1991

*(January 16-17) Desert Storm. U.S. and coalition forces begin serial bombardment of Iraq

(February 24th) Ground troops. (February 27th) Kuwait is liberated. (March 3rd) Iraq accepts terms of a cease fire.

*Anna, Jake and Emilia's daughter, gets married and moves from the farm.

1992

*Monday, July 26th, 1992 Aban and Hakim are seen glued to the Television watching and listening closely to the latest world news. To their delight they listen to the news correspondent report:

"Iraq has announced they will not let the United Nation Inspectors to inspect military records held in the Iraqi Agricultural Ministry building. And we are waiting for President George Bush to address the nation on this development immediately following an ongoing meeting with his Secretary of Defense Dick Cheney, National Security Adviser Brent Scowcroft and General Colon Powell The Joint Chiefs of staff

Dead in the middle of this news report, in comes a special News report.

"We are live and taking you to President George Bush live at Camp David."

President George Bush

This morning we accomplished our goal and received confirmation from the Iraqi officials to back down from their effort to refuse inspection of military records held in the Iraqi Agricultural Ministry Buildings. "Iraqi's belated announcement that it will allow the United Nations special commission inspectors to carry out an inspection of the Agricultural Ministry building, DOES NOT! Alter the facts that for the last 3 weeks Saddam Hussein Has flagrantly violated the U.N Security Council's Resolution #687. Nor, this DOESNOT! Announcement change the fact that Iraq purposely and callously harassed t and abused the U.N inspectors.

RED ALERT! Aban has been receiving communications from "The Wheel" with a message. *"Be prepared for highly classified information. The assassination of a Western World leader".* For the 1ˢᵗ time in a long while, Aban and Hakim are anxious and completely prepared for the information of the offence. Late December the wheel delivers.

THE BEGINNING 1993 WILL MARK A TRIUMPH OF THE INCREADABLE PROGRESS IN THE COMPLETION OF OUR COMPLICATED MISSION. APRIL 14th, PRESIDENT GEORGE BUSH Sr. WILL ARRIVE IN KUWAIT TO BE HONERED FOR HIS VICTORY IN THE PURSION WAR. ON THAT DAY. HE WILL DIE ON OUR SOIL.

1993

*Movies-Schindlers List

April 13th, 1993. Aban receives a devastating communication from the wheel.

"Today, one day before the arrival of United States President George Bush Sr., a Toyota Landcruiser which contained between 80 and 90 kilograms of plastic explosives connected to a detonator, and 10 cube plastic explosive devices connected to a detonator was found in Kuwait."

To make things worse in this Iraqi camp, Future President Bill Clinton, in retaliation to the Iraqi plot to assassinate former President George Bush Sr. during his visit to Kuwait, orders war ships to fire Tomahawk cruise missiles at Iraq Intelligence Head Quarters in downtown Baghdad.

1994

* Yasser Arafat wins the 1994 Nobel Pease prize for his efforts to create Peace in the Middle East.

*U.S. sends troops to the Persian Gulf.

*Saddam Hussein becomes Prime Minister.

It's June and the children are on their summer break. The entire family travels back home

To Iraq together for the first time. This is the first time Amira (66) and Abido (64) see their love ones since 1960. Although they have been in contact in the beginning from the day the left Iraq. They will be home during the end of Ramadan. The food cuisine includes both woman's favorites including cabals, (any kind almost) Abidos favorite and on the menu, starts with a grilled whole lamb stuffed with rice, almonds, cinnamon, cloves, nutmeg, cumin, coriander and paprika. Abido and Amira share some American dishes they brought with them much to the dismay of the village idiots. While shopping with their old friends they hear no English for the first time in 34 years. Aban and Hakim are both in their mid-60's. Aban Has carefully lived his life in preparation to become head of the family.

He and Hakim have schooled themselves by now to produce, deliver and implode a manure bomb. They in detail discuss details with Iraqi patriots while paying tribute to all martyrs, past, present and still to arrive. Aban and Hakim are told the Indiana comrades Aasera (42), Malik (42) and Raheem (44) jobs are going well but they miss home. Back here in Iraq, it is clear through communications that they are frustrated. This has not been an easy year for them. This year almost brought, for the first time, a collapse of the mission. Apparently the three living in Indiana were overheard discussing matters of the mission by two fellow employees. The red flags went flying. After a federal investigation, the three men were cleared". Lead investigator Frank Gage 28, was in complete disbelief. He felt the investigative team consisted of some who abused the real meaning of first amendment rights. Accused some of them as over the top with dangerous liberal ideals who treated these three suspects with kid gloves. The investigating team turned their head to lead investigator Gage's concerns of their secluded life styles with no spouse or significant other, their application for their pilot license, and their completion of the course all simultaneously. Boom, Boom, Boom. The fact that all three have been cited by their own trucking company (one of the largest in the State of Indiana) for habitual violations for keeping company trucks over the weekends. But most importantly, their reluctance to come clean when investigated. And, their stories didn't match. But…They were cleared! They have a strong will as comrades and are sadly enough, aware of the fact that there is no turning back. In the coming years, they will completely accept their mission and become resigned to the facts. There still has not been face to face contact with anyone in the United States other than themselves. They are dependent on each other and the Wheel.

While in Boston, Jamel is 29, Yusof is 34, Raheem is 35 and Uda is 36. All four works in the capacity of warehouse loading and trucking and are always winning employee of the month and other accolades.

Mother and father are still alive, retired and keeping house. Jamal still lives at home with his parents. Yusof and Raheem share an apartment. Uda is on his own in an upscale high rise. He has been known to be impressed with the Boston elite. He's even been accused of becoming too liberal by his brothers.

In Iraq, being too liberal and allowing western culture to consume parts of your life is problematic. Back home in Iraq, the communication wheel is just that. Remember, its old school. The wheel has been in existence long before 1957. Its operational responsibilities have been passed on from generation to generation. The wheel has always been operated by (Man Power) with only 20 or so close, loyal and committed martyrs. As in any operation like this comes the normal day to day drama. In this case, Amjad who is 25 years old and Bousaid, 27 find themselves somewhat a novelty amongst their fellow operators who are churning this informational wheel, younger, thinking they know it all and drip with western cultural aura. They aspire of becoming top operators of the wheel and open all the doors to unbridled jealousy and competition. They both show signs of disloyalty. Amjad and Bousaid are "Cut Throat"

Remember, cutting is their culture. No Problem.

And, these two morons are getting on everyone's nerves too boot.

That takes us back to this years most recent family trip back home to Iraq. It was decided with calculation, to have their values decimated, and then ordered to move to America. (Indiana Area) as future Martyr resurgence. (NEW BIRTH)

It is a reality Aban and Hakim may not live until Doomsday

ABAN WILL WAIT

1995

*150 million people watch as the not guilty verdict is read on the O.J. Simpson case.

Three years before the United Nations special commission weapons inspectors were forced to pull out of Iraq, Iraq admitted it had produced 2,000 gallons of anthrax. The UN destroyed most of that, but officials believe that Bagdad hid over 4 times as much as was discovered.

On April 19th, 1995, at 9:02 a manure packed truck exploded in front of the Alford P. Murrah Federal building in Oklahoma City, Oklahoma, leaving 168 people dead and hundreds injured. Manure explosive comes to the forefront and Aban does not miss a detail. He enlists Hakim to begin to bring some trucks he is driving while at work to the farm as a proto type rehearsal. On & On. That's when ammonium nitrate comes into play. Remember, that is CHEAP. He continues to experiment with much success.

The Oklahoma horror caused an up-swing in profiling Middle Eastern nationalities. Even though Timothy McVeigh, who is a white Caucasian, American, blue eyed ex-Marine is responsible for executing the bombing.

The United States of America executed him.

1996

*Iraqis strike Kurdish enclave (August 31) After warning, U.S. attacks Iraq's southern air defenses.

*Mancha at the age of 44 dies of a heart attack. Condolences by Hakim's family were channeled through the Wheel as were the Indiana three. He was cremated and sent home.

The freshly ordered Amjad now 27 and Bousaid 29 land on American soil. While they settle in the Indiana area, they immediately set off alarms., They do not live a low-key life as all comrades have been living for this mission in America for the last 4 decades. They talk too much, their seen too much, provocative and both want to be big shots. But it's their dark side they transcend that has effortlessly been observed by others. Their social life does not last long. There is no knowledge of the location and or identities of any fellow comrades living in America

Then comes a major concern communicated thru the wheel to Aban and Hakim.

It has been confirmed Amjad and Bousaid are being investigated by the Federal Borough of Investigation.

They fueled their suspicion after making a few careless remarks while abbreviated at a local bar called the Papadopoulos.

This, just a few years after Asera, Malik and Raheem were innocent of any suspicion of terrorism. Amjad and Bousaid start living their lives more and more like the role of some dice.

1997

*Titanic hits the Theaters.

*Saddam Hussein awarded Taha the medal of scientific achievement.

An un-said rule has been for the boys not to date a girl who is not of the Muslim faith. Ali Jared who is now 18 has been dating a young lady who has been an exchange student where he attends High School named Diana whom also 18 and is from Sydney Australia. Tawfeek has in every respect given Ali Jared his blessing. Tawfeek has been showing more and more discord toward his family more and more. Tony's death was a turning point. Although he will not allow himself to recognize it may have been an "Honor Killing", he does see the resentment and or jealousy by members because his wife Beth and son Ali Jared are not 100% Muslim. Tawfeek unconditionally loves his family. But has distanced himself when his family's actions are indefensible. He will expose this close-knit family to dissociation and detachment. A mortal defiance.

1998

*Iraq ends cooperation with United Nations Arm inspectors.
President Clinton orders air strikes.

January- The four brothers Jamal 33, Yusof 34, Raheem 35 and Uda 36 meet with Aban and Hakeem for the first time on American soil. The crew from Boston travel to the farm.

Their discussions were short and to the point and focused on the mission. They, for the first time, drew a draft of their targets. This included Washington, DC, the Lincoln and Holland Tunnel and nuclear power plants. And on their personal note, oil refineries. Regarding security concerns, we will see them all but disappear as the story unwinds.

February-Aasera 46, Malik 46 and Rahim 48 fly into the St. Petersburg Airport to meet with Aban and Hakim for the first time on American soil. All three hold a pilot's license. The meeting generally mirrored the one they had with their Boston patriots.

March-Aban and Hakim call together Tawfeek 45, son of Aban, and Darzi 50, sons of Hakim.

This meeting is obviously the hardest for Aban and Hakim. For the first time, they will come entirely clean regarding the mission. The explanation alone takes nearly an hour. The expressions and body language of each one is different. Neither show complete surprise. They have always treated the knowledge of what was taking place like a story book fantasy. But now it is real. Not just make believe. Tawfeek literally looks scared as hell. He is the only one that has a wife and child. Darzi already looks like a patriot. His shoulders back and a face that seems to have no emotion. Darzi has always been harder to read, but not now. Before even given a choice Tawfeek said he will not take a martyr's role. Tawfeeks fears of what really happened to Tony Abdullah separates him from any of this kind of life. Darzi gives Aban and Hakim a salute and is on board.

Aban and Hakim are now in a position where they will inform their wives of where the mission stands. Aban's side of the story is short. Their son Tawfeek will be returning home if the mission is complete while still alive. As will Amira. Hakim's story is much harder. He tells Abido Darzi is a comrade and joins the fight till death. Amira tries to show acceptance. She has never fully recovered from losing her son Tony to what was called suicide or her other beloved son Amirmoez to a drug overdose. Now, to hear her only son has pledged to die.

"And for what"! she yells

Hakim very softly lays his hand on her mouth and says,

"You were not heard" Period

She finally shows all the signs of defeat, she leaves the room making no sounds and closes the door quietly behind her.

1999

According to a DIA report, the normally mild-mannered Rihab Taha was questioned about

al-Hakam, Iraqis top secret biological-warfare facility. Taha exploded into violent rages. Shouting, screaming and storming out of the room, before returning and smashing a chair. Later, documents obtained by the United Nations principal weapons inspector Dr. Rod Barton showed Taha and the Iraqi regime had just purchased 10 tons of growth media from a British company called Oxoid. Iraqis hospital consumption of growth media was 200 kg a year, yet in 1988 Iraq imported more than 39 tons of it. Although this is wide spread talk in the terrorist's cells in Iraq, any chance of coming close to being any part of that world are impossible, unless you have Millions in cash to back up your terroristic plans. And with that, contact is easy.

This year a report commissioned by the Defense Intelligence Agency named Taha as the most dangerous woman in the world.

Dr. Rihab Rashida Taha ranks among the most important and new breed of third world weapon designers who were highly nationalistic, western-educated and willing to violate all international norms or scientific ethics. It was Taha who sold the idea of an Iraqi biological weapons program.

Ali Jared Marries Diana. In a small non-denominational chapel. 2 family members and 2 friends attend. Ali Jared and Diana move to Diana's Home land of Australia and start a new life. A decision they make to distance themselves from future association of what the future may hold.

2000

*Reformists win control of Iranian Parliament for the first time 1979 Islamic revolution.

Movie Gladiator

Frank Gage who is now 34 and climbing the ladder in the F.B.I. investigative world. jumps on board the Amjad and Bousaid investigation. Lieutenant Gage still to this day, can't get rid of that lump in his stomach because of what he considered a sad cry of justice in the investigation reading involving brothers Aasera. Malik and Raheem. Gage takes his investigation to the front door of Amjad and Bousaid. There is no evidence shed of any connection with any mission.

Amjad and Bousaid agree to give Lieutenant Gage enough bullcrap intended to convince him they are willing to co-operate. The year is "2000" and Iraqi cells are everywhere. Including the FB.I. The message reaches the wheel. Amjad and Bousaid again show they have no "loyalty".

NOTE: The year "2000" was the year of the end. They said planes will crash. They Didn't.

2001

The twin towers are attacked

The April 19th Alford P Murrah bombing became the 2nd worst terrorist attack on U.S. soil

Only second to the Twin Towers.

Anthrax attacks the United States of America following the September 11 attacks. Occurring over a period of several weeks

beginning on September 18th. Letters containing anthrax spores were mailed to several news media offices and two Democratic US Senators, killing five people and infecting 17 others. The intelligence community focused on Iraq as the source of anthrax used in the bio-terroristic attacks in America.

One of the letters read:

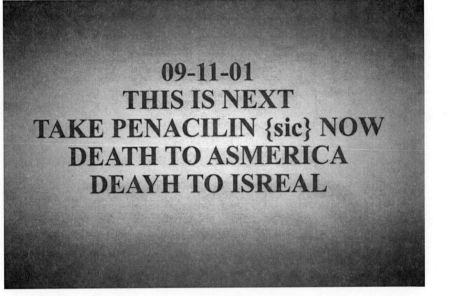

09-11-01
THIS IS NEXT
TAKE PENACILIN {sic} NOW
DEATH TO ASMERICA
DEAYH TO ISREAL

Following the Twin tower attacks, experts at John Hopkins Center for Civilian Biodefence Strategies concluded that one of the nineteen 9/11 hijackers, Ahmed al-Haznawi had likely been exposed to anthrax. If the 9/11 hijackers were involved in the anthrax attacks, they would have had to have an accomplice to mail the tainted letters since the four recovered anthrax letters were postmarked on September 18th and October 9th. Not only was this information known to Aban and Hakim, but they also had knowledge, maybe not in full, of the 9/11 attack well before it took place. The communication wheel does not stop churning.

They will continuously update the players on the top most trusted Iraqi tentacles of terrorist's who reside in the U.S., including names and contact information.

*U.S. and Britain carry out bombing raids to dismantle Iraq's defense network.

*Ariel Sharon wins election in Israel.

*Jake, Owner of the farm, Dies at the age of 59. His sons Mark who is now 31 and John who is 33 years of age take over ownership of the farm.

2002

*Israeli tanks and war planes attack West Bank towns Nablus, Jenin and Bethlehem and others in response string of Palestinian suicide attacks

After nearly two years of investigation Lieutenant Gage has associated Amjad and Bousaid with several reasons of suspicion connecting them to terrorism. The wheel should have done more research as to what might be available to American Federal borough of investigation. (Dirty Laundry) Gage is determined to brake them down and be relentless in his quest to find out all the information they know. December29th 2002, arrest warrants are issued for both men. In a calculated move by Lieutenant Gage to win over Amjad and Bousaid trust, He releases them following their booking.

2003

*Saddam Hussein is captured in Tikrit.

*British UN weapons inspector Dr. Kelly is murdered. It was well documented Dr. Kelly interrogated Dr. Taha so pitilessly that she was "reduced to tears"

Amjad and Bousaid are beginning to unravel. They begin to become careless. They cross the line when they personally try to contact Aban and Hakim. Instead of going thru the chain of command, which is the very *wheel* back in Iraq they spent years being part of Its operation. Amjad and Bousaid have not only become a threat. But, a threat to Iraq. The wheel begins to churn in motion to eliminate the threat.

January 4th, 2003, Bousaid is found hanging in his apartment. They are calling it suicide.

Amjads where a bouts are unknown.

2004

*Saddam Hussein is transferred to Iraqi legal custody.

*U.S. hands over power to Iraq interim government. Lyad Allawi becomes prime Minister.

*U.S. troops launch attack on Falluja, Strong hold of Iraqi insurgency.

*U.S. media releases graphic photos of American soldiers abusing and sexually humiliating Iraqi prisoners ae Abu.

*On September 18th, Tawhid and Jihad Islamic group kidnapped Americans Eugene Armstrong and Jack Hensley, and British engineer Kenneth Bigely, threatening to kill them if Iraqi woman prisoners were not released. Armstrong and Hensley were killed in the first 72 hours. But, Bigley was kept alive for three weeks. The only Iraqi prisoners being held at the time were Dr. Taha and another woman scientist, Huda Salih Mahdi Ammash, a bio-tech researcher who on the U.S. list of the 55 most wanted members of Sadddam's regime and Knick named Mrs. Anthrax by U.S. officials

Emilia, Jakes wife. Dies at the age of 73.

2005

*Iraq has an upsurge in car bombings. Iraqi Ministries put the death toll 672 in May. Up from 364 in April.

*(December) Iraqis vote for the first, full term government and Parliament since the U.S. invasion.

*Two days after the election, Dr. Taha and Huda Salih are released without charges.

*Former Iraqi President Saddam Hussein goes on trial for killing 143 people in the town of Dujail, Iraq.

2006

*In Iraq, a Coalition of Shiites and Kurds dominate the government. Sectarian violence engulfs the country. Killing tens of thousands. Because of the high casualty's, some exports describe the situation as a civil war between Sunnis and Shiites.

2007

*The U.S. begins its surge of nearly 30,000 troops to Iraq to stem increasingly deadly attacks by insurgents and militants.

2008

*Iraqi Parliament approves a security pack with The United States under which all U.S. troops are due to leave the country by the end of 2011.

2009

*All U.S. troops withdraw from Iraq. Security duties are handed over to new Iraqi Forces.

*January 20th, 2009, The United States swears in their first black President, Barack Obama.

*Aasera-Indiana Martyr dies of Cell cancer.

2010

*March 7<u>th</u>, Explosions disrupt general election day in Iraq when 2 bombs kill 38 people.

2011

*Tawakel Karman wins the Nobel Peace Prize for her non-violent struggle for the safety for woman and women's rights for full participation in Peace building work.

2012

*Taliban members shoot 14-year-old Malala Yousafzai in the head and neck. The shooting occurred on the way home from school in a bus filled with children. She was targeted for her outspoken against the Taliban and her determination to get an education.

2014

*Malala Yousafzai, Pakistani wins the Nobel Peace Prize for her struggle against the suppression of children and young people and the right of all children to education.

Malala is the youngest person awarded the Peace prize.

*Iraq announces the complete closure of Abu Ghraib, the infamous prison in which members of the U.S. military physically and sexually abused Iraqi prisoners

2017

*Malala Yousafzai is accepted to study at Oxford University

Donald J. Trump is sworn in as the 45th U.S. President. Kicking off his Presidency by encouraging a Muslim profiling frenzy.

*Thursday, August 24, 2017. Lottery officials say one winning ticket was sold in Massachusetts, for a staggering $758.7 million Powerball jackpot Powerball is played in 44 states, as well as Washington D.C., Puerto Rico, and the Virgin Islands.

This year will be the assumed last visit home to Iraq for Aban and Hakim while still alive. While there, reality begins to set in with the brothers that their mission will most likely come to fruition during the next generation

Aban explains with some regret the mission will most likely be completed within our next generation. He meets a new wave of seven young martyrs who have pledged their lives to complete the mission. Ahamed, Albaf and Alfars are in their young 20's. They have previously visited the United States, have pilot training under their belt and their Visa's in hand. Karimi, Zaman, Samara and Nejem are younger and will be taught and learn their duties and become part of the future. He explains with a smile on his face, "There will be little to no transition in your living quarters and/or your jobs. The farm jobs will be waiting with housing in place. Your transition in Indiana and Boston will be the same". He takes them meticulously through the manure, trucks and pilot license instructions. He emphasizes, "There is an underestimation among the terrorist world as to the amount of damage manure can do if done correctly. This will not be an amateur job. WE ARE READY! All preparations have been made. Your mission is waiting for you". This entire mission is without a doubt still under the radar with the exceptions of a few Federal investigations by the United States Government in 1994 which ended up leaving all suspected squeaky clean.

The discussion of anthrax always is in the conversation. They have all followed closely the progress, over the last few decades. They have ample anthrax contact information, all the way to the top including Taha's camp, but as always said., That world of terror can only be yours with 10's of millions of dollars.

The ground work has been laid. A new wave of young martyrs will be able to complete the mission. Aban explains, The St. Petersburg Airport is ours operate from. The Indiana mission is in place waiting and Boston is ripe. WE ARE READY! All preparations have been made. We vision it to take place in the next 10 years". Aham, Albaf and Alfars nod with approval and total commitment.

November 15th, 2017. Aban, now 87 and Hakim, 85 are boarding their connecting flight from the J.F.K. Airport to Philadelphia. While in flight Aban looks at his brother with a dazed look, he asks him, "What is todays date? Hamik looks at Aban and forgets the question he was just asked because the look in his eyes. Hakim asks, "What's wrong? You don't look good. Aban repeats his question. This time, slow and with conviction. "What is todays date?" Hakim reply's,

November 15ᵗʰ, 2017

Aban says calmly and in a whisper
"I just won 763 Million Dollars!"
763 Million Dollars
An unprecedented Danger to Our National Security
Imagine if Timothy McVeigh had won this.
Or anyone else wearing these terroristic shoes.
It's a fact future terrorist's live in the U.S.
From many countries and home grown.
Completely under the Government's radar
"All you need is a van" And win the lottery.
Yes, this is fiction
FOR NOW!
This Mission has a new time frame!
It will happen during Aban's and Hakims life time

The 1ˢᵗ person he calls is Wendel Bowman. Yes, the rat is still with us. Wendel is now 68 years old and still works at the airport. Aban easily convinces Wendel to claim the winning ticket and buy the airport. The Petersburg Airport is one of the smaller airports that survived the changing times. Still home to up to 25 planes. Having worked at the airport for 40 years, it was no surprise Wendel would do just that. The present owners received an offer they could not refuse. With a 763 million budget, the price is right. No red flags. The limited Government investigation which takes place when an individual wins this amount of money is focused on Wendel. And, only Wendel. Again, no red flags. Of course, there is a national spotlight on Wendell, He just won 763 million dollars. The spotlight will be short lived though. Wendell never had any friends and didn't want any. He went into hiding on the farm and lived under the shroud of the real winners. And was treated like a king. Wendel moves swiftly to satisfy Abans next wish/ *order*, Wendell purchases the trucking company where Hakim was employed to hire Jamel, Yusof, Raheem and Uda to "Operate the Trucks" when they arrive on the farm. Wendel inhales his assumed status of being wealthy.

Aban also arranges Wendel to begin to up the ante regarding the money laundering back to Iraq. Very substantial amounts! Now, by all accounts, Wendel will continue his soul selling ways under the watchful eyes of Aban and Hakim. He has now created a money trail and put himself in a position that makes it impossible to backtrack his role as a terrorist.

An immediate casting call goes out to Aham 20, Albaf 22 and Alfars 24. They will arrive with in the US in expeditiously. They've traveled to the U.S. before and are prepared with all their papers in order. Directly to the farm for the physical work required, as much as driving a truck.

As for the other four young men, Karini, Zaman, Samara and Nejen, their time will surely be just around the corner.

Mallik 66 and Raheem 66 fly themselves into the Petersburg airport from Indiana and then off to the farm. They both have pilot's licenses. And, will fly.

Jamal 52, Yusof 53, Reheem 54 and Uda 55 Bus it into Pennsylvania from Boston. They have lived a life in the trucking world. Strength and knowledge. The trucks are waiting.

The farm, for the first time, begins to produce manure at an industrial rate. Amounts they never dreamed of with in their life time.

Aham will fly as will Raheem 89. Hakim 87 and Aban will both fly. Darzi 68 will die in the plane by his father Hakims side.

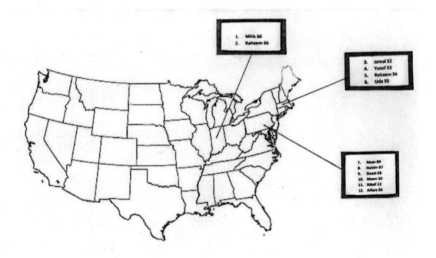

Wendel Bowman does not have to work anymore. Just play the role of "Their Jeannie", in other words, Channel the money where ever Aban and Hakeem wish. Wendel has been promised a one-way ticket anywhere he wants to go with a bundle of cash to boot. (Days before the first explosion.)

2018

January 2nd, 2018, Wendel Bowman Buys the Farm, literally, From Mark and John, who are now 47 and 49 years old respectively. They now own a farm that is literally and exclusively to harvest explosives. Unprecedented. This may seem trivial, but imagine learning the path most of the 763 Million takes.

Not only has tens of millions of dollars go to flame the mission in the U.S., including the mailings of cash in the millions to those trusted top Iraqi terroristic tentacles living in the U.S. so they have the capital to continue like a deadly virus. And, even more 10's of millions has been channeled over to the Iraqi network to bolster future unthinkable havoc in the future.

In short fashion, $50 million dollars' worth of jewels are bought by Wendel. It's what huge lottery winners do. And 763 million is huge. Then sent back home to Iraq to fuel future destruction earmarked *Anthrax. And they will arrive at the right location.* It's not the most difficult to launder such large amounts when you have enough to buy anyone who stands in your way. Just an extra when you win that kind of amount. They even Channeled at the last minute, Millions of dollars to hate groups across the country including, the Ku Klux Klan, Neo-Nazi and other "general hate groups" to bolster their cause. We must keep in mind. The money will have no meaning when there are dead.

Because of this Lottery win, the Iraqi devil will be fed. And he will Eat!

The US is in store to endure decades of misery, destruction and death.

January 15th, 2018, two months after the win, what's left of what was once healthy family, will be embarking back home to Iraq. They will never return. And they are ready to go.

Amira 87, Abido 85, Tawfeek, Beth and Shada 65 begin their Exodus home.

They leave quietly.

They arrive quietly.

Ali Jared 33 and his wife Diana, Move to Australia immediately.

Aban, now 86 embraces the fact that the mission is to be carried out during his life time by senior martyrs and backed up by a younger wave of martyrs. The Iraqi culture is known to be ageless and resilient.

January						
Su	Mo	Tu	We	Th	Fr	Sa
	1	2	3	4	5	6
7	8	9	10	11	12	13
14	15	16	17	18	19	20
21	22	23	24	25	26	27
28	29	30	31			
1:O	8:◐	16:●	24:◑	31:O		

Fellow martyrs from Indiana, Boston and the 3 young men who just arrived from Iraq to be new farm hands, have been split up working between the farm, trucking Co. and the St. Petersburg Airport And are under the employment of Wendell. They pay taxes and stay under the radar. They all live on the farm. There is more than enough sufficient housing considering the many family members who lived there before but made their own exodus to anywhere but the United States of America.

Wendell has been seen and heard boosting to anyone around town who will listen," Hey, with Abans help, I have brought to compliment my work force at the farm, trucking Company and the airport with Hard working Men." (All of whom were born in Iraq) It's nothing but another big cover-up. He also has promised nearly 20 to 30 different people and organizations they will have a place in his will. (With no intent) It isn't his money,

The wives miss their husbands excruciatingly. When the wives call, they will continue to only speak in their Iraqi tongue. They keep their cover, Amira begs Aban to visit. The martyrs refuse to return home to visit for fear of raising red flags. Hakim reminds everyone, "With President Trump, who knows what is going to happen next regarding his immigration policies. I am afraid we may not be able to return".

The debate between Aban and Hakim continues well after they are done speaking with their wives. Aban is leaning toward a visit to Iraq. Aban challenges Hakim to convince him the dangers of not being able to return.

That's when once again, Darzi steps in. Remember Darzi? He is now in his late 40's and has not missed a beat while watching President Trump change his immigration policy's like we change our sox. Darzi states with the authority he has earned: "If we think for one second? we can rely on the stability of President Trump when it comes to his immigration policy, we're wrong. This year alone, starting with January 27,

Trump signed an executive order that suspended entry for citizens of seven countries for 90 days, including ours.

On September 24, the executive order was repudiated by Trump.

On October 25ᵗʰ, President Trump altered once again, his immigration policy by altering 11 high risk nations including Iraq again with "NO ENTRY"

On June 26, Trump administration's travel ban, was deemed unconstitutional. And,

On March 6, Trump signed a revised executive order, excluded Iraq from the list of NO ENTRY

We can't not go home! We have come to far". January also marks the beginning of a year that will be their last. This team of martyrs believe they will still be alive even in death, living in a place Allah has waiting for them. This year we will experience all the male comrades/martyrs, lost souls etc., celebrate with piety for the last time all their religious and State holidays. This ain't no dress rehearsal. We also watch as Darzi is evolving into the full time cook. Sometime cafeteria style or whatever schedule he needs to work around. He is a good cook and accommodating to anyone's schedule.

Starting with Army Day. Saturday, January 6ᵗʰ. This day Iraq honors the Iraqi Army, Navy and air force. Aban and Hakim (the Elders) Explain in detail to their fellow martyrs that these forces are the most important element to counter insurgence fights.

```
        February
Su Mo Tu We Th Fr Sa
             1  2  3
 4  5  6  7  8  9 10
11 12 13 14 15 16 17
18 19 20 21 22 23 24
25 26 27 28
    7:○ 15:● 23:◐
```

Now that the countdown to their final day on the earth (Which is February 14th, 2019) has begun. Aban and Hakim discuss one of their toughest challenges. To keep Wendell happy. By no fault of his own, Wendell holds the purse strings. Ever since Abans big Lottery win, Wendell has been receiving a generous allowance to keep him the dishonest banker. Aban and Hakim being the bank customers. Wendel likes casinos, alcohol and call girls. Wendel is a pig and always has been.

As far as the rest, the only outside activity these terrorists is a bowling alley down town. We've coma a long way from 1957 when this cell 1st arrived here in the United States. While there are no red flags, Profiling because of their Muslim Nationality is in the air

```
          March
Su Mo Tu We Th Fr Sa
             1  2  3
 4  5  6  7  8  9 10
11 12 13 14 15 16 17
18 19 20 21 22 23 24
25 26 27 28 29 30 31
1:○ 9:◑ 17:● 24:◐ 31:○
```

March 14th, the Stoneman Douglas High School shooting over shadows the term "Foreign Terrorists" This terroristic attack was home grown.

Wendell gets thrown out of a casino. Red flags fly, and the fear that he may get careless ingulf the family of martyrs. There has been talk amongst them regarding their fears that he will just fuck-up one time and speak carelessly. Aban and Hakim call in the troops to help. From Indiana, Malik and Raheem. Their fellow comrade Aasera, succumbed to cell cancer in 2009. From Boston, Jamal, Yusof, Raheem and Uda. And the three last-minute recruits, Aham, Albaf and Alfars. Who just arrived from Iraq and moved immediately to the farm. Wendell needs a chaperone. And, the above will be his chaperone. They will keep an eye on Wendell, report back to Aban and Hakim and treat

Wendell with kid gloves. We will witness way too many times one of Wendell's probation officers hanging outside of a seedy hotel room waiting for the slug to finish. It goes without saying Wendell is romping with one of his many call girls. But Aban reminds them of the goose that laid the golden egg. Wendell is the egg. Be careful. Aban then explains. "We can't kill this virus until we have no need for it."

April						
Su	Mo	Tu	We	Th	Fr	Sa
1	2	3	4	5	6	7
8	9	10	11	12	13	14
15	16	17	18	19	20	21
22	23	24	25	26	27	28
29	30					
8:◑ 15:● 22:◔ 29:○						

Their wives surprise Aban and Hakim with a visit. Aban is livid. Not for the mission's sake, but for his beloved wife Amira's safety. He looks in her eyes with tears and says, "You both must return immediately. This is the first time Amira becomes aware she is No#1. There is something more important than the mission and their country. (to late) Hakim and Abido show no passion. But, signs of despair and/or one who is lost. Abido sits beside her son Darzi. Darzi's arm stretched around his mother's waist while she holds his hand firm. Abido does not acknowledge, look at or hold Hakims hand. She has already lost to much. And stands to lose the rest. The wives return less than 3 days after they arrived.

May						
Su	Mo	Tu	We	Th	Fr	Sa
		1	2	3	4	5
6	7	8	9	10	11	12
13	14	15	16	17	18	19
20	21	22	23	24	25	26
27	28	29	30	31		
7:◔ 15:● 21:◑ 29:○						

May 1st Aban, Hakim and Darzi, along with their fellow martyrs will celebrate "Labor Day."

An Iraqi state holidays. Also known as May Day. This holiday is most commonly associated as a salute to the achievements of the Iraqi labor Movement,

June						
Su	Mo	Tu	We	Th	Fr	Sa
					1	2
3	4	5	6	7	8	9
10	11	12	13	14	15	16
17	18	19	20	21	22	23
24	25	26	27	28	29	30

6:◐ 13:● 20:◑ 28:○

On Saturday, June 16th, Eid al-Fitr begins. The festival of fast breaking.

And marks the end of Ramadan. The Muslim belief is that during Ramadan the text of the Qur'an was revealed to the prophet Muhammad. On these major religion holidays. We will see everyone gather and worship together. The Elders are usually at the pulpit. Although, they have all visited the local mosque separately or in groups.

On Saturday, June 23rd, Iraq announces that it had launched an air attack on the gathering of Islamic State Leaders in neighboring Syria killing about 45 members of the Islamic group. Also known as ISIS.

The Iraq's ministry credits Russia for their military airstrikes success.

July						
Su	Mo	Tu	We	Th	Fr	Sa
1	2	3	4	5	6	7
8	9	10	11	12	13	14
15	16	17	18	19	20	21
22	23	24	25	26	27	28
29	30	31				

6:◐ 12:● 19:◑ 27:○

Saturday July 14th will mark the observance of "Iraqi Republic Day"

A commemoration of the over throw of the Hashemite Monarchy on June 14th, 1958.

(Note) 1958 is just 1 year one year after the 1957 Eisenhower Doctrine was signed. And shows clear evidence that

Russia's offering of military and economic aid to Iraq has quickly influenced Iraq's ability to "strike, and strike hard, with continued success.

August						
Su	Mo	Tu	We	Th	Fr	Sa
				1	2	3	4
5	6	7	8	9	10	11
12	13	14	15	16	17	18
19	20	21	22	23	24	25
26	27	28	29	30	31	

4:◐ 11:● 18:◐ 26:○

Eid Al Adha begins Tuesday August 21st. Also known as the "Feast of Sacrifice",

Ironicly, Hakim (the Elder) Explaines to the brew that these 3 days commerates the willingness of (Abraham) to obey God by sacrificing his son. Hakims son Darzi listens.

And, in his own way, preparing to be sacrificed.

There will be two dry runs of the mission. The 1st dry run will take place Wednesday August 8th, Albof, Alfars, Raheem and Uda, who's February 14th, 2019 mission will be to plow their explosive packed truck's thru both entrances and exits of the Lincoln and Holland tunnels will leave the farm at 6:00 A.m. sharp. They'll drive an empty truck to Jersey City, New Jersey. They will check into their individual hotels at 3:00 P.M. sharp. They will leave their Hotel the next morning, Thursday August 9^{th,} at 3:45 A.M. sharp, and proceed to their targets in which are both less than one mile.

Yusof's target will be the Marcellus Shale gas wells and Storage tanks located in Tioga County Pennsylvania. Yusof is also scheduled to check into his hotel Wednesday 3:00 P.M. sharp. He too will complete his dry run by leaving his hotel Thursday morning at 3:45 A.M. sharp. Yusof's target is 0.8 mile from hotel.

Reheem, Aham and Malik, who's mission will be deliver their explosive packed planes to The Cooper Nuclear Power Plant with 4 reactors located in New England, The Davis-Besse nuclear power plant with 3 reactors located in Ohio and the Braidwood Nuclear power plant with 3 reactors located in Illinois respectively. Their 1st dry run will begin with departing from the St. Petersburg Airport fly round trip to their target area's and log the time to co-ordinate a 4:00 A.M. Thursday February 14th arrival.

Aban, Hakim and Darzi are planning on spending the last second of their Live's on February 14th, 2019 in New York City. Aban, in the middle of Time Square. And, Hakim and his son Darzi, will be landing on top of the Twin Tower Memorial. They will not take part in the 1st or last dry runs. They have been there and back more than enough.

Friday, August 10th everyone will meet in the farm house at 5:00 A. M. and deliver their reports in which everything went off like clockwork. Reheem remarks, "If I wanted too, I could have landed on the Cooper nuclear grounds and hardly been noticed. Albof and Alfars both agreed that with enough speed neither of them would have a problem entering the exits of the two tunnels and penetrate enough to do the job. "With not much resistance.

September						
Su	Mo	Tu	We	Th	Fr	Sa
						1
2	3	4	5	6	7	8
9	10	11	12	13	14	15
16	17	18	19	20	21	22
23	24	25	26	27	28	29
30						

2:◐ 9:● 16:◑ 24:○

Again, we are reminded that Wendell hasn't changed. We see Jamel, one of Wendell's many body guards hanging outside a seedy hotel again, waiting for the slug to finish. There will always be concerns regarding Wendell getting looseliped. And, it is their job to make sure it does not happen.

Tuesday September 11th, That's right. "9/11" The Islamic New Year is observed. This family

Celebrates as they hoot and holler with joy as they watch the television coverage of the Twin Tower attacks. An event that sadly enough, gives them hope. And the hooting and hollering just may be heard by President Trump.

October						
Su	Mo	Tu	We	Th	Fr	Sa
	1	2	3	4	5	6
7	8	9	10	11	12	13
14	15	16	17	18	19	20
21	22	23	24	25	26	27
28	29	30	31			

2:◐ 8:● 16:◑ 24:○ 31:◐

In early October Wendell crosses the line. As Jamal, one of Wendell's chaperones is in waiting at the, "Let Me Bop You" Motel, 2 police vehicles swarm into the parking lot. They approach

Jamal who is leaning up against room 12, they inform him that they have received a call concerning domestic abuse in room 12. When the Police Officers enter the room, they immediately know who they are dealing with. They are very familiar with who and what Wendell Bowman is about.

The lady does not press charges. She just takes a gift of $130.000.00 and is gone.

Aban and Hakim come up with a new plan to keep Wendy Bowman busy without the drama. Aban is going to arrange for Wendel to begin making generous contributions to his and surrounding Communities. Wendell will soak in that adulation like a sponge soaks in water. For the first time these residents will begin to like Wendell. But, unknown to them, it's all because of a deceitful order from Aban to give these generous contributions in efforts to keep everyone off guard and have them blinded by the light of the contributions so that they cannot see any red flags. One of Wendell's," oh, I mean" Abans contributions of $200.000.00 has been earmarked for a library. To be completed in late November, early December. Wendell will attend the Opening

October will be the celebration of Iraqi Labor Day. It marks Iraqs independence from Britain in 1932. There is no red, white and blue for the Iraqi Independence Day. Not unless you add a bon fire to do some burning.

November

Su	Mo	Tu	We	Th	Fr	Sa
					1	2	3
4	5	6	7	8	9	10
11	12	13	14	15	16	17
18	19	20	21	22	23	24
25	26	27	28	29	30

7:● 15:◑ 23:○ 29:◐

On Tuesday, November 20th Iraqi's celebrate Muhammad's birthday. The Martyrs will for the 1st time, celebrate this religious Holiday completely out of character. They will, party hardy, and they will drink like a Roman fish.

As the evening unravels, there is another 1st, we begin see the other side to these humans no one could have imagined. "Cries for help" All except Wendell, that piece of shit has only one side to him. And it screams, "What's in it for me!

Malik at the age of 66 from Ind. & Uda, being 46 from Boston have never consumed liquor in their lives. They abstain. Raheem, 45 years old, used to drink a lot. He went sober when his brother Aasera died at the age of 57 of a cocaine overdose in 2009. Jamal at 43, and Yusaf 44 respectively get trashed. Aban 90, and Hakim 88 have a taste for Araq. An alcoholic beverage. Araq meaning perspiration. The beverage is served in a cup of ice. The ice must be in the cup before the Araq is poured. Made from the strains of anise. Both Aban and Hakim are sitting back and trying to take this all in. The reality of what seems like a crash landing with no notice. It all had to do with some numbers on a little piece of fucking paper. It will have become a full circle on Thursday February 14th, 2019. Aham 22, Albof 21, and Alfars 24 will take advantage of a rare November warm front coming thru the central Pennsylvania area. They'll sleep under the stars. These young Martyrs are from a different generation. Alcohol is not their choice. They enjoy their own incense, Darzi joined the young comrades. Darzi has so many questions about his home land. "Does average Iraqi Country men and woman back home know about our mission"?

All three without any hesitation said, "NO ONE! We've never even got to know the operators of the wheel. In fact, we just learned about the wheel two days before we left home for America. Ever since we were very young, and, in our childhood, we have been in training and waiting for our mission to serve our country and give our lives for Allah."

"Are the woman as beautiful as I am told?

"Is America hated as much as I am told?

"Is our homeland as beautiful as they say, ETC.

Hakim & Aban for the 1st time in memory, feel complete calm. They both call it a night before midnight. And, for the 1st time since they were young toddlers slept in the same room on a set of bunk beds. Their life has come full circle. No words, they never forgot that comfort they knew so well.

Malik and Uda, Sober when it comes to alcohol., have taken the role of a shepherd watching over their sheep. They squash any animosity among the drunk. Raheem who has been sober for several years joins the Young recruits and Darzi outside. Alfars decides to build a bon fire.

Reheem announces "it's time for me to get off the wagon"

Jamal and Yusaf will be heard thru the night singing old time Iraqi songs. Yusaf goes so far as to streak around the farm. It does not last long. He passes out by the bon fire before midnight.

They danced, they sang, some cried, some laughed. But together there was a mutual bond. As evident the next day. It seems they had immortalized the meaning of comrades'.

December						
Su	Mo	Tu	We	Th	Fr	Sa
						1
2	3	4	5	6	7	8
9	10	11	12	13	14	15
16	17	18	19	20	21	22
23	24	25	26	27	28	29
30	31					

7:● 15:◑ 22:○ 29:◐

Sunday, December 16th, The Community who at one time had no time for Wendell. Honor him at the opening of the new W. Bowman county Library.

Tuesday, December 25th, Christmas, all over the world.

The "FAMILY" meaning all, will follow the Muslim Customs of religious worship. Beginning with "the night before Christmas."

Held usually in the courtyard, in this case, the spacious acreage of the well-groomed farm. The children would then read the story of the Nativity from an Arabic Bible while those present hold lighted candles.

DARZI READS OUT LOUD. For everyone to hear.

JANUARY						
S	M	T	W	T	F	S
30	31	1	2	3	4	5
6	7	8	9	10	11	12
13	14	15	16	17	18	19
20	21	22	23	24	25	26
27	28	29	30	31	1	2
3	4	5	6	7	8	9

FEBRUARY						
S	M	T	W	T	F	S
27	28	29	30	31	1	2
3	4	5	6	7	8	9
10	11	12	13	14	15	16
17	18	19	20	21	22	23
24	25	26	27	28	1	2
3	4	5	6	7	8	9

<u>Monday January 5th</u>, the 2nd and last dry run will take place. This will be an exact replica of the 1st dry run in and again, go off without a hitch.

<u>On Friday February 1st</u> Hakim and Aban call in Wendell to give him his one-way tickets to Switzerland. Scheduled to leave with in the week. Aban tells Wendell "You will be meeting with a gentleman tomorrow who will create his new identity. Including a new birth certificate, Switzerland State I.D., A new Social Security Number etc.". Hakim hands Wendell his swiss bank account that reflects the 10 million Wendell himself transferred. Wendell has become like a big piece of putty in the two man's hands. And Wendell is stupid as hell to boot. A soft-spoken Hakim convinces Wendell to wright a suicide notes and leave it for the authorities to find to throw them off track and have them assume that "you, Wendell, may already be dead". Wendell writes his own suicide letter. As Wendell hands Hakim his suicide letter, Aban immediately wraps a hang noose around Wendell's neck. What a show!!!!!!! Both Aban and Hakim immediately begin to carry out the brutal hanging of Wendell Bowman. Starting with the brothers walking out the kitchen door of their farmhouse, pulling a rope that is tied around Wendell's neck and dragging

him across the porch, and down a flight of stairs. You hear him squealing for mercy as he is drug nearly 100 feet into the barn. Hakim decides to take a short cut and drags him thru a portion of the corn field. Wendell' for some stupid reason, keeping a grip on his airline tickets and his Swiss bank account. After in the barn, we continue to hear Wendell's screams for about 30 seconds more. It is a grounding scene as he hangs in a hidden and concealed shaft out of view from almost every angle of the barn. Aban lies Wendell's suicide note below his dangling feet. They will all call it suicide. Rumer has it that Wendell left hanging for 2 weeks before they took him down.

Hakim couldn't help but to remember his own wife Abido, and the heart wrenching look on her face of total disbelief and heartache at the image of their own son Tony Abdyllin hanging Even though that was 38 years ago, it seemed to Hakim, just like It was yesterday.

On Saturday February 2nd Aban and Hakim are seen having a cup of coffee together in the farm house kitchen like nothing happened yesterday.

On Sunday February 3rd, everyone takes time to clean house. Their purpose is to destroy all their personal belongings so not to leave a trace of their human side.

On Monday February 4th, 10 days until their dead. Alfars, Albaf, Aham and Darzi begin their daily work routine on the farm. This week they will very carefully prepare the more than enough lethal explosive materials to go around. Raheem and Malik head off to the airport and spend their last working hours there making sure the runway is ready and preparing the planes for a very important last-minute load of high density explosive material. Yusof, Jamal,

Reheem and Uda head to their job at Wendell's produce trucking company. They will be rotating trucks back and forth to and from the farm this final week in preparation of their mission. All this while never giving anyone a clue there is much more than meets the eyes. Their focus and mission obedience make it look almost effortless.

On Tuesday, February 5th Wendell is never missed. He's been known to be out of for a week or more at times. No one keeps track. No one really cares.

Wednesday February 6th, we watch as Reheem and Malik empty any unwanted cargo from the planes and begin to systematically, while wasting no space, replacing it with a staggering amount of devastating explosive material.

Thursday February 7th, Yusof, Jamal, Reheem and Uda fill up the 7 trucks With gas, then Systematically, while wasting no space, with more of the same staggering amount of devastating explosive material.

On Friday, February 8th, still, no one is missing Wendell. Even the farm hands don't acknowledge he hasn't been seen in a few days. They assume he's in his room on another drinking binge.

On Saturday Feb 9th, Alfars and Albaf complain of a sickening smell in the barn.

They describe the smell as if it was a cellar full of dead rats.

Sunday February 10th, a few of the men living on the farm begin to question where Wendall is. Not that they even care one iota. To them, it's like losing a matching sock.

<u>On Monday February 11th</u>, Wendel is found hanging in the barn. For the second time, he bought the farm. They called it suicide. They found a suicide note. We all know that he was left hanging for two weeks before he was taken down. His wake is scheduled Thursday February 14th, 2019

It does not take lone for everyone who knows nothing, think they have a handle on all the details regarding Wendell's will. (To everyone's surprise) Wendell named Darzi as the executor of his will and left him the bulk of the winnings that were left. The money has no significance because Wendell's will not be read until after Wendell's wake. And, by then after the dusts settles, the mission will be complete. What is significant? Wendell's three companies, The St. Petersburg Airport, the produce Trucking and the farm will operate as usual for the time being. Enough time to complete the mission.

<u>On Tuesday February 12th</u>, Raheem, an Indiana boy, has been known to experiment in the drug world. When he gets busted for cocaine, investigators smell a rat. The investigation uncovers he spent most of his life in Indiana. The authority's call Frank Gage into the picture, Gage is a retired lead F.B.I. agent who investigated terrorism in the Mid-Western United States. Including the State of Indiana. He visits the farm. He sees Raheem! Raheem sees Frank Gage. Frank's gut sinks. Frank remembers, like it was yesterday he saw that face. In 1994 Raheem was one of those Frank investigated only to have the system slam the door in his face. Agent Frank Gage immediately relays the following message to the Federal burau of Investigations division on terror. and the heads of Homeland Security.

"WE GOT A PROBLEM ON THE FARM!"

On Wednesday morning, February 13th at 6:00 A.M. sharp. Yusof is the 1st Martyr to leave and complete his mission and die for Allah. He drove off with his truck filled with cataclysmic destructives. With very few words spoken, at 7:00 A.M. sharp, Albof, Alfars, Raheem and Uda follow suit. There was nothing to be said. On to Jersey City, New Jersey. They separated ways forever.

The heads of the F.B.I. and Homeland Security meet with Frank Gage, local Law Enforcement, and federal agents. They spend less than 24 hours investigating the brew that live at the farm and uncovered enough evidence and were immediately granted the warrants they need to go in.

Back at the farm, Aban is walking by Hakim and says, "I am going to take my last shower." Hakims head goes down for a second. Then immediately he snaps it back up straight. Even with his spine, back straight and says to Aban, "I think I'll go do the same".

Back at the war room, Frank is reminding everyone of the red flags the Government ignored and the abuse his departments dealt out in the name of "First amendment rights". This scene is difficult for Agent Frank Gage, who will forever remember his own investigators having over the top, dangerous liberal ideals and treating the three suspects with kid gloves. Frank describes how the investigating team turned their heads to most of his concerns back in in 1994. Those concerns included their secluded life styles with no spouse or significant other, their application for their pilot license, and their completion of the course all simultaneously. Boom, Boom, Boom. The fact that all three have been cited by their own trucking company (one of the largest in the State of Indiana) for habitual violations including keeping company trucks over the weekends. But most importantly, their reluctance to come clean when investigated. And, their stories didn't match.

And now, the airport, trucking Company and a farm to boot.

The decision is made, and it was clear. The F.B.I. and Homeland Security agree they will go in tomorrow, Thursday February 14th, 2019 with an early morning raid. "We want them sleeping!" one agent is heard saying. Agents prepare thru the night and the beginning of the early morning.

That same night between the hours of 11:00 P.M. Wednesday night February 13th and 1:00 A.M. Thursday morning February 14th, Malik, Raheem and Hakam take off from the St. Petersburg Airport for the last time.
Aban, Hakim and darzi are all that remains. They hug and are all in flight by 1:00 A.M.

2:00 A.M. Thursday February 14th, 2019. There is no sign of life on the farm.

Thursday February 14th, 2:00 A.M. There is no sign of life on the farm. 4;00 A.M. this calculated full fledge morning raid on the farm is executed by the F.B.I. and Homeland Security! F.B.I. Agent Frank Gage finally sees a means to an end. An empty farm.

For Frank Gage, it's 3 strikes you're out. The news of the terror strike comes quickly to the agents.

DOOMSDAY

*There has been a single attack

*The first Plane hit a nuclear power plant, Braidwood 1 IL. 3 reactors. (Millik)

*Then another one crashed into Cooper nuclear Power Plant, N.E. 4 reactors (Raheem)

*Then another one, Downed at the Davis-Besse nuclear Power Plant, OH. 3 reactors (Hakim)

*A plane lands dead center in Time Squares, N.Y. (Aham)

*Then the last plane, piloted by Hakim and Darzi, shot down, exploding somewhere below in the New York skyline. Short of their target. The Twin Tower memorial building. Darzi will be sacrificed in the same plane by his father's side.

*Two trucks ram through the Lincoln and Holland Tunnels in the middle of the night entering the wrong way at tunnels exits with little to no flow of traffic or security (Albof, Alfars)

*Two trucks ram through the Lincoln and Holland Tunnels in the middle of the night accessing the entrance. With no to little traffic or security (Raheem, Uda)

*A truck Rams through the Philadelphia Independence Hall (Jamal)

* A final truck rams thru Marcellus Shale gas storage tanks in Western Pennsylvania' (Usof)

*Within minutes air traffic control towers and Homeland Security see the red flags.

* How many planes? Where are they going? How many trucks? Where are they going?

Back at Wendell's wake. All those people and organizations he had promised to put in his will show up. Not one could care less about the man himself. Their presence stood for only one thing. They have become just like the piece of shit laying out in the coffin. What's in it for me, and where's my money. The service is interrupted by the news of a U.S terror strike that has taken a grip of the entire World's attention. As the news filters in, they realize who the terrorists are and there is complete shock. Then you start hearing from a few "know it all" attendees, "I knew something was wrong, "he told me he had a big secret" I told people not to trust them. etc.

*President Trump orders with the unanimous approval of Congress

*A COMPLETE OVERHAUL OF THE LOTTERY SYSTEM!

Dedicated
to
The Innocent

1957

1. Abdyllin - The Patriarch of the Family. His age is unknown. Longest grey beard in the village. Father of 10 Children. His eldest son is 40 years old. Abdyllin passes in 1662.
2. Gabir - 58 Wife of Abdyllin – Liberal in the eyes of the Muslim faith. Gabir passes in 1963.
3. Aban - 28 son of Abdylln – his goal is to become Patriarch. Dies February 14th, 2019.
4. Amira - 28 wife of Aban – is most enamored of Western culture. Returns to Iraq, 2017.
5. Tawfeek - 3-year-old son of Aban – born the year of the Eisenhower Doctrine. Returns to Iraq, 2017.
6. Hakim - 26 son of Abdyllin – more focused on family than the other men. Dies February 14th, 2019.
7. Abido - 26 faithful wife of Hakim – she relishes the role of mother. Returns to Iraq, 2017.
8. Amirmoez - 6-year-old son of Hakim – always trying to keep up with older brother, Darzi. Passes of a cocaine overdose, 1989.
9. Darzi - 8-year-old son of Hakim-very intelligent. Dies February 14th, 2019.
10. Zaid – early 20's - Tutor/Translator. Continues to teach.

1960

11. Ajam - gentleman lawyer in Philadelphia helps Iraqis come to America, cuts through red tape and does it pro bono. Returns to Iraq in 1963.
12. Fr. Michael – Priest at St. Gertrude's, ahead of his time, very nice. Retires in 1999.

1962

13. Beth- child of an illicit affair. Attends school with Tawfeek and becomes his wife. Returns to Iraq with Tawfeek.

1967

14. Tony-Son of Hakim & Abido. Passes 1980.

1970

15. Wendel Bowman-A piece of shit that will sell out his Country for$$$. Dies January 13th, 2018.

1971

16. Jake-Father of three. Owner of the farm where Aban and Hakim find employment. Passes 2001.
17. Emilia-Jakes wife. Passes 2004.
18. Mark-Son of Jake and Emilia. Alive and well.
19. Anna-Daughter of Jake and Emilia. Alive and well.
20. John-Son of Jake and Emilia. Alive and well.

1975

21. Shada -Returns with Aban and Hakim, shortly after arriving she will marry Amirmoez. Son of Hakim. Returns to Iraq, 2017.

1976

22. Aasera-Arrives in the U.S. as a martyr and part of the mission. Passes 2009. Cell Cancer.

23. Milik -Arrives in the U.S. as a martyr and is part of the mission. Dies February 14th, 2018.
24. Raheem Arrives in the U.S. as a martyr's and part of the Mission. Dies February 14th, 2018.

1978

25. Moncha -Father of 4 boys-Who are to be brought up to be martyrs and part of the mission. Passes 1996. Heart attack.
(A proud day for his parents?)
26. Sabeen-Wife of Moncha. Returns to Iraq, 2017.
27. Boy 1 Jamal 3 Years old. Dies February 14th, 2018.
28. Boy2 Yusof 4 Years old. Dies February 14th, 2018.
29. Boy 3 Reheem 5 years old. Dies February 14th, 2019.
30. Boy 4 Uda 6 years old. Dies February 14th, 2019.

1979

30 ½.Ali Jared-Moves to Australia. Walks away and refuses the violence.
The Hero.

1985

31. Sanaa – mother of Shada. Lives in Iraq.
32. Jamail – father of Shada. Lives in Iraq.
33. Shatha – sister of Shada, daughter of Jamail. Lives in Iraq.
34. Leyla – sister of Shada, daughter of Jamail. Lives in Iraq.

1994

Frank Gage-Lead F.B.I. agent investigating this terroristic cell sees it come full circle. 3 strikes you're out.

1997

Diana 18 Will marry Ali Jared. Moves home to Australia with husband Ali Jared.

2017

35. Aham- Last-minute Martyr-All due the LOTTERY. Dies February 14th, 2019.
36. Albaf- Last Minute Martyr-All do to the LOTTERY. Dies February 14th, 2019.
37. Alfars- Last-minute Martyr-All do to the LOTTERY. Dies February 14th,2019.
38. * Sign of the times
39. <u>A complete waste of time</u>
40. 5th Wheel - Amjad – still missing.
41. 5th Wheel - Bousaid – suicide by hanging. Rumor has it he remained hanging for five minutes before being taken down.

A little about the author

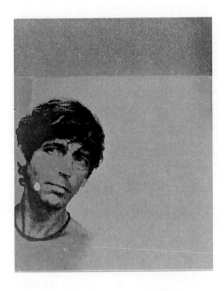

Tony Matula was born May 25, 1957

He watched the formation of the first interstate Lottery. Which scared the hell out of him.

- Favorite shade is burlesque. Favorite book is, "One Month to LIVE.
- Is Tony's life full circle? Not even close.

To learn more about the Author: Go to: www.tonymatula.com

D0681463

At Issue

Is Organic Food Better?

Other Books in the At Issue Series:

At Issue

Is Organic Food Better?

Ronald D. Lankford, Jr., Book Editor

GREENHAVEN PRESS
A part of Gale, Cengage Learning

GALE
CENGAGE Learning·

Detroit • New York • San Francisco • New Haven, Conn • Waterville, Maine • London

GALE
CENGAGE Learning

Christine Nasso, *Publisher*
Elizabeth Des Chenes, *Managing Editor*

© 2011 Greenhaven Press, a part of Gale, Cengage Learning.

Gale and Greenhaven Press are registered trademarks used herein under license.

For more information, contact:
Greenhaven Press
27500 Drake Rd.
Farmington Hills, MI 48331-3535
Or you can visit our Internet site at gale.cengage.com

For product information and technology assistance, contact us at

Gale Customer Support, 1-800-877-4253
For permission to use material from this text or product, submit all requests online at www.cengage.com/permissions.

Further permissions questions can be e-mailed to permissionrequest@cengage.com.

Articles in Greenhaven Press anthologies are often edited for length to meet page requirements. In addition, original titles of these works are changed to clearly present the main thesis and to explicitly indicate the author's opinion. Every effort is made to ensure that Greenhaven Press accurately reflects the original intent of the authors. Every effort has been made to trace the owners of copyrighted material.

Cover image copyright Debra Hughes 2007. Used under license from Shutterstock.com.

LIBRARY OF CONGRESS CATALOGING-IN-PUBLICATION DATA

Is organic food better? / Ronald D. Lankford, book editor.
    p. cm. -- (At issue)
  Includes bibliographical references and index.
  ISBN 978-0-7377-5157-4 (hardcover) -- ISBN 978-0-7377-5158-1 (pbk.)
  1. Natural foods. 2. Natural foods industry. I. Lankford, Ronald D., 1962- II. Series: At issue (San Diego, Calif.)
  HD9000.5.I814 2011
  641.3'02--dc22

                                   2011000871

Printed in the United States of America
1 2 3 4 5   15 14 13 12 11

ED084

Contents

Introduction

In recent years, organic food has generally become more popular, increasing its market share against traditional food sold in discount grocery stores (like Safeway or Kroger). This growth has been evident in the increase of chain stores such as Whole Foods, Earth Fare, and Trader Joe's that specialize in organic products, but also in the decisions of more mainstream grocers like Wal-Mart to carry organic food. The rise in importance of organic food is also evident in the increased involvement of federal agencies like the United States Food and Drug Administration (FDA) in regulating organic food. With a growing customer base, wider availability, and official regulators, many observers believe that organic food will continue to become increasingly popular in the future.

The number of organic food offerings, however, is inequitable with the choices offered in traditional food markets. While there may be multiple reasons for this, one is cited most often: organic food is generally more expensive than traditional, non-organic food. The extra expense of organic food becomes even more problematic during difficult economic times, as with the economic downturn in the United States and Europe that began in 2007. When consumers who are inclined to purchase organic food have less money, they can save by switching to non-organic.

Because of the worldwide recession, social commentators have wondered whether recent trends in organic food sales will be maintained or reversed. Will organic food reach a greater number of consumers in the near future? Or will organic food, as long as it remains more expensive, never reach more than a limited niche group?

Market Shares for Organic Food

According to the Organic Trade Association, organic food purchases have trended upward since 2000. Between 2000 and

2009, sales of organic food in the United States grew from one billion dollars to nearly $25 billion. This increase is also reflected in the amount of land reserved for organic agriculture, equaling 4.8 million acres of crop land and pasture in 2009. According to the Organic Trade Association, sales increased 5.1 percent from 2008 to 2009. While these statistics are impressive evidence of the growth of the organic food market, they should be measured against other organic food trends and changes.

Even as organic food sales grow, they remain a small part of the overall market share in the United States. Organic food and beverages equaled 3.7 percent of the nation's sales on these types of items, while organic farm land equaled only .7 percent of all American farmland. Likewise, organic pasture for livestock only equaled .5 percent of all American pasture. Even while organic food continued to reach more consumers, then, it captured a relatively small portion of the overall market.

In Great Britain, both the land used by organic farmers and the number of organic producers decreased slightly between 2008 and 2009. On the international level, sales of organic food increased by 1.7 percent. While this last statistic shows an increase in the organic food market, it is a significant drop from the 26 percent growth in organic food sales registered over the last several years. This drop suggests that the overall growth of organic food sales on an international level has—at least temporarily—stalled.

Specialty Grocers and Co-ops

The organic food market has experienced other changes and setbacks over the last two or three years. During the recent economic downturn, some specialty grocery stores have lost sales to more mainstream grocers like Safeway and Harris Teeter. This seems to indicate that while a number of consumers continue to buy organic food, they tend to purchase those foods at discount grocery stores rather than specialty stores in a less robust economy. In 2009, for instance, sales at natural food stores had dropped at least 12% from the previous year.

Traditional natural-organic grocery stores have also lost ground to increasingly popular co-ops. With co-ops, a number of people buy-in to a grocery store for a set price, allowing them to own and operate the store. Co-ops specializing in organic food frequently attempt to buy products locally. While co-ops typically only serve a small number of customers (the people who own the store), these stores have less overhead and can provide organic food cheaper than many chain stores. As a result, many people have started local co-ops as a way to avoid the higher costs of grocery chains.

While economic setbacks and co-ops have offered significant challenges to natural food chains like Trader Joe's and Whole Foods, these specialty companies have nonetheless continued to stay profitable and build new stores during the current economic slump. Unlike many traditional grocery chains, they have also been able to remain profitable without cutting prices.

Wave of the Future or Small Niche?

As the growth of organic food markets has slowed, observers have debated the reasons for this slowdown. A key reason is the ongoing economic crisis, squeezing consumers who formerly chose to buy organic food. According to this line of thought, organic food sales will resume growth and steadily increase market share once the US and other world economies begin to recover. It is also possible that current trends, such as the growth of co-ops, will pose less prominent competition.

Others have suggested that organic food levels will remain fairly steady, continuing to capture a niche market of upper middle class consumers, but little more. In other words, these critics have suggested that organic food has reached as many people as it can reach as long as the cost of these products remains significantly higher than traditional groceries. In fact, the argument states, affluent customers are the very reason that the organic market has remained steady during the recent economic downturn: these upper middle class customers have been less affected by the crisis than those with lower incomes.

Other changes, however, may point to future areas of new growth. Companies have begun offering organic baby food and organic pet food, potentially expanding sales to new customers or expanding sales to current customers. How these new products or other trends will affect the organic food market, however, will probably remain unclear until the current economic crisis passes.

Organic Food: An Overview

Katherine J. Chen

Katherine J. Chen is a writer majoring in English at Princeton University.

Organic food has become a worldwide trend. While debate continues on whether or not organic food is healthier than non-organic food, consumers find a number of benefits to organic food. For instance, organic vegetables are grown without pesticides, and animals on organic farms are allowed to graze in a natural environment. Also, many consumers believe that organic food tastes better. Despite these advantages, there are problems with organic food from a consumer's point of view. Standards for organic foods are sometimes confusing and many shoppers complain that organic food is too expensive. Despite these outstanding issues, consumers continue to purchase more and more organic food.

The purchase of organic food has become nothing short of a global trend, as consumers aim to spend money on products they feel they can relate to and trust. This means knowing exactly what food is made of, how it is processed and its country of origin.

While millions of shoppers continue to flock to grocery stores and farmers' markets, investing their faith (and dollars) in the promise of healthy organic foods, the debate surrounding the true value of "organic" has yet to reach a definitive conclusion. The return to a so-called "natural diet" piques

Katherine J. Chen, "How Organic Is Organic Food?" *Earth 911*, March 8, 2010. Reprinted with permission.

shoppers' interests—enough to generate a global organic market valued at an estimated $48 billion in 2007.

Is Organic Food Healthier?

In July 2009, researchers in London claimed that customers only purchase organic food because they believe it is healthier for their bodies. Scientists at the London School of Hygiene & Tropical Medicine, however, were not convinced.

After a review of 162 scientific papers published in the last 50 years, the research team concluded that there was simply no notable difference between reportedly healthier organic food and conventionally processed food products.

"There is currently no evidence to support the selection of organically over conventionally produced foods on the basis of nutritional superiority," says Alan Dangour, one of the report's authors.

On the other side of the debate, the Soil Association, an international charity whose primary activities involve campaigning for public education on nutrition and health and participates in the certification of organic food in the U.K., disagrees.

In order to make educated decisions about the benefits of organic food, shoppers must first understand what sets organic products apart.

In response to the July 2009 report on the lack of additional health benefits in organic food, the Soil Association's Policy Director Peter Melchett stated in a press release, "We are disappointed in the conclusions the researchers have reached. The review rejected almost all of the existing studies of comparisons between organic and non-organic nutritional differences."

"Although the researchers say that the differences between organic and non-organic food are not 'important', due to the relatively few studies, they report in their analysis that there are higher levels of beneficial nutrients in organic compared to non-organic foods."

Despite in which camp your opinions lie, the implied power of eating organic still holds sway over shoppers' decisions.

What Does the Label Mean?

In order to make educated decisions about the benefits of organic food, shoppers must first understand what sets organic products apart from their conventional counterparts and what qualifies as "organic" in the U.S.

"Organic refers to the way agricultural products are grown and processed," says Jennifer Rose, new media manager and staff writer of the Organic Trade Association (OTA). "It includes a system of production, processing, distribution and sales that assures consumers that the products maintain the organic integrity that begins on the farm."

"This system which is governed by strict government standards," Rose explains, "requires that products bearing the organic label are made without the use of toxic and persistent pesticides and synthetic nitrogen fertilizers, antibiotics, synthetic hormones, genetic engineering or other excluded practices, sewage, sludge or irradiation."

Jack Hunter, spokesman for the U.K.-based Soil Association, says, "Certain standards for animal welfare, avoidance of chemicals and harmful food additives form the basis for the trade term 'organic.' This is enshrined in European law, but many organizations set their standards above this level, including ours. The Soil Association is considered one of the highest standards in the world, so consumers seeing our distinctive logo can be sure of high standards, policed by our inspectors who visit all levels of the production chain on an annual and unannounced basis."

According to Hunter, many of the benefits of organic food are even overlooked by consumers who believe that these products are better only in the sense that they contain no chemicals, antibiotics, traces of pesticides or fertilizers.

"Organic is a package of really worthwhile things," he says. "This often makes it hard to understand and is why most people think organic equals no chemicals. Organic is all about producing food in a way that doesn't harm people or the environment."

Given the environmental benefits of eating organic, it is no shock that many consumers find organic food more pleasing to the palate.

Sustainable Farming

Organic food is tied directly to the concept of sustainable farming, which covers every part of the food production process from the way animals are fed and their living conditions to the types of amendments that can or cannot be added to the soil in which products are grown.

"So where a worrying amount of pigs, chickens and cows can be reared in miserable conditions, grow faster than their bodies can cope with, are fed things they have not evolved to eat and get a liberal dose of drugs, organic farming does not allow such abuses in the name of profit," Hunter says.

Rose shares a similar sentiment on the overall benefits of organic farming and says that in addition to the environmental benefits, which include soil health, carbon sequestration, clean water supplies and the many personal health advantages organic food has to offer, organic farmers are required by law in the U.S. to "provide their animals with access to the outdoors and pasture, quality organic feed and safe, clean living conditions" without the use of antibiotics or synthetic growth hormones.

"Because organic farms are less intensive, they are far better for wildlife, both in terms of diversity and sheer numbers," Hunter says. "Fields growing wheat one year will need to replace the lost nitrogen through manure and growing clover, for example."

Given the environmental benefits of eating organic, it is no shock either that many consumers find organic food more pleasing to the palate. Nutritionists around the world have also revealed that organic food contains higher levels of several important vitamins and minerals, including vitamin C, calcium, magnesium, iron, and chromium, in addition to cancer-fighting antioxidants and omega-3 fatty acids. According to Hunter, a good example is organic milk, which has on average 68 percent more omega-3 essential fatty acids than conventionally produced milk.

Organic Food Standards

Despite the progressive move towards organic products around the world, there are still some confusing aspects of organic food, such as why standards vary from country to country and also—from an ecological point of view—whether organic food outweighs the benefits of buying local, conventionally grown food from community farmers.

Rose explains that the difference in organic standards exists simply because the development of these laws originates at the national versus international level.

Despite the progressive move towards organic products around the world, there are still some confusing aspects of organic food.

"Some may be very similar as they may have followed direction from an international body, such as the International Federation of Organic Agriculture Movements (IFOAM)," she says. "OTA is supportive of equivalence or trade agreements with other countries, and there has been some progress on this front, such as the equivalence agreement between the U.S. and Canada signed last year [2009]."

"However, in order to be sold as organic in the U.S., products, regardless of their origin, must meet U.S. standards. Thus, it doesn't matter where they were grown. They must be certified by USDA [United States Department of Agriculture] accredited certifying agents or by agencies within their countries that have been recognized by USDA as meeting the requirements of the National Organic Program."

When asked which is more beneficial, buying local produce from farmers or purchasing organic food from the supermarket, Rose says, "It's great if you have a personal relationship with a local farmer whose production methods you can trust. It is important to remember, though, that only products bearing the organic label afford government-backed assurance about how they were grown and processed. So, if you want to be sure that what you buy has indeed been grown and processed according to strict production and processing standards, organic is the best choice."

When it comes to organic foods, sentiments and opinions run strong.

Organic Food's Carbon Footprint

Hunter, on the other hand, advises consumers to do a little bit of both when grocery shopping.

"Local food is going to be fresher than anything you can buy in the supermarket, organic or not," he says. "Because many nutrients break down with time, local food is often more nutritious, too. But unless it's organic, it may have been grown with pesticides and on farms that are a disaster for wildlife. If you can afford it, buy local and organic. Often, local is the cheapest way of buying organic. It's significantly cheaper to get through box schemes than at the supermarket and sometimes even cheaper at a farm shop or farmers' market."

Yet another issue that researchers have raised in the past is whether or not the benefits of organic food outweigh the extra costs in shipping or fuel. In terms of fossil fuels, is an organic apple traveling from Washington state to Pennsylvania really worth the extra mileage?

Rose says organic food actually helps to reduce our carbon footprint and combat climate change by preventing organic farmers from using fossil fuel-based fertilizers. She believes that shipping organic products, even from a distance as wide as California to New York, makes no difference since non-organic products are usually shipped the same way.

Hunter, however, sees it differently. "The benefits and pitfalls of flying produce around the world is a complicated one involving third world development, consumer choice and the balancing of competing environmental issues," he says. "Some products can't be grown in colder climates and need to be transported long distances. This isn't much of an issue where these are shipped, but are problematic when flying is involved. Some of this is undoubtedly organic."

Is Non-Organic Food Really Cheaper?

When it comes to organic foods, sentiments and opinions run strong. While researchers such as those at the London School of Hygiene & Tropical Medicine believe that the alleged benefits of organic food are negligible, other organizations are campaigning in countries around the world to promote the consumption of organic produce and meat.

"The basic message is that in the race to make food cheap—which is a good thing—there has been these unintended consequences which mean that really, it's not that cheap at all," Hunter says. "Not if you consider that so many of us are becoming obese, in large part because of the rubbish many of us are now eating. It's also not cheap on the animals that suffer or the environment that is trashed."

Whatever the opinion of these organizations or campaigns, the ultimate choice is still left to the consumer, who must determine whether the extra financial costs of organic food are worth the health benefits so frequently debated by researchers for nearly an entire century.

2

National Standards for Organic Food

United States Department of Agriculture

The United States Department of Agriculture (USDA) oversees farm product standards by conducting inspections and enforcing federal laws. The USDA's oversight includes the development and implementation of the National Organic Program.

In 1990, Congress passed an organic food act, allowing the USDA to regulate organic farms and organic food standards. These standards include setting criteria for production and handling, labeling, certification, and accreditation of organic products. While these standards are designed to regulate domestic organic food production, they also apply to any imported organic food.

Congress passed the Organic Foods Production Act (OFPA) of 1990. The OFPA required the U.S. Department of Agriculture (USDA) to develop national standards for organically produced agricultural products to assure consumers that agricultural products marketed as organic meet consistent, uniform standards. The OFPA and the National Organic Program (NOP) regulations require that agricultural products labeled as organic originate from farms or handling operations certified by a State or private entity that has been accredited by USDA.

The NOP is a marketing program housed within the USDA Agricultural Marketing Service. Neither the OFPA nor the NOP regulations address food safety or nutrition.

USDA, "National Organic Program," April 2008. Reprinted with permission.

How Was the NOP Developed?

The NOP developed national organic standards and established an organic certification program based on recommendations of the 15-member National Organic Standards Board (NOSB). The NOSB is appointed by the Secretary of Agriculture and is comprised of representatives from the following categories: farmer/grower; handler/processor; retailer; consumer/public interest; environmentalist; scientist; and certifying agent.

Organic crops are raised without using most conventional pesticides, petroleum-based fertilizers, or sewage sludge-based fertilizers.

In addition to considering NOSB recommendations, USDA reviewed State, private and foreign organic certification programs to help formulate these regulations. The NOP regulations are flexible enough to accommodate the wide range of operations and products grown and raised in every region of the United States.

What Is in the NOP Regulations?

Production and handling standards address organic crop production, wild crop harvesting, organic livestock management, and processing and handling of organic agricultural products. Organic crops are raised without using most conventional pesticides, petroleum-based fertilizers, or sewage sludge-based fertilizers. Animals raised on an organic operation must be fed organic feed and given access to the outdoors. They are given no antibiotics or growth hormones.

The NOP regulations prohibit the use of genetic engineering, ionizing radiation, and sewage sludge in organic production and handling. As a general rule, all natural (non-synthetic) substances are allowed in organic production and all synthetic substances are prohibited. The National List of Allowed Synthetic and Prohibited Non-Synthetic Substances, a section in the regulations, contains the specific exceptions to the rule.

Labeling standards are based on the percentage of organic ingredients in a product. Products labeled "100 percent organic" must contain only organically produced ingredients. Products labeled "organic" must consist of at least 95 percent organically produced ingredients. Products meeting the requirements for "100 percent organic" and "organic" may display the USDA Organic seal.

Products labeled "100 percent organic" must contain only organically produced ingredients.

Processed products that contain at least 70 percent organic ingredients can use the phrase "made with organic ingredients" and list up to three of the organic ingredients or food groups on the principal display panel. For example, soup made with at least 70 percent organic ingredients and only organic vegetables may be labeled either "made with organic peas, potatoes, and carrots," or "made with organic vegetables." The USDA Organic seal cannot be used anywhere on the package.

Processed products that contain less than 70 percent organic ingredients cannot use the term "organic" other than to identify the specific ingredients that are organically produced in the ingredients statement.

A civil penalty of up to $11,000 for each offense can be levied on any person who knowingly sells or labels as organic a product that is not produced and handled in accordance with the National Organic Program's regulations.

Certification standards establish the requirements that organic production and handling operations must meet to become accredited by USDA-accredited certifying agents. The information that an applicant must submit to the certifying agent includes the applicant's organic system plan. This plan describes (among other things) practices and substances used in production, record keeping procedures, and practices to prevent commingling of organic and non-organic products. The certification standards also address on-site inspections.

Producers and handling (processing) operations that sell less than $5,000 a year in organic agricultural products are exempt from certification. They may label their products organic if they abide by the standards, but they cannot display the USDA Organic seal. Retail operations, such as grocery stores and restaurants, do not have to be certified.

Accreditation standards establish the requirements an applicant must meet in order to become a USDA-accredited certifying agent. The standards are designed to ensure that all organic certifying agents act consistently and impartially. Successful applicants will employ experienced personnel, demonstrate their expertise in certifying organic producers and handlers, and prevent conflicts of interest and maintain strict confidentiality.

Imported agricultural products may be sold in the United States if they are certified by USDA-accredited certifying agents. Imported products must meet the NOP standards. USDA has accredited certifying agents in several foreign countries.

In lieu [instead] of USDA accreditation, a foreign entity also may be accredited when USDA "recognizes" that its government is able to assess and accredit certifying agents as meeting the requirements of the NOP—called a recognition agreement.

3

Consumers Should Not Support Organic Foods

Rob Johnston

Rob Johnston is a doctor and science writer.

While organic food is a popular trend, many of its supposed benefits are myths. It is assumed, for instance, that organic food is good for the environment and creates sustainable agriculture. In truth, organic produce and livestock often require more carbon energy to sustain production than standard agriculture. Likewise, organic farmers declare that they do not use pesticides, but nonetheless use non-degradable copper-based solutions to treat funguses. There is also no evidence that organic food is healthier or more nutritious than non-organic food. In fact, even the belief that organic food is becoming more popular is false. In truth, less farm land is being used for organic agriculture today than in 2003.

Myth One: Organic Farming Is Good for the Environment

The study of Life Cycle Assessments (LCAs)[1] for the UK, sponsored by the Department for Environment, Food and Rural Affairs, should concern anyone who buys organic. It shows that milk and dairy production is a major source of greenhouse gas emissions (GHGs). A litre of organic milk requires

1. A Life Cycle Assessment determines the possible environmental impact of a product, process or service.

Rob Johnston, "The Great Organic Myths," *Independent*, May 2008. Reprinted by permission.

80 percent more land than conventional milk to produce, has 20 percent greater global warming potential, releases 60 percent more nutrients to water sources, and contributes 70 percent more to acid rain.

Also, organically reared cows burp twice as much methane as conventionally reared cattle—and methane is 20 times more powerful a greenhouse gas than CO_2 [carbon dioxide]. Meat and poultry are the largest agricultural contributors to GHG emissions. LCA assessment counts the energy used to manufacture pesticide for growing cattle feed, but still shows that a kilo of organic beef releases 12 percent more GHGs, causes twice as much nutrient pollution and more acid rain.

Life Cycle Assessment (LCA) relates food production to: energy required to manufacture artificial fertilisers and pesticides; fossil fuel burnt by farm equipment; nutrient pollution caused by nitrate and phosphate run-off into water courses; release of gases that cause acid rain; and the area of land farmed. A similar review by the University of Hohenheim, Germany, in 2000 reached the same conclusions (Hohenheim is a proponent of organic farming and quoted by the Soil Association).

Myth Two: Organic Farming Is More Sustainable

Organic potatoes use less energy in terms of fertiliser production, but need more fossil fuel for ploughing. A hectare of conventionally farmed land produces 2.5 times more potatoes than an organic one.

Food scares are always good news for the organic food industry.

Heated greenhouse tomatoes in Britain use up to 100 times more energy than those grown in fields in Africa. Organic yield is 75 percent of conventional tomato crops but takes twice the energy—so the climate consequences of home-grown organic tomatoes exceed those of Kenyan imports.

Defra [Department for Environment, Food and Rural Affairs] estimates organic tomato production in the UK releases almost three times the nutrient pollution and uses 25 percent more water per kg of fruit than normal production. However, a kilogram of wheat takes 1,700 joules (J) of energy to produce, against 2,500J for the same amount of conventional wheat, although nutrient pollution is three times higher for organic.

Myth Three: Organic Farming Doesn't Use Pesticides

Food scares are always good news for the organic food industry. The Soil Association and other organic farming trade groups say conventional food must be unhealthy because farmers use pesticides. Actually, organic farmers also use pesticides. The difference is that "organic" pesticides are so dangerous that they have been "grandfathered" with current regulations and do not have to pass stringent modern safety tests.

For example, organic farmers can treat fungal diseases with copper solutions. Unlike modern, biodegradable, pesticides copper stays toxic in the soil for ever. The organic insecticide rotenone (in derris) is highly neurotoxic to humans— exposure can cause Parkinson's disease. But none of these "natural" chemicals is a reason not to buy organic food; nor are the man-made chemicals used in conventional farming.

Myth Four: Pesticide Levels in Conventional Food Are Dangerous

The proponents or organic food—particularly celebrities, such as Gwyneth Paltrow, who have jumped on the organic bandwagon—say there is a "cocktail effect" of pesticides. Some point to an "epidemic of cancer". In fact, there is no epidemic of cancer. When age-standardised, cancer rates are falling dramatically and have been doing so for 50 years.

If there is a "cocktail effect" it would first show up in farmers, but they have among the lowest cancer rates of any group. Carcinogenic effects of pesticides could show up as stomach cancer, but stomach cancer rates have fallen faster than any other. Sixty years ago, all Britain's food was organic; we lived only until our early sixties, malnutrition and food poisoning were rife. Now, modern agriculture (including the careful use of well-tested chemicals) makes food cheap and safe and we live into our eighties.

Myth Five: Organic Food Is Healthier

To quote Hohenheim University: "No clear conclusions about the quality of organic food can be reached using the results of present literature and research results." What research there is does not support the claims made for organic food.

Disease is a major reason why organic animals are only half the weight of conventionally reared animals.

Large studies in Holland, Denmark and Austria found the food-poisoning bacterium Campylobacter in 100 percent of organic chicken flocks but only a third of conventional flocks; equal rates of contamination with Salmonella (despite many organic flocks being vaccinated against it); and 72 percent of organic chickens infected with parasites.

This high level of infection among organic chickens could cross-contaminate non-organic chickens processed on the same production lines. Organic farmers boast that their animals are not routinely treated with antibiotics or (for example) worming medicines. But, as a result, organic animals suffer more diseases. In 2006 an Austrian and Dutch study found that a quarter of organic pigs had pneumonia against 4 percent of conventionally raised pigs; their piglets died twice as often.

Disease is the major reason why organic animals are only half the weight of conventionally reared animals—so organic farming is not necessarily a boon to animal welfare.

Myth Six: Organic Food Contains More Nutrients

The Soil Association points to a few small studies that demonstrate slightly higher concentrations of some nutrients in organic produce—flavonoids in organic tomatoes and omega-3 fatty acids in organic milk, for example.

The easiest way to increase the concentration of nutrients in food is to leave it in an airing cupboard for a few days. Dehydrated foods contain much higher concentrations of carbohydrates and nutrients than whole foods. But, just as in humans, dehydration is often a sign of disease.

The study that found higher flavonoid levels in organic tomatoes revealed them to be the result of stress from lack of nitrogen—the plants stopped making flesh and made defensive chemicals (such as flavonoids) instead.

Despite the "boom" in organics, the amount of land being farmed organically has been decreasing since its height in 2003.

Myth Seven: The Demand for Organic Food Is Booming

Less than 1 percent of the food sold in Britain is organic, but you would never guess it from the media. The Soil Association positions itself as a charity that promotes good farming practices. Modestly, on its website, it claims: ". . . in many ways the Soil Association can claim to be the first organisation to promote and practice sustainable development." But the Soil Association is also, in effect, a trade group—and very successful lobbying organisation.

Every year, news outlets report the Soil Association's annual claim of a big increase in the size of the organic market. For 2006 (the latest available figures) it boasted sales of £1.937bn [billion].

Mintel (a retail consultantcy hired by the Soil Association) estimated only £1.5bn in organic food sales for 2006. The more reliable TNS Worldpanel, (tracking actual purchases) found just £1bn of organics sold—from a total food sector of £104bn. Sixty years ago all our food was organic so demand has actually gone down by 99 percent. Despite the "boom" in organics, the amount of land being farmed organically has been decreasing since its height in 2003. Although the area of land being converted to organic usage is scheduled to rise, more farmers are going back to conventional farming.

The Soil Association invariably claims that anyone who questions the value of organic farming works for chemical manufacturers and agribusiness or is in league with some shady right-wing US free-market lobby group. Which is ironic, considering that a number of British fascists were involved in the founding of the Soil Association and its journal was edited by one of [British politician] Oswald Mosley's blackshirts [Associated with British Union of Fascists] until the late 1960s.

All Britain's food is safer than ever before. In a serious age, we should talk about the future seriously and not use food scares and misinformation as a tactic to increase sales.

4

Non-Organic Foods Are Coated with Pesticides

Vegetarians in Paradise

Vegetarians in Paradise *is a Los Angeles–based magazine, distributing vegetarian information to the broader community.*

In 2003 the Environmental Working Group identified the "dirty dozen," a list of fruits and vegetables that had the most pesticide residues. The Environmental Working Group found numerous pesticides that were potentially harmful to consumers. Even traces of DDT (dichlorodiphenyltrichloroethane), a pesticide banned in the United States since 1972, were identifiable in certain vegetables. The dangers of pesticides are numerous. Some contain carcinogens, or cancer-causing agents, while others cause birth defects in animals. Although pesticide residue may seem small in an individual serving of fruits or vegetables, eating the five to nine recommended servings of fruits and vegetables each day will lead to greater risk. The best way to avoid pesticide contamination is to switch to organic produce.

You don't want to know what's in the next bite of that juicy peach you're devouring on that hot, summer day. If someone told you that it contained Iprodione, Azinphos methyl, and Phosmet, you might respond with a puzzled look before asking for an explanation. As few of us know, the three chemicals are designed to make sure no other creatures eat that peach before you do. In fact, they are the most common

Vegetarians in Paradise, "Dirty Dozen May End Up on Your Dinner Plate," January 1, 2006. Reprinted with permission.

of 45 different pesticides discovered in laboratory tests on peaches. Those tests revealed that pesticides were present in 94% of peaches examined.

The three pesticides are problematic for both humans and animals. Iprodione is an animal carcinogen [cancer-causing agent]; Azinphos methyl interferes with hormones; Phosmet is a triple threat by being an animal carcinogen, damaging the human reproductive system, and interfering with hormones.

Peaches seem to win the pesticide prize, but 11 other fruits and vegetables are close behind to make up the dirty dozen cited by the Environmental Working Group [EWG]. According to the *EWG Pesticides in Produce* issued in 2003, peaches, apples, bell peppers, celery, cherries, imported grapes, nectarines, pears, potatoes, red raspberries, spinach, and strawberries are the leading pesticide-laden produce items.

Measuring Pesticides in Food

In the *Food News Report Card* the Environmental Working Group ranked 46 common fruits and vegetables for pesticide contamination. Their ranking chart was based on an analysis of over 100,000 tests for pesticides on those foods, conducted from 1992 to 2001 by the US Department of Agriculture [USDA] and the Food and Drug Administration.

The EWG produced a composite score based on six measures:

- Percent of the samples tested with detectable pesticides

- Percent of the samples with two or more pesticides

- Average number of pesticides found on a sample

- Average amount (level in parts per million) of all pesticides found

- Maximum number of pesticides found on a single sample

- Number of pesticides found on the commodity in total

Being at the bottom of the rating scale is not necessarily bad, especially when the scores rank the amount of pesticide contamination. The twelve lowest pesticide purveyors are asparagus, avocados, bananas, broccoli, cauliflower, sweet corn, kiwis, mangos, onions, papayas, pineapples, and sweet peas. Being on this list did not mean the fruits or vegetables were pesticide free, just that they were least likely to have pesticide residues on them.

Eight of the dirty dozen were fruits. Over 90% of nectarines, peaches, and pears tested positive for pesticides, while nectarines, peaches, and cherries were likely to have multiple pesticides on a single sample (over 75%). Peaches and raspberries had the most pesticides on a single sample (9) with strawberries and apples close behind with 8.

Leading the dishonor roll of vegetables were celery, spinach, bell peppers, and potatoes. Celery was most likely to have multiple pesticides and had the highest percentage of samples (94%) test positive for pesticides. It almost edged out spinach for most pesticides in one sample. Spinach counted 10 pesticides with celery registering 9. Bell peppers surpassed both with 39 pesticides, the most overall.

DDT was banned because it caused significant damage to wildlife around the world.

DDT Residues

Although 70% of potatoes were found to have pesticides and its total of 29 pesticides ranked it below celery and spinach, one of those pesticides was DDT [synthetic pesticide, dichlorodiphenyltrichloroethane], which was banned in the United States after December 31, 1972. Samples of spinach also contained DDT.

According to the Natural Resources Defense Council [NRDC], "In soil, DDT lasts for a very long time because it binds strongly to soil particles. Once attached, DDT and its byproducts can persist for as long as 15 years. Moreover, when bound to soil particles, DDT can begin to bioaccumulate, building up in plants and in the fatty tissue of the fish, birds, and animals that eat the plants. Despite a longstanding ban in this country, the United States exported more than 96 tons of DDT in 1991."

The NRDC reported the presence of DDT in breast milk, although there has been a decline in countries that have banned or restricted this chemical. DDT was banned because it caused significant damage to wildlife around the world and was a suspected link to breast and liver cancer. It was also believed to hinder embryo development and reproduction. . . .

Pesticide Dangers

In looking at the test results of the dirty dozen of fruits, one notices that there are other chemical pesticides that have more dangers associated with them. Benomyl and Carbaryl, for example, have five pronounced effects. They are animal carcinogens and cause birth defects in animals. In humans they damage the reproductive system, interfere with hormones, and damage the brain and nervous system. Benomyl and Carbaryl are also found in spinach. Benomyl is also present in peaches and strawberries, while Carbaryl is evident in peaches, strawberries, raspberries, nectarines, imported grapes, cherries, bell peppers, and apples.

Another pesticide heavy hitter is Captan, a carcinogen that causes birth defects in animals. In humans it damages the reproductive system, the brain and nervous system, and the immune system. Captan has found a home in peaches, strawberries, raspberries, pears, imported grapes, and apples.

Since the National Cancer Institute and Produce for Better Health Foundation recommend eating 5 to 9 servings of fruits and vegetables and the Centers for Disease Control and Prevention recommend 5 servings, wouldn't this mean that people would be consuming more pesticides? Not necessarily, if people cut back on eating the items on the dirty dozen list. But that eliminates many vegetables that contribute nutrients beneficial to the human diet.

Going Organic

The best way to scale back pesticide consumption is to go organic. In its annual survey released in 2004, [the Organic Consumers Association] revealed that 68% of Americans have tried organic fruits and beverages compared to 54% in the two previous years. The survey also reported that 27% indicated that they consumed more organic foods and beverages than they did the year before.

The three principal reasons people gave for purchasing organic were avoidance of pesticides (70.3%), freshness, (68.3%), and health and nutrition (67.1%). Avoiding genetically modified foods was the reason given by 55% of the respondents. "Better for my health" was the answer of 52.8% while "better for the environment" was the statement of 52.4%.

The best way to scale back pesticide consumption is to go organic.

The chief obstacle to more purchases of organic items is price with 74.6% of those polled giving that as a reason for not buying more. As a positive sign more Americans (40%) now recognize the organic logo and labeling on their purchases, up 19% from 2003.

Washing Fruits and Vegetables

In response to those who suggest thorough washing of fruits and vegetables to remove pesticides, the Environmental Working Group reminds them that in the tests conducted by the USDA the produce was washed before being analyzed.

"While washing fresh produce may help reduce pesticide residues, it clearly does not eliminate them," says EWG. "Nonetheless, produce should be washed before it is eaten because washing does reduce levels of some pesticides. However, other pesticides are taken up internally in the plant, are in the fruit, and cannot be washed off. Others are formulated to bind to the surface of the crop and do not easily wash off. Peeling reduces exposures, but valuable nutrients often go down the drain with the peel."

In VIP [*Vegetarians in Paradise*] visits to farmers' markets we have noted an increase in the number of farmers selling organic produce during the last seven years. In many cases the fruits and vegetable prices are the same or even less than those in supermarkets. As more and more people purchase and demand organic the prices will come down.

VIP commends the Environmental Working Group for their efforts to make the public aware of pesticides in our food. We agree with their goal of encouraging people to eat a varied diet, wash their fruits and vegetables, and select organic whenever possible.

5

Organic Fertilizers Pose More Health Risks than Pesticides

Stanley Feldman

Stanley Feldman is a medical professional and the author of several text books, including Scientific Foundations of Anesthesia.

Organic food has been promoted as a healthier and tastier alternative to non-organic foods that are reported to be covered with dangerous pesticides. In truth, there is no such thing as non-organic food: all food is made up of organic substances. Whether a farm uses conventional or organic fertilizers, both products provide the same nutrients to soil. Organic fertilizers, however, can contain potentially hazardous bacteria. The use of natural pesticides is likewise misleading: unlike organic pesticides, conventional pesticides are monitored by the government and are completely safe. Despite many inconsistencies and half truths, the organic food market has nonetheless become successful.

*T*HE MYTH: *Non-organic foods are covered in harmful pesticides.*

THE FACT: *One of the pesticides deemed 'safe' by organic producers carries a warning that it is harmful to fish.*

As I look back to my childhood, it seems that every summer's day was sunny and filled with joy. I cannot remember it raining so hard that it spoiled a day out in the country. The food tasted better, the tomatoes were juicier, the strawberries tasted sweet and succulent and the peas that came from

Stanley Feldman, "Organic Food," *Panic Nation: Exposing the Lies We're Told About Health and Food*. London: John Blake, 2005, 47–55. Reprinted by permission.

the pods were so delicious that many were eaten raw before my mother could cook them. I realise that my memory is highly selective—there must have been rainy days, rotten tomatoes, sour strawberries and worm-infested peas, but somehow things today never seem quite as good as they were in our youth.

It is the same rose-tinted nostalgia that is used to promote organic food. The cult of natural 'organic food' is based on a belief that, while the sun may not always have shone in days gone by, the food was better and healthier before the advent of modern farming and horticulture, when the crops were liberally fertilised with manure from animal faeces or rotting vegetable waste, in the form of compost.

This belief has been energetically reinforced by the scare stories of the eco-warriors who have blamed every ill—from heart disease and cancer to global warming, pollution, less biodiversity and the rape of the countryside—on the perceived evils of modern farming.

As soon as one spurious claim is disproved another scare is invented. So vociferous and well funded is the propaganda that they have caused many otherwise sensible people, and some government agencies, to embrace the organic bandwagon, although no one has produced any evidence in its favour. By scaring the public, the organic lobby has created a billion-pound market in the UK for food that is up to 40 per cent more expensive than that produced by conventional farming and from which it is indistinguishable.

Organic vs. Nonorganic

The term *organic food* is in itself misleading. The separation into 'organic' and 'nonorganic' was based on the belief that some substances contained a life-giving property: these were originally called 'organic'. In recent times it has come to mean chemicals containing molecules based on a carbon atom. So all food is organic (with the technical exception of water).

There is no such thing as inorganic food. Whenever a pressure group resorts to a nonsense name, in order to suggest that it has nature on its side, that it has the monopoly on what is good, or that it is the only path that faithful followers of purity and truth can take, one should smell a rat.

The Soil Association, the high priests of this cult, believe that chemicals, whether organic or inorganic, are bad, a danger to the consumer, and will possibly bring death to the planet. Natural substances, by contrast, are apparently good. Yet all infections are caused by natural, organic bacteria; many organic substances produced in plants and berries, such as the belladonna of the deadly nightshade and the prussic acid in almonds, are highly poisonous; the 'natural' copper sulphate that is recommended as an organic treatment for fungal infections is so toxic to marine life that copper-based antifouling of boats has been banned in many countries. If a fungicide is not used and the ergot fungus infects cereal crops, then the unsuspecting organic consumer may end up with gangrene of fingers and toes.

In all fairness to the Soil Association, it does permit the use of pesticides provided they come from an approved list. Some have reassuringly innocent names such as 'Soft Soap', which turns out to be octodecanoic acid and carries a label warning that it is dangerous to fish.

Organic Fertiliser

The main thrust of the argument used by adherents of this cult seems to be that organic fertiliser, by which it is implied that it is produced from animal excreta or rotting vegetable waste, is necessary in order to produce food that is both nutritious and safe. This supposition is difficult to support. Manure is teeming with bacteria, many of which are pathogenic, and a few lethal. Compost rots because of the action of these bacteria, and, while they are in the main less harmful than those in manure, most sensible consumers would be reluctant to ingest them in the produce they purchase.

The root systems of plants can absorb only those nutriments that are in solution. They cannot take up particulate matter. Before the plant can use any fertiliser, organic faeces, rotting vegetable waste or chemical additive, it must first be broken down and rendered soluble in water. This necessitates reducing organic matter to its basic chemical form. It is true that in organic fertiliser these are usually more complex chemicals, but they must be rendered into the same simple basic chemicals in the plant before they can be used to encourage its growth.

There is absolutely no rational reason why all the breakdown products of organic fertiliser should not be supplied in a basic chemical form rather than leaving it to the bacteria in the soil to produce them from compost. At the end of the day, the plant uses both chemical and organic fertiliser in the same way in the same chemical processes that are essential for its growth. The main difference is that chemical fertiliser is produced with a standardised value of its content, and does not contain the dangerous bacterial pathogens present in organic waste.

The level of pesticides in our food is carefully monitored and kept below a very conservative safety level.

It was reportedly Prince Albert [husband of British monarch Queen Victoria] who started the vogue for using natural, organic household waste to fertilise the kitchen garden at Osborne House on the Isle of Wight. Prince Albert died of typhoid fever, a disease caused by ingesting food contaminated with the faeces from a carrier who may not have exhibited symptoms of the disease.

Pesticides vs. Natural Compounds

The other canon of organic law is the avoidance of known effective pesticides and the preference for naturally occurring compounds such as sulphur and copper-based chemicals to control infestations. This again is illogical. It is based on the belief that the organophosphate pesticides [those containing phosphorus] are poisonous and naturally occurring chemicals are not. This ignores the fact that sulphur and copper-based ones are also poisonous. Both organophosphate pesticides and naturally occurring chemicals can be poisonous; it is all a matter of dose. The German-Swiss doctor and chemist Paracelsus (1493–1541) pointed out 'nothing is without poison; it is the dose alone that makes it so'. When one looks at those parts of the world where pesticides are not freely available (usually because of cost), it is found that over a third of all the food produced is eaten by pests, whereas in the Western world, where pesticides are used, the loss is reduced by 41 per cent.

The level of pesticides in our food is carefully monitored and kept below a very conservative safety level. The chemicals have a short half-life and have not been shown to accumulate in the body. Their level in food is way below that at which it is likely to cause symptoms, even in the most sensitive individual. Although pesticides in food have been blamed for a variety of ill-defined syndromes, including cancers, extensive medical studies have failed to implicate them as the cause of any known clinical condition. There are no mysterious unknown disease states caused by the prolonged intake of small doses of these chemicals. Since they do not accumulate in the food chain or in the body, chronic toxicity is improbable. As Sir John Krebs, the former chairman of the Food Standards Agency, pointed out in *Nature* in 2002, 'a single cup of coffee contains natural carcinogens equal to at least a year's worth of synthetic carcinogenic residues in the diet'.

The various conditions that have been attributed to these chemicals by the food faddists bear no relationship to any of the known effects of the pesticides. There have been sufficient cases of self-induced organophosphate poisoning to recognise the symptoms of poisoning (pesticides are a common form of suicide in Third World countries). It starts with excessive salivation and lachrymation [tear production] and is invariably followed by painful gut cramps and an uncontrollable twitching of the muscles. Pesticides are not commonly associated with any allergic conditions.

Virtually all the chemical pesticide residue that occurs in food is found on the outside of fruit and vegetables and is easily washed off. If the choice has to be made between pest-infected food, food exposed to bacterial pathogens and minute harmless amounts of pesticide, then to choose not to use them is the equivalent of a patient with pneumonia refusing antibiotics in favour of leeches and bleeding.

There are many mysteries about what constitutes organic food.

Organic Standard

The inconsistent approach of the advocates of organic food becomes apparent when one considers organic eggs. These have to come from organically reared chickens. To be an organically reared chicken, the bird has to eat 80 per cent organic food for six weeks. No effort is made to control the other 20 per cent, which may contain potential carcinogens or toxic material. At the end of that time, any eggs it lays will be deemed organic and therefore much more expensive. Organic eggs and chickens should not be confused with free-range chickens, which can roam more freely and eat whatever they like. Organic chickens are not kept in battery cages. To conform with the organic requirements, they must be allowed 1 square metre of space per 25 lb of chicken.

There are many mysteries about what constitutes organic food. If a banana is squashed and its juice extracted to produce 'banana flavouring', it can be analysed and shown to be the chemical amyl acetate. However, if one produces amyl acetate by adding vinegar to amyl alcohol it cannot be called 'organic'. It is the same chemical, it tastes the same, it smells the same but it is not natural and it is therefore presumed to be bad. The same logic suggests that acetic acid is somehow different from the acid in vinegar, or citric acid from that of lemon-juice extract.

A walk around the organic shelves of a supermarket leaves one amazed at the gullibility of its patrons.

It has been suggested that prepackaged, cleaned lettuce is dangerous, as it is washed in a solution containing chlorine. The initiates of this scare fail to point out that the amount of chlorine residue in the product is less than that found in most swimming-pool water and in some drinking water.

Does Organic Food Taste Better?

A walk around the organic shelves of a supermarket leaves one amazed at the gullibility of its patrons. The produce is not particularly inviting in its appearance, and its taste is, for the most part, identical to that of the normal produce. A ten-year, obsessively controlled trial of foods grown in similar positions, on the Boarded Farm study in Essex [England], compared organically grown crops with those produced by conventional farming, using integrated farm management. The study revealed that the best results, judged by soil quality, effect on bird life, biodiversity and yield, came from the integrated farm management fields. Blind tasting of the crops from these studies failed to reveal any consistent difference between organic and nonorganic produce. This is hardly surprising, since taste is largely a result of the genetic makeup of the particular strain of the crop that was planted, the time it has spent maturing before being picked and the climatic conditions during its growth.

Today, the zealots of the cult of organic food are making ever more irrational inroads into the way we live.

Although most produce, be it organic or not, tastes better when freshly picked, the use of preservatives can prolong the freshness of some produce. Some preservatives are available for use in organic foods but they are seldom used in organic vegetables and fruits, which consequently have a short shelf life—as evidence by wilting lettuces and bendy cucumbers.

The Future of Organic Food

Today, the zealots of the cult of organic food are making ever more irrational inroads into the way we live. They are promoting organic clothing and toiletries with the implied assurance that these are somehow less likely to cause allergies and skin disease. There is no evidence to support this claim, which plays on the fears of parents with children who suffer from skin allergies.

So why do people pay up to 40 per cent more for organic products? Is it a cynical confidence trick to exploit consumer ignorance? Is it the belief that, should little Johnny turn out to have allergies/asthma/autism or a brain tumour, this might have been prevented if he had been brought up on organic food and worn pyjamas made from organic cotton? Or is it simply a matter of choice? It is difficult to believe that the proponents of organic produce are all part of an evil conspiracy to defraud the public, although they often use unworthy, unscientific scare tactics, conjuring up all sorts of disasters to frighten the nonbelievers. Most just seem to be victims of their own propaganda, who yearn after bygone days when the sun shone all the time.

However, there is another side to the story. The food industry has to accept some of the blame. It has too often put cost before quality, marketed fruit picked before it has had time to ripen and mature on the tree, and encouraged the production of food that looks good on the supermarket shelf rather than produce that tastes good when eaten. I believe that our memories of apples picked straight from the tree, tasting crisp and juicy, of strawberries that were sweet and succulent and peas that one could not resist eating raw have some factual basis. It is our desire to get back to the days of real, fresh, ripe fruit and vegetables that has encouraged the spurious market for organic food.

6

The Mass-Marketing of Organic Food Presents an Ethical Dilemma

Katherine Mangu-Ward

Katherine Mangu-Ward is a senior editor for Reason *magazine, and her work has appeared in the* Washington Post, Los Angeles Times, *and the* New York Times.

An original tenet of the organic food movement emphasized the importance of local markets. The mantra, buy local, defined the ethics of many organic food consumers. Over time, however, the buy local tenet would be challenged as larger grocery chains began selling organic food. Many of today's consumers easily accept buying organic food from Wal-Mart and Whole Foods, and express little concern over the need to support local farmers. Organic TV dinners purchased at Wal-Mart may not be what the original organic food movement envisioned, but it is nonetheless a development that consumers are embracing.

Consider, if you will, the dilemma posed by the organic TV dinner.

Such microwavable paradoxes are hardly what ethical eating pioneers of the 1970s envisioned when they founded cooperative farms and tiny dairies. But in the decades since, organic food has become cautiously, steadily more industrialized. More outlets sell organics every day—organic milk is now the fastest growing sector in the beverage market—and grocery

Katherine Mangu-Ward, "Food Fight," *Wall Street Journal*, June 9, 2006. Reprinted with permission.

chains like Whole Foods are expanding so quickly that many suppliers have adopted the techniques of mass production, using trucked-in fertilizer and harvesting machines to keep up with demand.

Still, old-school ethical eaters held onto the notion that, however indirectly, buying pre-washed vacuum-packed organic "baby" carrots shipped from California somehow helped to protect the kind of small traditional farmers who started the movement. But when Wal-Mart announced plans to introduce more than 1,000 new organic products in its stores [in 2006], denial was no longer possible. And that's when the organic compost hit the fan.

Competing for Organic Customers

Michael Pollan, author of *The Omnivore's Dilemma*, calls industrial organic food a "contradiction in terms." Of Wal-Mart's promise to sell organics at a relatively small markup he has written: "To say you can sell organic food for 10 percent more than you sell irresponsibly priced food suggests that you don't really get it."

As the ethical-eating movement falls apart, old allies are fast becoming new enemies. They're competing for customers, market share and legitimacy. Small farmers, their marketers and food gurus have started exhorting ethical eaters to "eat local," "eat seasonal" or to get "beyond organic."

Ground zero for the struggle to decide who owns ethical eating in Manhattan is the shiny new 50,000 square-foot Whole Foods staring across 14th street at the Union Square Greenmarket Farmers Market. The food fight is just starting, with trash talk by both sides recently reported, and it's only a matter of time before the Greenmarket farmers start lobbing locally grown vine-ripened tomatoes and balls of fresh Hudson Valley mozzarella across the street at the new megastore. Hundreds of Whole Foods employees (perhaps with support from nearby Trader Joe's) will retaliate by tossing frozen organic pizzas like ninja death stars and smashing bottles of organic Chilean wine to use the fragments as shivs. Their battle cries will ring out in the early morning air: "Eat Local!" vs. "Eat Organic!"

The Organic Dilemma

How did we get here? Early in the organic movement, participants wanted to opt out of the modern capitalist food supply and try something more, well, groovy. But as the movement grew, more justifications were added. Some eaters got onboard because they were concerned about health—they feared that pesticides, hormones and mercury were taking a toll on our physical well-being. Others liked the idea of supporting family farms and the picturesque landscape they create. Still others decided that food tasted better and fresher when it wasn't part of the culinary-industrial complex.

Early in the organic movement, participants wanted to opt out of the modern capitalist food supply and try something more, well, groovy.

But as justifications for eating ethically proliferated, so did the modes of ethical consumption, creating all sorts of new allegiances, not to mention more chances for sanctimony from certain elitist ethical eaters. For those worried about the effect of chemical pesticides and hormones on their children's development, organic TV dinners are a quick, easy way to do the right thing for their kids. But for consumers who fret about over-reliance on fossil fuels, those same meals—assembled from ingredients grown in a dozen countries, heavily packaged and shipped in freezer trucks—miss the point entirely. Free-range cows don't appease vegetarians concerned about the sustainability of our food supply. And people who campaign for humane treatment of farm animals don't care much about the vast amounts of energy required to import grapes from Chile.

When organics hit the big time, a few movement purists realized factory farms weren't the only enemy. They began to shun industrial organic and its big-store purveyors, instead favoring farmers markets. As a result, these small growers who were initially afraid that Whole Foods would steal their customers are doing a booming business—the number of farmers markets in the U.S. has—more than doubled in the last decade.

Local vs. Organic

Most Americans, of course, remain happily oblivious to the local vs. organic debate. Organics are still a small proportion of overall food sales ($20 billion out of a trillion dollars). But certain celebrities are trying to draw more attention to the issue.

Primatologist Jane Goodall recently published a manifesto called "Harvest for Hope" in which she laments that "we have been hypnotized into believing that it is perfectly reasonable to walk into a supermarket and find any kind of food, from anywhere, anytime of the year." She would prefer us to "think about meals the way our ancestors did," to "preserve the local harvest by freezing fresh fruits and vegetables and leftovers," to "better endure the lean months of winter and early spring."

Organic is now an agricultural method that includes winter blackberries, TV dinners and plastic-wrapped spring greens able to travel 3.000 miles without wilting.

These purists, who apparently think "lean months" build character or something like that, blame Wal-Mart (and Whole Foods and small organic farmers who sold out to big conglomerates) for defining organic down while giving customers a false impression of what organic really means. The happy leaping cow on the label of a gallon of Horizon Organic milk, they say, is no longer representative of the real lives Horizon's cows are leading.

In fact, much of the blame rests with the federal government. When the USDA [United States Department of Agriculture] released revised labeling guidelines for organic foods in 2000, a bare minimum was established. And it turned out that what Uncle Sam wanted farmers to do to earn an organic label (and thus garner a 50% premium, on average, over conventional foods) wasn't all that difficult. Additives like xanthan gum are permissible in processed foods, and many spray-on pesticides with organic precursors are completely kosher. Cows needn't be allowed to wander over photogenic green pastures; dumping organic corn into the feed trough is just as legit. By regulating organics fairly loosely, government stepped into the middle of a contentious moment in the movement's history—and wound up picking winners.

Convenient Organic Food

For better or worse, organic is now an agricultural method that includes winter blackberries, TV dinners and plastic-wrapped spring greens able to travel 3,000 miles without wilting. Advocates of local eating find themselves back on the fringes where they started in the 1970s and speak angrily about industrial organic as "selling out." And perhaps there's truth to that allegation. But as with most sectarian splintering, the opposing sides have more in common than they like to admit.

"We don't think you should have to have a lot of money to feed your family organic foods," Wal-Mart's CEO [chief executive officer] has said. To some, this sounds like a threat—especially to the ethical eating elites who will have to find new ways of distinguishing themselves from the hoi polloi [the masses]—but for most of us it sounds like good news about better food.

7

Large Companies Compromise the Values of the Organic Food Movement

Family Farm Defenders

Family Farm Defenders (FFD) is an organization that supports the small farmer against encroaching agribusiness. Founded in 1994, FFD supports independent family farms and sustainable agriculture. John E. Peck, current executive director of Family Farm Defenders, states that while the information in this viewpoint is relevant, it is also important to know that it is dated, and chain-store practices may have changed.

With large chain stores like Whole Foods, selling organic food is primarily another way to make a profit. While the chief executive officer of Whole Foods, John Mackey, refers to his employees as team members, he has fought worker unionization. He has introduced a variety of specialty organic foods, products that appeal to an upscale market. Ironically, while customers are buying upscale organic foods, the wine, cheese, beer, and bread they fill their carts with may not be that healthy. Even Whole Foods' donations to charities are based on marketing plans designed to bring more customers into the company's stores. Finally, Whole Foods has worked against many local organic markets, preferring to buy organic products from around the world.

Whole Foods is the largest retail giant in the natural food sector in the U.S. with 168 stores nationwide (plus in Canada and Britain) and annual gross sales now exceeding

Family Farm Defenders, "Welcome to Whole Foods: The Walmart of Organic," May 24, 2010. Reprinted with permission.

$4.6 billion. In fact, Whole Foods has grown twice as fast as the leading corporate grocer, Walmart, over the last four years. Started in a humble storefront at the corner of 8th and Rio Grande in Austin, TX back in 1978 by self-described "free market" libertarian and current CEO, John Mackey, Whole Foods grew parasitically throughout the 1990s by absorbing its competitors: Bread & Circus, Fresh Fields, Merchant of Vino, Mrs. Gooch's, Bread of Life, and Wellspring Markets. "If someone had been ruthless enough, or opportunistic enough—or, really, just smart enough—we could've been crushed," Mackey noted in a 2004 interview, "But I don't fear that anymore. We're not that vulnerable anymore. Our culture is too strong. Our locations are too good. And we know so much more than we used to." Today [in 2010], the only contenders left in the ring to challenge Whole Foods are Wild Oats and Trader Joes [sic].

Back in 1992, a year after Whole Foods made its first public stock offering, Mackey proudly declared "we're creating an organization based on love instead of fear." A devote admirer of Star Trek's United Federation of Planets (with a framed poster of the starship Enterprise on his wall), Mackey styles himself a democratic renegade when it comes to corporate management. The Whole Foods' "Declaration of Interdependence" includes such high-minded principles as "satisfying and delighting our customers" and "team-member happiness and excellence."

Most Whole Foods shoppers are kept blissfully ignorant of the labor strife behind the deli counter.

Resisting Unions

Like Walmart's "associates," Whole Foods doesn't have workers—instead they are called "team members." Whole Foods employees are hired on a provisional basis, and after four months co-workers get to decide whether or not someone stays on their "team." Bonuses beyond the base wage rate are pegged according to performance, so just like the televison series "Survivor" a climate of competitive efficiency is internalized. If you're not good enough, it's your "team" that will vote you off the Whole Foods island, not the boss. This type of propaganda and conditioning is supposed to ensure company loyalty.

At the same time, Mackey's personal antipathy towards labor unions and workers rights has become rather notorious within the business world. He once said, "The union is like having herpes. It doesn't kill you, but it's unpleasant and inconvenient and it stops a lot of people from becoming your lover." As early as 1998, Whole Foods refused to endorse the United Farm Workers (UFW)'s campaign on behalf of better conditions and higher wages for California's 20,000 strawberry pickers. In 2000 the U.S. Dept. of Labor even went to court against Whole Foods over $226,000 in overtime wages that had not been paid to obviously disgruntled "team members."

In July 2002, when employees at the Whole Foods in Madison, WI, dared to organize under the auspices of the United Food and Commercial Workers (UFCW), they incurred the wrath of Mackey, who flew into town for a three hour long mandatory "employee presentation." Nonetheless, workers still voted for the union two days later. One of the organizers behind the Madison drive, Debbie Rasmussen, was later terminated for having given a botched latte to a co-worker, Julie Thayer, another union supporter who was also fired. Whole Foods ultimately crushed the fledgling union through persistent NLRB [National Labor Relations Board] challenges (with the help of business union incompetence according to more radical union activists), sending a clear message to "team members" throughout the rest of Mackey's empire. . . .

Most Whole Foods shoppers are kept blissfully ignorant of the labor strife behind the deli counter. According to grocery retail analyst, David Livingston, quoted in the Sept. 15th, 2005 issue of the *Capital Times*, "Whole Foods is so different from conventional grocery stores. They tend to have their own loyal customer base." The apolitical high status nonchalance that pervades Whole Foods can be appealing. To quote Livingston once again, shopping there is sort of "like being part of a cult." Prof. Jerald Jellison of the Univ. of Southern California puts it a slightly different way: "Whole Foods offers a psychological absolution of our excesses. After filling your cart with sinful wine, beer, cheese and breads, you rationalize it's healthy, so that cancels out the negatives."

Whole Foods thinks shopping should be fun.

The "Yuppie" Market

Whole Foods does cater to a largely college educated "yuppie" clientele with incomes of $50,000+, clearly reflected in the pricey vehicles that crowd the parking lot, whether SUVs or hybrids. These so-called "foodies"—people interested in high-quality, gourmet foods and an overall organic lifestyle—are the main customer base for Whole Foods, accounting for about three quarters of all its sales. Indulgence and convenience often go hand in hand, which is why the typical Whole Foods now devotes two-thirds of its shelf space to more lucrative prepared foodstuffs—hence the derisive nickname "Whole Paycheck."

Whole Foods also highly touts its corporate policy of earmarking 5% of net profits towards philanthropy each year. For instance, Whole Foods has been a top rung corporate sponsor of the Food for Thought Festival in Madison, WI. Each Whole Foods outlet can also donate to community non-profit organizations, with an obvious silver lining for company investors. As Mackey explained in an Oct. 2005 "Reason on Line" article: "In addition to the many thousands of small donations each Whole Foods store makes each year, we also hold five 5% Days throughout the year. On those days, we donate 5 percent of a store's total sales to a nonprofit organization. While our stores select worthwhile organizations to support, they also tend to focus on groups that have large membership lists, which are contacted and encouraged to shop our store that day to support the organization. This usually brings hundreds of new or lapsed customers into our stores, many of whom then become regular shoppers. So a 5% Day not only allows us to support worthwhile causes, but is an excellent marketing strategy that has benefited Whole Foods investors immensely."

Hapless organic supporters are now buying Chinese asparagus, New Zealand peas, and Mexican broccoli at their local Whole Foods outlet.

In a March 8, 2005, *USA Today* article, Mackey lamented that "Americans love to eat. And Americans love to shop. But we don't like to shop for food. It's a chore, like doing laundry. Whole Foods thinks shopping should be fun. With this store, we're pioneering a new lifestyle that synthesizes health and pleasure. We don't see a contradiction." While other grocery chains are downsizing, seeking to replicate the feel and appeal of the neighborhood "mom and pop" grocery. Whole Foods is unveiling 80,000 square foot "Super Size Me" behemoths costing $15 million. Within this decadent themepark one can almost imagine Walt Disney and Willy Wonka skipping down the aisles. Lucky visitors will be able to dip a fresh strawberry into a chocolate fountain ($1.59), have junior try on an organic cotton onesie ($14.00), get a 25 minute massage ($50), and even take home a vat of almond butter ($89.99)—all in a hard day's shopping.

Expanding Organic Markets

The new and improved 50,000 square foot Whole Foods superstore now in the works on University Avenue near Segoe Road in Madison, WI, is modeled on a similar big box Whole Foods in Omaha, NE, which boasts an in-house meat smoking station and a wine kiosk where customers can read reviews by [wine critic] Robert Parker simply by scanning the bottle. Other features that Whole Foods is banking will entice in even more well-heeled foodies into the fold include sushi bars, brick oven pizzerias, wi-fi hotspots, walk-in beer coolers, hot donut makers, and gelato stations.

With the skyrocketing popularity of organic—increasing by 20% per year—the organic USDA [United States Department of Agriculture] label no longer means "Grown in the U.S.A." When a Whole Foods outlet opened in Pittsburgh, local organic farmers were told they could not sell to the store direct, but would have to negotiate with a regional warehouse as far away as Maryland. Though no official figures are kept on organic imports, the USDA estimated that over $1.5 billion worth entered the U.S. in 2002. Hapless organic supporters are now buying Chinese asparagus, New Zealand peas, and Mexican broccoli at their local Whole Foods outlet not realizing that their dollars are going elsewhere. Just like Walmart, Whole Foods' interest in the wellbeing of workers and consumers does not translate into respecting their rights, especially when the bottom line comes first.

8

Large Companies Play an Important Role in the Organic Food Movement

Samuel Fromartz

Samuel Fromartz is a business journalist who began his career at Reuters in 1985. His work has appeared in Fortune Business Inc., BusinessWeek, *the* New York Times, *and other publications.*

The Whole Foods grocery chain succeeded by offering a number of organic food products that combined health and taste. This combination of health and taste became part of the organic food trend. Consumers began to define eating organic as healthy, even when they were eating rich, organic chocolate truffles. Whole Foods learned that they could move beyond the standard health food market by offering beer, wine, meat, seafood, and coffee. Whole Foods also focused on making the shopping experience more enjoyable, while continually searching for new products to expand the company's customer base. This included offering a broad range of product lines, including a variety of organic food choices.

Walking though the sliding glass doors into the Whole Foods Market on P Street recently, I perked up upon seeing the bright displays of produce, but noticed that the early romance I felt toward the store had mellowed. I had acquired the slightly jaded mien of the seasoned shopper who

Samuel Fromartz, "Consuming Organic: Why We Buy," *Organic Inc.: Natural Foods and How They Grew.* New York: Harcourt, 2006, pp. 237–45. Reprinted with permission.

could find exactly what he wanted and get out, leaving the more expensive enticements for novices. Since I owned only five shares of Whole Foods stock (I kept them to receive the annual reports), my rationalization that buying whatever I wanted would swell the company's bottom line and thus my own no longer held water. Now more knowledgeable and with a young child, I had become more price conscious and my shopping venues had splintered.

Health food historically meant bug-eaten organic produce, hardy beans and grains, and badly prepared tofu.

My voluminous purchases of Whole Foods's fresh produce slowed between May and October, when I bought at the local farmers' market; in the winter, I shopped for Earthbound organic salad mix at Costco, which priced it about a third less than Whole Foods. I heard about a smaller local supermarket, My Organic Market (MOM's), which stocked a lot of organic goods and had a business model largely premised on undercutting the prices of its bigger rival. ("We don't mark prices up from wholesale, we mark them down from Whole Foods," Scott Nash, MOM's CEO, told me.) Employees also carried your grocery bags to the car—a big plus with a child in tow. Occasionally, I shopped at Trader Joe's, the cheaper, smaller, eclectic food chain. I largely avoided Whole Foods's artisan bread and sprung instead for superior loaves from local bakers and didn't buy much of their high-end cheese, since I discovered a far better artisan shop in nearby Alexandria. But, as Ellen said one day, "We can't shop at a hundred stores!" Whole Foods still ranked as our main supermarket, since it stocked the most of what we wanted in one venue. I also found if I shopped smart and bought its private-label products, I could avoid emptying my wallet. Still, compared with the giddiness I felt a few years back, my loyalty had diminished.

Pleasure and Health

Whole Foods initially hooked me by satisfying two primal impulses articulated by William Grimes in a *New York Times* review of Whole Foods's mammoth supermarket in Columbus Circle [New York City], which opened in 2004. Whole Foods, he wrote, "subscribes to a religion that might be called moralistic hedonism. With an eye to pleasing presentation and attractive packaging, it offers a Venusberg of gustatory temptations, often rarefied, and all guaranteed to be good for you." These two traits—pleasure and health—for too long stood in opposition to one another in the same way that desire clashes with restraint.

Simply presenting organic produce in an attractive setting became a slam dunk against tough, bland supermarket fare.

Health food historically meant bug-eaten organic produce, hardy beans and grains, and badly prepared tofu—their health quotient rising as palatability declined. On the other extreme, gourmands consumed, say, a milk-braised pork loin, butter-whipped potatoes, and yet another plate of chocolate truffles—delicious, but full of cardio-challenging saturated fat and calories. Instead of viewing these camps as opposed and static and choosing one, Whole Foods saw a dialectic and came up with the synthesis; it made healthy food delicious and marketed the perfect meal. Foods with artificial preservatives, colors, flavors, sweeteners, and hydrogenated oils were verboten; so, too, were the agro-industrial brands like Kraft, General Mills, and Coca-Cola. They were replaced with offbeat natural and organic producers like Hain, Eden Foods, Spectrum, and Amy's Kitchen; natural and organic brands like Boca, Cascadian Farm, and Odwalla, owned by the agro-industrial giants; and artisan fare that could run the full gamut of possibilities. Customers could find tofu or a cheeseburger in this world because it was up to them to find the balance, but as retailing consultant Willard Bishop Jr. told me, Whole Foods "did the editing," setting the boundaries of feel-good food.

Whole Foods was hardly alone in this marriage of health and taste, since chefs such as Alice Waters repositioned organic food to emphasize its high quality. Others, like Deborah Madison, showed how spices, fresh herbs, and ethnic techniques could make a vegetarian dish the center of a fabulous meal. The restaurant movement had by the mid-1980s rebelled against stuffy, elite, saucy French fare, coming up with simple dishes made with the freshest ingredients often bought at the farmers' market. Service at the most popular fine-dining restaurants became friendly, rather than haughty, in the same way that Whole Foods's high-end comestibles [food] enticed rather than excluded the customer. At the same time, the organic movement's historic antipathy to artificial and highly processed food dovetailed with a broader perception that "fresh" meant "healthy." The long-winded arguments about soil biology and organic agriculture could never match the visceral appeal of a perfect tomato or peach. Simply presenting organic produce in an attractive setting became a slam dunk against tough, bland supermarket fare, creating the largest segment of the organic marketplace and, not accidentally, the entryway to Whole Foods. A twenty-foot stroll through the pampered produce section convinces the customer of the high quality of organic food and articulates the values of the store, even if only a portion of what it sells is organic.

It should not be surprising that health and nutrition motivate 70 to 80 percent of all organic shoppers, reaching 90 percent among frequent buyers.

Bishop told me Whole Foods's merger of quality goods with a concept of health created a niche in the grocery industry. "One of the reasons they've been so successful is that they are quite clear and consistent about who they are and what they deliver to the customer," he said.

Organic Food and Health

The timing was right because health had become increasingly important to shoppers, even if they had trouble following any consistent regime. Fifty-five percent of Americans cited health as a key motivation in food purchases in 2004 (up from 45 percent in 2000), and 59 percent said they tried to eat healthy food to avoid illness later in life. These consumers weren't looking at food as medicine but as a way to avoid medicine, doctors, and hospitals in the future, just as J. I. Rodale [early advocate of sustainable farming] had in the 1940s. Even among those on a diet (six in ten Americans), the biggest motivation was health (cited by 77 percent). Pesticides, antibiotics, and hormones also played a role in these decisions, since seven in ten Americans report they are "somewhat concerned" about the risk posed by these substances in the food supply. The 28 percent who view them as a "high risk" roughly mirrors the percentage of people who buy organic food regularly.

With this backdrop, it should not be surprising that health and nutrition motivate 70 to 80 percent of all organic shoppers, reaching 90 percent among frequent buyers. Freshness, taste, environmental benefits, and helping small farms are also cited, with those reasons becoming more important as purchases increase.

Organic food persisted and grew precisely because the movement defined organic *as a production method rather than a prescriptive diet.*

But ordinary consumers wouldn't begin to care about these benefits if organic food remained unpalatable, unavailable, or too closely associated with a fringe diet. Indeed, organic food persisted and grew precisely because the movement defined *organic* as a production method rather than a prescriptive diet such as Atkins, South Beach, the Zone, or Weight Watchers. The benefit came from eating the food, not from avoiding foods or counting calories. In this way, organic food became associated with a "healthy lifestyle," which meant you ultimately decided what made you feel good. Whole Foods's organic chocolate truffles epitomize this for me; they taste good because they contain chocolate, sugar, and saturated fat—not the healthiest mix. Yet by making them organically, Whole Foods tempered the "bad" quotient and transformed them into something "good."

"For years, people said, 'Consumers don't know what organic means,'" said Harvey Hartman, head of the Hartman Group marketing firm, whose clients include Whole Foods. "We knew that. But we also knew that consumers didn't care! They just wanted to feel good that they were doing the right thing."

Expanding the Organic Market

When the cofounder and CEO of Whole Foods, John Mackey, opened the original store, called Safer Way, in Austin, Texas, in 1978, it was a typical counterculture venue that sold only vegetarian fare. But then Mackey and his friends realized if they wanted to grow, they had to loosen their grip on granola and sell meat, seafood, beer, wine, and coffee. "We didn't think they were particularly healthy products, but we were a whole food store, not a 'holy food' store," he told one interviewer.

This brought in consumers of various persuasions beyond the company's core market. Now vegetarians are just one small segment of a wide base that includes health-and-nutrition devotees, fitness fanatics, foodies, environmentalists, and core organic consumers. Since their concerns overlap to a degree, Whole Foods can feed them all, so long as its message remains consistent. Selling meat, for example, might alienate vegans and vegetarians, but Whole Foods is now developing a program to ensure its meat, which is free of antibiotics and hormones, will be raised to "animal-compassionate" standards. While Mackey publicly dismissed the animal-rights activists who initially pressured the company on this issue, he also looked into their arguments, switched from a vegetarian to a vegan diet, and then began a dialogue. He was not about to ban meat in Whole Foods stores, but he decided if animals must be eaten, the ones the company sold would at least be raised humanely. This would further differentiate Whole Foods's meat from the factory-farm fare in conventional supermarkets, and create a common ground for consumers as divergent as vegans and high-protein dieters. The company won the endorsement of People for the Ethical Treatment of Animals (PETA) in 2004, giving the meat, in effect, a vegetarian seal of approval.

As it has grown, Whole Foods has continued to improve the customer's experience.

Making Grocery Shopping Fun

The company's broader success lay in selling this enhanced food in an enticing setting, with a lot of customer coddling—adding another dimension to the idea that healthy food could be pleasurable rather than puritanical. Mackey has said that Whole Foods capitalized on a paradox: Americans loved food and loved shopping, but hated shopping for food. So the stores, in retailing lingo, became "an experience," wowing customers who had long associated grocery shopping with a loathsome taste. As it has grown, Whole Foods has continued to improve the customer's experience. In the late 1990s, when the company gobbled up regional natural-food chains such as Fresh Fields on the East Coast, Mrs. Gooch's Natural Foods Markets in Los Angeles, and Bread & Circus in New England, each of these acquisitions brought much more than real estate; they brought expertise—which was given a chance to flourish in a culture of autonomy.

Mackey allowed each region and store to make decisions and compete so that the best ideas would win. Bonuses reflected a team's performance in the store, so that all had a stake in making the model hum at the ground floor. Mackey envisioned a company that took care of customers first and employees second; then shareholders, the community, and the wider environment. Profit, in short, was the result of a highly competitive and localized customer focus, not the dictates of a control freak at the top.

When I popped into stores in Berkeley, Seattle, Portland, Denver, Boulder, western Massachusetts, New York, and Washington, they looked similar but never alike. Unique offerings at one would later appear at another. Boulder [Colorado] had a stunning Eden-like fresh flower display at the entrance that I soon saw replicated in other stores, even if they did not quite hone theirs to the same effect. Seattle [Washington], a top store, boasted a highly theatrical prepared-foods area all abuzz at dinnertime, with customers mingling as cooks worked an open grill. Whole Foods's store in Columbus Circle took this to the extreme, rolling out Asian, Latino, and Indian food; brick-oven pizza; and sushi. In the mid-Atlantic region, I noticed the company renovated and reconfigured often, expanding meat sections and playing up thick cuts of aged beef once high-protein diets took off. This refinement demanded engagement, which made the stores fun.

Attracting Customers

Whole Foods soared high and dove low to capture more varied customers. Its lower-priced 365 brand of natural and organic food products sold alongside premium artisan fare. This made eminent sense since few brands dominated the organic and natural-food marketplace, leaving it to Whole Foods to, in effect, become a top brand. Reaching high, it slapped an Authentic Food Artisan (AFA) seal on products deemed worthy of discriminating customers. A shopper seeking value might snap up the perfectly acceptable 365 pasta ($0.79) or choose the organic version ($1.29); if less concerned about price, she could reach for the Montebello brand ($2.99), made from wheat grown on the grounds of a former hilltop Italian monastery that has been farmed free of chemicals since 1388, earning the AFA seal. Or, if she sought an even more rarefied plate of spaghetti, she could buy the Rustichella d'Abruzzo offering ($5.29), crafted by a third-generation Italian master using stone-ground, local organic wheat extruded through handmade bronze dies and dried exceedingly slowly. Each product has a slightly different appeal for a particular occasion, such as feeding the kids or impressing a date.

Making Organic Foods Profitable

Mackey has described this work as marrying love and creativity, which might translate to passion and innovation in a more traditional business context. Whole Foods has no employees, only team members; no managers, but team leaders. The company believes the communal character of the tribe gives its workers more than a union ever could, which is why it trumpets a 100 percent union-free shop (a plus on Wall Street). When an organizing drive at its Madison, Wisconsin, store succeeded in 2002, Mackey e-mailed employees that "the temptation to contract into fear and anger is very powerful. Love and forgiveness are the more difficult choices to make." A year later, two organizers said they were unfairly fired and a pro-union Web site claimed Whole Foods played hardball, but the union was out. Perhaps this was tough love, for Mackey's libertarian, New Age vision—as in much of the organic food industry—never included a place for industrial-era unions. In his view, they impeded the team. To dismiss this as corporate greed would be simplistic, however, since the company also limits salaries and bonuses of the highest paid to no more than fourteen times the average and donates 5 percent of after-tax profits to charity, both of which are unusual in corporate America, union shop or not.

If you were an organic or local food purist, vegan fundamentalist, or union agitator, the store might irk you, but for Mackey, losing these customers was the price of success. "What if we only sold organic stuff? We'd . . . cease to exist because not enough of our customers want us to just sell organic," Mackey said in one interview. "They would find it would be too expensive for them; they wouldn't be willing to buy it." To succeed, the business had to connect with an audience beyond the core by offering a wider palate of attributes.

Again, this wasn't unique in the organic food market. Salad mix and soy milk didn't win in the marketplace solely because they carried an organic label, or any other single attribute. The appeal of salad mix derived from the trendy taste of baby greens, the cleanliness of triple washing, the convenient package; for soy milk, it came from the health benefits and improved palatability of soy and a chilled-shelf placement that implied "fresh." As with Whole Foods, an array of overlapping attributes and connotations—along with the ORGANIC label—made these products attractive to a broad customer base. It was the only way to prevail in the marketplace.

9

Organic Food Is Worth the Extra Expense

Alex Johnson

Alex Johnson is an advocate of organic living and writes for Organic Guide.

Many people note that organic food is more expensive than conventional groceries. The reasons are multiple. Organic farming is often more labor intensive, and small organic farms cannot practice economy of scale by spreading costs across a large agricultural output. Organic farms must also follow strict government guidelines to qualify for the National Organic Program. Finally, once organic products have been sold to retailers, the farmer has little control over the price. Although each of these factors increases the cost of organic food, consumers should also calculate the potential health problems caused from eating conventional agricultural products. When one considers the health of one's family, organic food is worth the extra cost.

One of the first questions I'm asked when I let people know that I prefer to consume organic food is, "How can you afford to eat organic food on your salary?" Okay, so I'm the first to admit it, my annual income only places me marginally above the official poverty line. But that isn't to say that I don't have priorities in my life. I have a young family—a wife and two children to be exact. And having spent quite a bit of time in the food processing industry, I know what goes on behind the scenes. And let's just say, I'm not prepared to

Alex Johnson, "Is Organic Food Too Expensive?" *Organic Guide*, September 29, 2007. Reprinted with permission.

accept the routine shortcuts that conventional food processors are forced to take by the large supermarket chains they are subservient to. Call me nuts, but I don't want my daughter growing breasts at seven years old as a direct consequence of the hormones that were routinely pumped into the battery hens whose eggs she ate. And I'm not overly keen for my son to undergo minor surgery at our local hospital only to discover that, due to the rampant overuse of antibiotics in our food chain leading to yet another outbreak of antibiotic resistant staphylococcus aureus [which causes staph infections], they'll have to amputate his leg below the knee in order to save his life. Am I alarmist? No. I'm just a dad with priorities.

Personally, I'd rather spend a few extra dollars to feed my family a small quantity of high quality organic produce. The alternative, as I see it, requires subjecting my family to the constant moving target of what constitutes "acceptable" parameters for human safety. Does that mean I have to stick to a budget? Yes, of course. Does it mean that my wife and I have to be creative in how we shop? Definitely. Okay, so I'm fairly certain that the extra cost associated with organic food is worth it. But why should it cost more you ask? Well, here are the reasons I believe it's reasonable for me to expect to pay a premium for organic food.

Personally, I'd rather spend a few extra dollars to feed my family a small quantity of high quality organic produce.

Labour—one of the downsides of organic production methods is that they tend to be labour intensive. Because there are no pesticides or herbicides used on an organic farm, more people are involved in undertaking routine tasks, such as the removal of weeds in between rows of vegetables. On the face of it, this might not seem like it should add much in the way of additional cost to your box of fruit and vegetables, but if you've ever spent more than a couple of hours in the garden pulling weeds, you've probably got some idea of how time consuming—and therefore expensive—weeding can be.

Scale—organic farms tend to be smaller than conventional farms. I don't think it necessarily has to be this way. In fact, if more consumers switched to consuming organic food, I'm sure we'd see many larger organic farms pop up. But at the moment, your average organic farm tends to be a small-scale operation. The small scale of organic farming operations means that the associated fixed costs and overheads must be distributed across much smaller produce volumes than conventional farms. Unfortunately, this increases the cost to you and me.

Compliance—both organic farms and organic processors must adhere to strict certification guidelines. Apart from the obvious fees associated with achieving and maintaining certification, an enormous amount of staff time, effort and energy is expended in ensuring all necessary specifications are adhered to. These are additional costs that are not incurred by conventional farms or conventional processors.

As consumers, what we need is strong Government that's prepared to stand up to corporate profiteering at the expense of human health.

Retailers—I've spoke directly with some retailers that have told me that organic lines don't move as fast as some conventional lines. For them, this equates to risk and therefore a price premium must be paid by all customers purchasing organic products. And I suspect that some, but by no means all, retailers are riding the wave of organic popularity all the way to the beach at our expense. But the party won't last indefinitely for these retailers. So, shop around.

Conventional lies—I believe that if we were to look at the true economic cost of conventional food, we'd find that the price society as a whole pays for it would be much higher than its shelf price. Pesticides, antibiotics, herbicides, additives, genetic modification—what is the true cost of the health care people require, and will in the future require, as a result of some of these nasties? After all, what is the cost associated with being told that GM [genetically modified] crops do actually cause bowel and colon cancer? Pretty high I would have thought! What was the cost for numerous Britains being told that, as a direct consequence of cows being fed the spinal tissue from other cows to facilitate cost savings, they had developed a rare from of bovine spongiform encephalitis, more commonly known as "Mad Cow Disease". Did the price of the beef mince they picked up from their local supermarket incorporate the real cost to society? No way. But did the artificially low price, and the cynical cost saving use of spinal tissue fed to ruminants, enable a few large corporates to benefit at the expense of both consumers and honest farmers? You're damn right it did!

As consumers, what we need is strong Government that's prepared to stand up to corporate profiteering at the expense of human health. In the interim, we need to make our own choices. So, next time you're agonising over the price of organic food, as I do from time to time, ask yourself what the true price of the conventional alternative really is. Is organic food really worth it? I think so. How about you?

10

Organic Food Is Not Worth the Extra Expense

Andrew Ellison

Andrew Ellison is the personal finance editor of the London Times.

In order to find out whether organic food was worth the extra cost, the Times *conducted an unscientific blind taste test of organic and non-organic food sold at UK grocery chains. While there were significant differences, organic selections were seldom chosen as the tastiest of the choices. Taste my be considered subjective, but the results of the test raised the question: is organic food really worth up to 60 percent more in price if the supposedly superior quality is not obvious? Other claims for organic food—that it is better for the environment or that "nature knows best"—are equally difficult to support. While there may be reasons to buy some types of organic food, overall organic items are not worth the extra price.*

Food marketers and estate agents have much in common. Both use words of inappropriate grandiosity to sell distinctly average products. Where most of us see a shed, estate agents see a Swedish-timber summer outhouse. Where most of us see a burger, food marketers see a grass-fed Highland-reared steak haché.

Usually found on the supermarkets' premium brands, these fanciful descriptions are designed to encourage us to part with

Andrew Ellison, "Organic Food Is a Waste of Money," *Times* (London), September 5, 2009. Reprinted with permission.

a little bit more of our hard-earned cash. But do these supposedly superior products offer anything more than fancy packaging? *Times* Money decided to investigate.

Over the past fortnight, we have been conducting a blind taste test to establish whether it is really worth paying extra for the supermarkets' standard, premium and organic ranges [product lines]. To ensure that we were unbiased, we chose foods that were hard to tell apart by appearance alone, such as chicken breasts, apples, broccoli, tea, white wine and yoghurt. The results are surprising, but perhaps not for the reasons that you might expect.

The idea that organic food is worth more because it is healthier is totally bogus.

Blind Taste Test

For a start, the difference in taste between the supermarkets' cheapest ranges was huge. Overall, Waitrose's Essentials range was judged to be by far the tastiest of all the ranges at all of the supermarkets. The Sainsbury's Basics range, however, was judged to be by far the worst of all. But the most revealing result is how badly organic food performed.

The organic brands at Tesco, Waitrose and Asda scored worse than each supermarket's basic, standard and premium ranges. Only at Sainsbury's did organic food not come bottom, and that was only because its Basics range is so bad. Hard though it may be to believe, Asda's standard range scored higher than Waitrose's organic range.

Remember, this was a completely blind test—we had no idea what we were tasting, we simply gave each food a mark out of ten based on how much we liked it. Of course, taste is purely subjective and our experiment did not have the scale or scientific rigour to be conclusive. Nonetheless, the results are fascinating and suggest that it is not worth paying extra for organic food. (Which? [a product testing website] estimates that organic food costs on average 60 per cent more than conventional produce).

Inevitably, the organic lobby will dismiss our findings. The Soil Association, which relies on brand organic for its livelihood, defends the industry with a passion that borders on blind faith. But the arguments that it uses are spurious at best.

Is Organic Food Better?

The idea that organic food is worth more because it is healthier is totally bogus. Only last month the Food Standards Agency, the unbiased government agency set up to protect the public's health, published a report concluding that organic food has no greater nutritional value than conventional produce.

The idea that organic food is better for the environment is also questionable. Organic milk, for example, generates more carbon dioxide emissions than standard milk and uses significantly more land.

Then there is the pesticide question. High doses can indeed cause cancer and birth defects. However, there is no evidence that the miniscule amounts found in conventional food are harmful. In fact, some studies have shown that the incidence of cancer among farmers, who are routinely exposed to relatively high levels of pesticide, is lower than in the wider population. In the past 50 years, since synthetic chemicals have come into wide use, average life expectancy has increased by more than seven years.

The origins of the myth that organic is somehow better are complex—in part a result of recent food scares that have made consumers suspicious of modern farming methods, and in part a result of tireless campaigning by pressure groups that exploit the media's desire for sensationalist headlines.

Organic Does Not Equal Quality

Support for organic farming seems based on the belief that "nature knows best". Sadly, this is little more than nostalgia for a golden age of small-scale and simple farming that never really existed. Before intensive agriculture, pesticides and artificial fertilisers, food supplies were constantly endangered by drought and disease. Agriculture was associated with grinding poverty, intensive labour and low yield.

Of course, this is not to say that all organic food should be avoided. The animal welfare standards of organic farmers are generally considered better than average. And as our test demonstrates, some organic foods, such as burgers, do seem to taste better. But consumers should be aware that with organic food in general, they are not paying a premium for real quality, just the perception of such.

11

Government Subsidies Could Lower the Cost of Organic Food

Christy Harrison

Christy Harrison has worked as a senior editor at the green lifestyle magazine, Plenty *and wrote for* Gourmet.

While organic food has become more popular, increased sales have not led to lower prices. Partly this is related to common organic farming practices: many organic farms are small. Unlike large commercial farms, many fruits and vegetables must be harvested by hand, leading to higher labor costs. Another factor centers on government financial assistance, in the form of subsidies: conventional crops are subsidized in the United States, while organic crops are not subsidized. In order for organic foods to reach more consumers, there must be a stable market for organic products. This could potentially be achieved by providing consumers with better information about organic food—in essence, educating shoppers on the benefits of organic products.

A recent study [in 2010] by researchers at the University of California [UC]-Davis reported that U.S. shoppers who consistently choose healthy foods spend nearly 20 percent more on groceries. The study also said the higher price of these healthier choices can consume 35 to 40 percent of a low-income family's grocery budget. That's bad news for public health. It's also bad news for the organic-food market, since organics usually carry the highest price tag of all the healthy stuff out there.

Christy Harrison, "The (Still) High Cost of Organic Food," *Earth Easy*, May 2010. Reprinted with permission.

Eventually, analysts keep telling us, demand for organics will set the wheels in motion that will drive prices down. But eventually never seems to come. Even though organics sales are growing by about 20 percent a year—almost 10 times the rate of increase in total U.S. food sales, according to the *Nutrition Business Journal*—these cleaner, greener products still carry a hefty premium.

How many shoppers have to jump on the organic bandwagon before we actually see prices fall? How long will that take? And what's the government's role in all this? It depends who you ask.

Today, roughly three-quarters of conventional grocery stores carry natural and/or organic food.

Be Fruitful and Multiply

The organic market we know today began evolving in the 1960s and '70s, when rising environmental awareness led to a backlash against pesticides and increased demand for "green" products. Over the last 20 years, the market has flourished, gaining enough stature to merit the introduction of nationwide U.S. Department of Agriculture [USDA] certification standards in 2002. (Those guidelines have been attacked by some for being too weak; some producers also cause confusion by claiming to be "natural" or "sustainable" without being certified.)

Today, roughly three-quarters of conventional grocery stores carry natural and/or organic food, according to a 2002 Food Marketing Institute study. Restaurants across the country, from the high end to the greasy spoon, are plunking organic ingredients onto their menus. Still, organics represent only about 2 percent of the food industry, both in the U.S. and worldwide. And less than 10 percent of U.S. consumers buy organic items regularly, according to survey data from

Nutrition Business Journal and the Hartman Group, a research firm specializing in the natural-products market. The $10.8 billion industry may be booming, but it's not even close to overtaking conventional sales.

This is in part because of plain old economics. According to basic economic principles, in the short term, as demand grows, prices climb along with it; this small supply and growing demand is what's now getting us, say, $4 quarts of milk. But in the long term, if the market continues to expand, consumption of organics should reach a higher plane where the cost per unit of processing, marketing, and distributing products is much lower. In other words, organic producers will build economies of scale. That price break, in turn, "could bring many more consumers into the market," says Thomas Dobbs, a sustainable-agriculture economist at South Dakota State University. Trouble is, no one seems to know for sure when that will happen.

That's because there are still so many exceptions to the rules, says Steven Blank, an agricultural economist at UC-Davis. Most organic farms in the U.S., for instance, are still small, often family-run operations that don't necessarily fit the economy-of-scale model, because they don't usually have high distribution costs that could be cut as demand rises. Many rely on farmers' markets, community-supported agriculture, and other small-scale distribution channels. "We're too local and hands-on for high distribution to change our costs significantly," confirms Sarah Coddington, co-owner of Frog Hollow Farms in northern California.

Small Farms, Intense Labor

And when the little guys grow delicate crops like peaches and plums that have to be handpicked, Blank says, they can't reach the same economies of scale as farmers who harvest mechanically—their labor costs are too high. "If we have a bumper crop [an unusually large harvest], everything costs more to do," says Coddington.

Frog Hollow's tree-ripened fruits have developed a nation-wide reputation, and a single, succulent peach can run more than $3. But generally, "it" fruits from small farms are not the ones causing a strain on the bank account. Most organic fruits and vegetables—the largest sector of the organics market—are only 10 to 30 percent more expensive than their convention-ally grown counterparts, and Dobbs says many people are willing to pay that kind of markup for better produce. Where economies of scale could really make a difference is in the world of frozen produce, processed foods, and animal prod-ucts.

Those items typically cost 50 to more than 100 percent more than their conventional counterparts, according to a 2002 USDA study. In a survey conducted by Colorado-based Walnut Acres—which bills itself as America's first organic-food company—price was a major barrier for nearly 70 per-cent of shoppers who didn't usually buy organic items.

So to win these folks over, do organic producers have to start offering cheap cheese and budget bonbons? Dobbs makes a surprising estimate: if just one-third of American shoppers bought organic foods on a regular basis, most prices would come down to that 10 to 30 percent markup we're seeing on produce today.

Still seems expensive, but Dobbs says a third of U.S. con-sumers could afford to buy at today's prices if we chose to. The reason we can afford more than we think? We're already paying that much—and more—for supposedly cheap food.

More than Meats the Eye

Conventional crops are heavily subsidized by the federal gov-ernment in the United States, making them artificially inex-pensive. Couple those subsidies—which have been in place since the New Deal [a domestic reform program from the 1930s]—with the cost of cleaning up pollution and treating health problems created by conventional farming, and we're paying a lot in taxes in order to pay a pittance at the grocery store.

"When we make the argument that low-income people can't afford organics, we're assuming that the prices of conventionals are the prices we should be paying," says a USDA economic researcher who asked to remain anonymous. "But those prices externalize a lot of costs, like pollution and higher energy inputs."

A study last year by Iowa State University economists showed that the annual external costs of U.S. agriculture—accounting for impacts such as erosion, water pollution, and damage to wildlife—fall between $5 billion and $16 billion. . . . And Michael Duffy, a coauthor of the Iowa paper, says his team's estimate is conservative.

Subsidizing Organic Farms

So will this drive frustrated consumers to the o-side? Hardly. If anything, the taxes consumers already pay to support conventional farming are a disincentive to paying "double" for organics. To encourage a shopping shift, as European agricultural researchers Stephan Dabbert, Anna Maria Haring, and Raffaele Zanoli write in *Organic Farming*, government has to throw farmers a bone.

"In Western Europe, most countries have decided that organic agriculture needs special support to bring production [and consumption] up to a significantly higher level," Dobbs notes. In countries including Denmark, Sweden, Germany, Austria, and Switzerland, and also at the European Union [E.U.] level, governments contribute to organic markets. In fact, many European policy makers treat organic farming as an instrument to help mitigate environmental problems, manage marginal lands, and address falling farmer incomes, according to Dabbert, et al.

Meanwhile, in the U.S., scant federal money is set aside strictly for organic farmers. The industry doesn't even have access to the type of pricing data and guarantees available to conventional farmers, says University of Georgia agricultural economist Luanne Lohr. "In order to induce producers to get into the [organics] market, they need to know what kind of prices and revenue they're looking at," she says. Without that information, "the producers are flying blind," at the mercy of large distributors who can set unfair prices. "A lot of people would be willing to go into organic, but they don't want to just throw away their investment [in their conventional farms] to get into a system in which they don't have price guarantees," says Lohr.

The success of the USDA's Natural Resources Conservation Service, which dispenses grants that help conventional farmers implement more sustainable practices, suggests subsidies are a key part of encouraging such changes. Deputy Chief Tom Christensen reports that so many farmers are interested in the $3.9 billion program that only one in four applicants is given funding.

In the U.S., scant federal money is set aside strictly for organic farmers.

Loaves and Wishes

Subsidies are a useful way to increase supplies, experts say, but they're only effective in conjunction with a well-run market. "Regulations that promote organic agriculture by encouraging supply are not ... sufficient to ensure the continuous growth of the organic sector," wrote Nadia Scialabba, a senior officer of environment and sustainable development for the U.N. [United Nations], in 2001.

Scialabba cited the case of Austria, which was the leading organic producer in the E.U. in the mid-1990s. About 10 percent of farmers in the country decided to go organic because of subsidies offered by the government, but this increase in supply was met with inadequate information, distribution, and marketing channels; as a result, many threw in the trowel. They had the money—they just needed a market.

Some other policies that would effectively increase supply have been contentious. For instance, the USDA has been criticized for allowing dairy farmers to be certified while still in the process of converting conventional cows to organic status. (Such status depends on the grain fed to the cows.) Somewhat ironically, a ruling this January that reversed that provision could hurt the market, at least temporarily. Some of the companies making "organic" products under the weaker standards might jump ship due to the higher production costs under the stricter guidelines, says Lohr. This could slow progress "as the industry reorients itself" around the new rules, she says.

The Future of Organic Markets

Such dilutions and confusion can cause consumers to lose trust in the organic label and stop buying, according to a 2002 report presented by German researchers to the U.N. Environment Program. Lohr predicts that the rules will continue to be challenged in years to come, "because if there's demand for organic, people want to make it easy for farmers to become certified."

One thing is clear: though organics have been around for a half-century, unknowns still rule. Long-range studies are few and far between, says UC-Davis' Blank. And most economists don't wager a guess on when pricing will change. For now, in the absence of federal support, they put their money on consumer education driving the market.

"It's a matter of the public really knowing what they get when they buy organic," Blank says. The necessary increase in demand, he adds, is likely to happen only if shoppers develop a pro-organic philosophy before they ever set foot in the store.

12

The Organic Food Market Faces Many Challenges

Kimberley Kindy

Kimberley Kindy writes for the Washington Post; *Kathleen Merrigan serves as the Deputy Secretary for the United States Department of Agriculture (USDA).*

In an interview with Kimberly Kindy of the Washington Post, *the deputy secretary of the USDA, Kathleen Merrigan, discusses the challenges that the National Organic Program and the organic food market are facing. First, Merrigan notes, the rules instituted by the USDA in relation to the National Organic Program are adequate, but need to be consistently enforced. Active enforcement would assure consumers of the quality of the organic food they purchase. Secondly, Merrigan believes that consumers need to be convinced that organic food does not have to be expensive. By active enforcement and consumer education, markets for organic products will continue to grow.*

Kathleen Merrigan, deputy secretary at the Agriculture Department, sat down with *The Washington Post* to discuss the agency's eight-year-old National Organics Program and the challenges ahead for the organics market, which is growing as much as 20 percent a year. In an investigation published last year, *The Post* pointed to several problems in the program, including the agency's failure to discipline violators and to properly test products labeled organic. The USDA's

Kimberley Kindy, "USDA's Deputy Secretary Discusses Challenges for the Organic Food Market," *Washington Post*, April 6, 2010. Reprinted with permission.

[United States Department of Agriculture] inspector general [IG] issued a report last month identifying the same problems and calling for changes.

Kimberly Kindy: *What is the greatest challenge you face implementing reforms recommended by the inspector general so consumers know they are getting high-quality organic products?*

Kathleen Merrigan: I like to call this the age of enforcement.... There is always that period of time when people are adjusting to a new rule. What are the laws of the land? How do I comply? It is 2010. There is no longer any question about what the rules are, and there is no longer any forgiveness of any significant amount in the system for lax enforcement, for failure to comply. Among the things that the inspector general report pointed out was that we need to upgrade our enforcement mechanisms, and we are very much doing so.

Organic foods can be found at farmers' markets, Wal-Mart and grocery stores like Safeway.

How much time do you think it will take?

We have already begun. We are already in the process of putting residue-testing expectations at a higher level ... so part of this is just getting our [organic] certifying agents that we accredit to do the job that they are supposed to do. We don't have to do big rulemaking. We don't have to get huge new budgets. We don't have to come up with huge new visions. We just need to do the job that was set forth in the law.

You helped develop the USDA's organic labeling rules in 1999–2001, but the program was largely shaped and implemented after you left. When you returned to the USDA last year, what was the most surprising thing you learned about what had happened with the program?

I left a pretty long to-do list when we published the final rule. Case in point: pasture.... What does it mean when we say "access to pasture," for ruminants, particularly dairy cows? ... Well, that was on the list when I left in 2001. ... There were a lot of things on that to-do list. I inherited that list right back.

The problems with the organics program cited in the IG report took place during the [George W.] Bush administration. What happened? Was it a lack of will? A lack of resources? Were they too friendly to big organic producers?

I assume it was not a priority.

What do you think is the biggest misconception that Americans have about organic products?

That organic has to be super expensive. I don't think it has to be, and with the growth in the industry we are seeing, some of those prices have come down. I think a lot of people think it is the white-tablecloth yuppies, the foodies who buy organic. ... But organic foods can be found at farmers' markets, Wal-Mart and grocery stores like Safeway.

If consumers are choosing to use their food dollar to support that environmental system [purchasing junk food], I think that's fine.

What would you recommend to consumers who want to find pesticide-free, organic products they can count on?

First, I'd tell them that organic is no guarantee that it is pesticide free. Organic farmers are allowed to use certain pesticides, and sometimes they are natural. I think one thing they can do is go to the [USDA's] Ag Marketing Service's pesticide-testing program (http://www.ams.usda.gov/pdp). We do supermarket sampling all over the country. We go into supermarkets just like Mom or Dad would do and we buy different produce, different foods, dairy, and we test them for pesticide residue. We put all our results on that Web site.

Do you buy organic products? What kind?

I do, but not exclusively. My husband does most of the grocery shopping. . . . We are more inclined to spend money on organic on the perimeters of the grocery store. So we are spending most of our time in the produce, meat, dairy aisles and not so much in the middle, where the processed foods are.

A small percentage of synthetic ingredients is allowed in products like organic cake doughnuts, marshmallows and macaroni and cheese. Should the USDA grant exemptions like this to find an organic path for junk and comfort foods?

I think yes. Obviously, I think so because it was in the law and in the final rule. Again, for me, organic has a very strong environmental connection, and people are always going to eat a certain amount of junk food, and if that junk food arrives in the supermarket and it has come from the most environmental, sound production regimes possible, I think that's great. So if consumers are choosing to use their food dollar to support that environmental system, I think that is fine. So you will sometimes see organic junk food in my basket as well.

As you look ahead, what important developments do you see for organic foods and the program?

I think consumers sometimes feel conflicted. Do I buy organic or do I buy local? . . . We are trying to find ways to grow domestic food markets to help rural communities. . . . And I think the extent to which we can expose [to the public] that overlap between organic and local/regional [producers] will help. I think there are some opportunities there that haven't been explored.

13

Organic Farming Offers Learning Opportunities for Volunteer Workers

Tracie Cone

Tracie Cone is an award-winning journalist and has won a Pulitzer Prize for her writing while working at the Miami Herald.

In recent years, hundreds of people have become organic farm hands through the organization World Wide Opportunities on Organic Farms USA. Known as woofers, these workers are assigned to organic farms around the world where they work for room and board. The program has allowed people to experience both rural living and a variety of ethnic cultures. While every woofing experience does not turn out perfectly, the program has offered hundreds of people the chance to travel and learn more about organic food production.

The morning sun lights up blue lupin and magenta owl's clover as Erik Ramfjord and Andrew Riddle scoop soured milk into a trough, drawing delighted squeals from a dozen free-range pigs.

A month ago [in March 2010], Ramfjord was an unmotivated biology major in Oregon, and Riddle didn't know what he wanted from Humboldt State University in northern California. Now they are energized, toiling from sun up to sun down for meals and a bunk on an organic ranch in central California, hundreds of miles from home.

Tracie Cone, "Organic Farm Volunteers: The New Beat Generation?" *Salon*, April 30, 2010. Reprinted with permission.

"I consider myself extremely lucky to have stumbled upon this," says Ramfjord, 20.

Ramfjord and Riddle each paid $20 to become part of World Wide Opportunities on Organic Farms USA, a group with 9,000 members known by a variation of its acronym, woofers. It's kind of a new millennium version of the traveling hobo willing to work for a meal.

The website allows willing workers to negotiate a non-paid work stint with nearly 1,200 U.S. farmers and ranchers. Every farm could use an extra hand, but the hosts also benefit from the parade of characters who become a part of their lives, if only temporarily.

Most [woofers] are young people from urban areas who want to experience rural life.

Experiencing Rural Life

"When I was younger, I used to hitchhike; it's not the same, but it is that idea," said Ryan "Leo" Goldsmith, executive director of WWOOF-USA, founded with former classmates at the University of California, Santa Cruz. "You have to have faith in humanity and that showing up at someone's house is going to be OK. The tie that binds is a shared interest in sustainable agriculture."

Most are young people from urban areas who want to experience rural life. Some are newly jobless, or don't have prospects. Membership has skyrocketed as the economy has plummeted, soaring from about 1,600 willing U.S. workers in 2005. More than a dozen other autonomous branches match workers with farmers around the globe.

After a year woofing across the U.S. with her boyfriend, Jennifer Makens of suburban Detroit plans to ditch her teaching career to farm for a living. But first the couple will woof on a farm in Pennsylvania, then California and Oregon, Costa Rica, Ecuador, Argentina, Japan and New Zealand.

"I had no idea we'd do this for so long," said Makens, 29, who travels with Charlie Ryan in a Saturn with 150,000 miles on it. "We're getting proud of all the calluses on our hands. It has really changed the way I feel about material possessions, as well. If it won't fit in my car, I don't need it."

Ramfjord heard about woofing while a student at Lewis and Clark College in Portland [Oregon], so he signed up while awaiting a guide job on the American River in California. Riddle will work this summer with the California Conservation Corps.

Making Worldwide Connections

On the Douglas Ranch, about 75 miles south of San Jose [California], they start their day with the pigs, move to milking Bonnie the cow and feeding horses and lambs, then take on whatever owners Don and Rani Douglas need done. It ends at sunset with the cow's second milking and another round of feeding.

The Douglases have hosted woofers since 2005. They've made connections with people from Italy, France, Belgium, South Korea, Scotland and England, and across the United States. Forty in all.

"Besides all the hard work that they do for us, it's been a wonderful experience meeting them all," Rani said.

At South Carolina's Utterly Awesome Goat Farm, the owners need someone to tend Nubians and build a barn addition. West Elk Ranch in Colorado wants help with a garden and vineyard.

Having woofers at Butternut Farms has allowed Patricia West-Volland to hang onto the 20-acre farm in Glenford, Ohio, since the death of her husband a year ago.

"I truly could not stay on this farm without their help," she said.

Not all experiences are good, so Goldsmith encourages woofers to make sure expectations are clear, including how long the visit will last. One left a Georgia farm when an emotionally unstable neighbor joined the crew. One host said a worker broke candlesticks when she asked him to leave.

But usually it works out.

Understanding Food Production

"The first night I was sketching out," Ramfjord said. "I was with people I never met. I thought, 'I'm a dead man.'"

One day an outbuilding needs a new roof, or Ike the pet buffalo has broken a fence, or the cow's eye infection needs medication. They talk excitedly about what they have learned.

"Oh, man, how to drive a tractor, how to use a chain saw, how to roof a house," Ramfjord began.

"How to milk a cow, how to brand, how to dehorn a cow," Riddle continued.

"How to fix a barbed wire fence," Ramfjord added.

"I've extracted a dead pig from Vicki, which was different," Riddle said, and they stop briefly because Vicki did not survive and left two orphans, a harsh reality of ranch life.

"Just being around a pig," Ramfjord offered, then adds: "How you can use a tractor for anything."

Both said they have a better understanding about the labor that goes into food production, and a new awareness about its origins.

"I definitely want to eat meat from a place like this, not a factory farm," Ramfjord said, then he paused and surveyed the green hills around him. "I consider myself extremely lucky to have stumbled onto this ranch."

14

Organic Farm Workers Are as Mistreated as Non-Organic Farm Workers

Jason Mark

Jason Mark co-manages San Francisco's Alemany Farm. He is the coauthor, with Kevin Danaher, of Insurrection: Citizen Challenges to Corporate Power.

Workers on organic farms are frequently treated as badly as workers on conventional farms. While consumers of organic food often assume that the United States Department of Agriculture (USDA) oversees labor, the organic label issued by the USDA only addresses food growth and production, not labor practices. Although the organic food market is growing, the growth has not aided the farm worker. Instead, organic market growth has encouraged corporate companies to enter the organic market, and these corporations have focused on profits, not wages. One solution to the farm labor problem is to create a "fair made" label for food in the same way that these labels are used to identify fair made products imported from other countries. A fair made label, however, would require time to put into practice. In the interim, organic farm workers will continue to work under difficult conditions.

When Elena Ortiz found a job on an organic raspberry farm after working for nine years in conventionally farmed fields, she was glad for the change. The best part about

Jason Mark, "Workers on Organic Farms Are Treated as Poorly as Their Conventional Counterparts," *Grist*, August 2, 2006. Reprinted with permission.

her new job was that she no longer had to work just feet away from tractors spraying chemical herbicides and pesticides. An added bonus was the fruit itself—"prettier," she said, and firmer, which made it easier to pick.

But when it came to how Ortiz was treated by her employers, little was different. Her pay remained meager: $500 a week at peak berry-picking season, but as little as $200 a week during much of the year, leaving her and her farmworker husband with little money to buy fruits and vegetables for their five children. The supervisors at her farm, Reiter Berry, were often "aggressive" and capricious. Rules were arbitrary; workers were sometimes closely monitored, but sometimes allowed to work independently. They were, said Ortiz, assigned to "better or worse rows"—all depending on the whims of the supervisors.

When organizers from the United Farm Workers [UFW] encouraged the Reiter employees to form a union, the company allegedly responded with intimidation and harassment.

"There was an atmosphere of fear. People were afraid they would be laid off," Ortiz said in a recent interview. (Elena Ortiz is not her real name; fearful of losing her job, she spoke only on condition of anonymity.) "I wish they would treat us better. What can the people do? Nothing."

Garland Reiter, one of the co-owners of the company, took objection to Ortiz's comments. "I think we're a leader in the industry, living by honesty, openness, and respect," he said.

While the [organic] seal covers a range of environmental practices, it says nothing about labor conditions.

Organic Farms and Conventional Wisdom

Nevertheless, it appears that worker abuse in the organic industry is widespread.

"There's a common conventional wisdom by a lot of consumers, especially at the higher-end stores, that just because it's organic the workers are treated better," said UFW spokesperson Mark Grossman. "And that's simply not true."

That disconnect between reality and public perception is of increasing concern to farmworker advocates, food activists, and some farmers, who worry that as the organic sector replicates the abusive conditions of conventional agriculture, it is sacrificing the founding values of the sustainable-food movement. The desire to return organic to its roots is driving a slew of initiatives to develop labor standards for organic farms. If successful, the new standards would establish the organic sector as the kind of fully sustainable industry—both socially responsible and environmentally sound—that could be a model for the entire economy.

Where Have All the Hippies Gone?

When you go to the supermarket and buy produce or packaged goods that carry the organic label, you can feel confident that the food was grown under rigorous environmental standards. The U.S. Department of Agriculture's [USDA] organic seal, which debuted in 2002, is a guarantee that your fruits and vegetables were cultivated without petroleum-based fertilizers or (with rare exceptions) synthetic chemicals, and that they aren't genetically modified. The organic label, however, goes only so far. While the seal covers a range of environmental practices, it says nothing about labor conditions.

Although comprehensive studies of conditions on organic farms are hard to find, complaints like Ortiz's are not uncommon. For example, Willamette River Organics, one of Oregon's largest organic operations, has been hit with several lawsuits charging violations of minimum-wage laws. A Human Rights Watch report on the exploitation of adolescent workers said the atmosphere at Arizona's organic Pavich Farms was "hostile, suspicious," with laborers apparently not permitted to speak to inspectors. Threemile Canyon, a large organic dairy and potato farm in Oregon, faces accusations of sexual discrimination in its hiring practices.

Workers get no consolation in the form of higher wages or better benefits, either. According to a report published last year by researchers at UC [University of California]-Davis, a majority of 188 California organic farms surveyed do not pay a living wage or provide medical or retirement plans. In fact, most organic workers earn the same as those in conventional fields—less (adjusted for inflation) than they were making in the 1970s, when the famous UFW boycotts occurred. "The exploitative conditions that farmworkers face in the U.S. are abysmal—it's a human-rights crisis," said Richard Mandelbaum, policy analyst at the Farmworker Support Committee. "In terms of wages and labor rights, there's really no difference between organic and conventional."

While organic's profitability would suggest that there is plenty of money to pay workers better, much of the profits go to retailers and wholesalers higher up the food chain.

If that doesn't seem to fit the organic movement's hippie and homesteader origins, the incursion of big business may be partly to blame. Reiter Affiliated Companies, where Ortiz works, is a perfect example of how the movement has shifted. With thousands of employees, Reiter is the biggest supplier to Driscoll Berry, one of the country's largest distributors of strawberries, raspberries, and blueberries. Driscoll sells both conventionally grown and organic berries—an indicator of organic's growing popularity, but also a sign of how some companies see organic more as a market niche than as a broad business philosophy.

Corporate Organic Farming

That niche is now a $14 billion industry in the U.S. Giant food-processing corporations, seeing opportunities for expansion, have become major players in the organic industry. For example, General Mills owns the organic brands Cascadian Farm and Muir Glen. Kellogg owns Sunrise Organic. Even agribusiness giant ConAgra is in on the act, recently introducing organic versions of its Orville Redenbacher popcorn and Hunt's tomato sauce brands.

And while organic's profitability would suggest that there is plenty of money to pay workers better—for those so inclined—much of the profits go to retailers and wholesalers higher up the food chain. Raising workers' wages is also complicated by the fact that organic labor costs are disproportionately high, since such operations often depend on hand weeding in place of chemical herbicides.

[One] obstacle toward improving conditions is that, simply put, the treatment of farm laborers doesn't rate high on most people's list of concerns.

Ultimately, paying workers more depends on paying farmers more, which appears unlikely in a country that has gotten used to cheap food. "People look down on farmers," said Tim Vos, one of the co-owners of California's Blue Heron Farm, which pays its 10 field workers about $12 an hour. "If you want to pay people well, you need high prices. What would it take to offer benefits? We would have to almost double our prices."

Workers' Rights

Another obstacle toward improving conditions is that, simply put, the treatment of farm laborers doesn't rate high on most people's list of concerns. At least, that's the conclusion of a recent consumer study conducted by researcher Phil Howard at UC-Santa Cruz. The survey found that workers' rights ranked fifth on a list of food-related issues that interested respondents—right behind the treatment of animals.

Farmer Jim Cochran put it bluntly: "Everybody cares about how the bugs are treated, but nobody cares about how the workers are treated."

Cochran knows what he's talking about. In 1987, his operation, Swanton Berry Farm, became the first organically certified strawberry grower in California. Eleven years later, Swanton became the first organic farm to sign a contract with the UFW. Today Swanton Berry remains the only organic farm in the country to have a collective bargaining agreement with the farmworkers' union. "I like the union label, because it means that the workers are saying, 'It's OK,'" Cochran said.

The 30 workers at Swanton Berry—who earn between $9 and $11 an hour—have a medical plan, a pension plan, holiday pay, and subsidized housing in a pair of well-kept bunkhouses with a view of the Pacific. If they need a loan to cover emergency expenses, workers can get an advance on their paychecks. Once workers have put in 500 hours on the farm, they can begin buying stock in the company.

"Fair Made" Label

While Cochran's commitment to social justice is laudable, being a union farm makes his costs 15 percent higher than those of other organic growers. Because union certification seems unrealistic for the small and medium-sized farms that still make up the bulk of organic growers, a range of organizations is working on proposals to create some kind of "fair made" label to encourage farmers to adopt better labor policies.

At least half a dozen projects are in the works. The Rural Advancement Foundation International and the Farmworker Support Committee have enlisted five farms in a pilot project demonstrating best labor practices. Growers in Canada have started a "fair deal" label. The organic soap maker Dr. Bronner's is implementing fair-trade standards to "improve the livelihoods of farmers and workers," while some dairy farmers have come together under the Wisconsin Fair Trade cheese initiative.

The slew of different programs demonstrates an energetic grassroots commitment to improving worker treatment. But there is a danger that having too many separate standards will be confusing to consumers and cumbersome for growers. So the various interests have come together in an ad-hoc coalition—the Domestic Fair Trade Working Group—to develop a single set of labor standards, a single monitoring process for farms, and one seal that consumers can trust to mean workers were treated right. The draft principles include a living wage for farmworkers, fair prices for farmers, transparent business practices, and family farm ownership.

Coming Soon-ish to a Supermarket Near You

Of course, another alternative would be to try to amend the existing USDA organic seal to include labor standards. But with advocates already busy fighting back efforts by the major food processors to loosen the organic rules, creating an independent label appears the best way to go.

"The government can't lead on this," said Cecil Wright, director of local operations at Organic Valley, a cooperative of more than 800 family-owned dairies, ranches, and farms. "We need to have the people who know what they're doing, who are entrepreneurial, to lead. We believe that at some point in the future we'll need a standard that goes above and beyond the USDA label."

When will that point be? Participants in the coalition agree it will be at least three years before shoppers can expect to see an independent label that certifies decent working conditions. In the meantime, advocates point out that there are a number of steps farmers can take to make their employees feel more valued. A recent [in August 2006] report by the California Institute for Rural Studies looked at best labor practices on 12 organic farms and identified several low-cost ways for cash-strapped farmers to improve workplace conditions. When interviewed, farmworkers said a slower pace of work, year-round employment, free food from the farm, flexible schedules, and plain old "respectful treatment" would make them feel like their work was important.

The stakes are high when it comes to the successful creation of a "fair labor" organic seal, and the importance of the struggle goes beyond the tight-knit sustainable-food community. If organic farmers can find a way to produce food without exploiting either the environment or their workers, advocates say, they can set an example for other industries to follow.

"For me, the big issue is in terms of progressive movement-building," said Ronnie Cummins, director of the Organic Consumers Association. "It's time to dovetail the health, sustainability, and justice movements. The potential is incredible. But it's going to take some real, hard organizing."

Organizations to Contact

The editors have compiled the following list of organizations concerned with the issues debated in this book. The descriptions are derived from materials provided by the organizations. All have publications or information available for interested readers. The list was compiled on the date of publication of the present volume; the information provided here may change. Be aware that many organizations take several weeks or longer to respond to inquiries, so allow as much time as possible.

American Council on Science and Health (ACSH)
1995 Broadway, 2nd Fl., New York, NY   10023-5860
(212) 362-7044
e-mail: acsh@acsh.org
website: www.acsh.org

ACSH provides consumers with scientific evaluations of issues related to food, pharmaceuticals, chemicals, and the environment, pointing out both health hazards and benefits. Its representatives participate in a variety of government and media events, testifying at congressional hearings and appearing on television and radio news programs. Its website includes relevant articles and reports.

Cato Institute
1000 Massachusetts Ave. NW, Washington, DC   20001-5403
(202) 842-0200 • fax: (202) 842-3490
e-mail: cato@cato.org
website: www.cato.org

The Cato Institute is a libertarian public policy research foundation dedicated to limiting the role of government and protecting individual liberties. It asserts that the concern over the possible health risks of pesticide use in agriculture is overstated. The institute publishes the quarterly *Cato Journal*, the bimonthly *Cato Policy Report*, and numerous books and commentaries.

Center for Science in the Public Interest (CSPI)

1875 Connecticut Ave. NW, Suite 300, Washington, DC 20009

(202) 332-9110

e-mail: cspi@cspinet.org

website: www.cspinet.org

Formed in 1971, the Center for Science in the Public Interest (CSPI) is a nonprofit education and consumer advocacy organization dedicated to fighting for government food policies and corporate practices that promote healthy diets. CSPI also works to prevent deceptive marketing practices and ensures that science is used for public welfare. It publishes *Nutrition Action Healthletter*, the most widely circulated health newsletter in North America.

Cornucopia Institute

P.O. Box 126, Cornucopia, Wisconsin 54827

(608) 625-2042

e-mail: cultivate@cornucopia.org

website: www.cornucopia.org

The Cornucopia Institute's mission is to promote economic justice for family scale farming. It supports educational activities that spread the ecological and economic principles that underlay sustainable and organic agriculture. Through research and investigations on agricultural issues, the Cornucopia Institute provides information to consumers, family farmers, and the media about organic food and farming.

Food and Nutrition Service (FNS)

1400 Independence Avenue, S.W., Washington, DC 20250

(202) 720-2791

website: www.fns.usda.gov

The Food and Nutrition Service is an agency of the US Department of Agriculture (USDA) and is responsible for administering the nation's domestic nutrition assistance programs. It provides prepared meals, food assistance, and nutrition education materials to one in five Americans. The agency also encourages children and teens to follow the healthy eating guidelines set by MyPyramid in its "Eat Smart, Play Hard" campaign.

Food First: Institute for Food and Development Policy

398 60th St., Oakland, CA   94618
(510) 654-4400
website: www.foodfirst.org

Food First, founded by the author of *Diet for a Small Planet*, promotes sustainable agriculture and seeks to eliminate causes of hunger. Its current projects include the Cuban Organic Agriculture Exchange Program and Californians for Pesticide Reform. Its website includes articles and press releases as well as audio and video postings addressing its various initiatives.

Food Safety Consortium (FSC)

110 Agriculture Building, Fayetteville, AR   72701
(501) 575-5647
website: http://www.uark.edu/depts/fsc

Congress established the Food Safety Consortium (FSC), consisting of researchers from the University of Arkansas, Iowa State University, and Kansas State University, in 1988 through a special Cooperative State Research Service grant. The FSC conducts extensive investigation into all areas of poultry, beef, and pork meat production.

Friends of the Earth (FoE)

1717 Massachusetts Avenue, Washington, DC   20036
(202) 783-7400
e-mail: foe@foe.org
website: www.foe.org

Friends of the Earth monitors legislation and regulations that affect the environment. The group's Safer Food, Safer Farms Campaign speaks out against what it perceives as the negative impact biotechnology can have on farming, food production, genetic resources, and the environment.

Organic Agriculture and Products Education Institute (Organic Institute)
PO Box 547, Greenfield, MA   01302
website: www.theorganicinstitute.org

The Organic Institute was created by members of the Organic Trade Association (OTA). Its mission is to educate the public regarding the attributes, benefits, and practices of organic agriculture and products for better environmental and personal health. Its website offers a downloadable guide for students who want to bring organic dining to their school or college campus.

Organic Trade Association
P.O. Box 547, Greenfield, MA   01302
(413) 774-7511
website: www.ota.com

The Organic Trade Association (OTA) is a membership-based business association that focuses on the organic business community in North America. OTA's mission is to promote and protect the growth of organic trade to benefit the environment, farmers, the public, and the economy.

Rodale Institute
611 Siegfriedale Road, Kutztown, PA   19530-9320
(610) 683-1400
e-mail: info@rodaleinst.org
website: www.rodaleinstitute.org

The Rodale Institute was founded in 1947 by organic pioneer J.I. Rodale. The Institute employs soil scientists and a cooperating network of researchers who assert that organic farming techniques offer the best solution to global warming and famine. Their website offers information on the longest-running US study comparing organic and conventional farming techniques, a study that forms the basis for Rodale's practical training to thousands of farmers in Africa, Asia, and the Americas.

US Environmental Protection Agency (EPA)
Ariel Rios Building, Washington, DC   20460
(202) 272-0167
website: www.epa.gov

The Environmental Protection Agency (EPA) is a government agency that, among other things, regulates pesticides under two major federal statutes. It establishes maximum legally permissible levels for pesticide residues in food, registers pesticides for use in the United States, and prescribes labeling and other regulatory requirements to prevent unreasonable adverse effects on health and the environment.

US Food and Drug Administration (FDA)
10903 New Hampshire Ave., Silver Spring, MD   20903
(888)INFO-FDA (888-463-6332)
website: www.fda.gov

The Food and Drug Administration (FDA) is a public health agency, charged with protecting American consumers by enforcing the Federal Food, Drug, and Cosmetic Act and several related public health laws. To carry out this mandate of consumer protection, FDA has investigators and inspectors cover the country's almost 95,000 FDA-regulated businesses. Its publications include government documents, reports, fact sheets, and press announcements.

Bibliography

Books

Alex Avery   *The Truth About Organic Foods.* Chesterfield, MO: Henderson Communications, 2006.

Denis Avery   *Saving the Planet with Pesticides and Plastic: The Environmental Triumph of High-Yield Farming.* Washington, DC: Hudson Institute, 2000.

Cindy Burke   *To Buy Or Not Buy Organic: What You Need to Know to Choose the Healthiest, Safest, Most Earth-Friendly Food.* New York: Da Capo, 2007.

Jeff Cox   *The Organic Cook's Bible.* Hoboken, NJ: Wiley & Sons, 2006.

Jeff Cox   *The Organic Food Shopper's Guide.* Hoboken, NJ: Wiley & Sons, 2008.

Tanya L. K. Denckla   *The Gardener's A-Z Guide to Growing Organic Food.* North Adams, MA: Storey, 2003.

Samuel Fromartz   *Organic Inc.: Natural Foods and How They Grew.* New York: Harcourt, 2006.

James McWilliams   *Just Food: Where Locavores Get It Wrong.* New York: Back Bay, 2009.

Joseph Mercola and Ben Lerner — *Generation XL: Raising Healthy, Intelligent Kids in a High-Tech, Junk-Food World.* Nashville, TN: Thomas Nelson, 2007.

Steve Meyerowitz — *The Organic Food Guide: How to Shop Smarter and Eat Healthier.* Guildford, CN: Globe Pequot, 2004.

Marion Nestle — *Food Politics: How the Food Industry Influences Nutrition and Health.* Los Angeles, CA: University of California, 2002.

Marion Nestle — *What to Eat.* New York: North Point, 2006.

Robert Paarlberg — *Food Politics: What Everyone Needs to Know.* New York: Oxford, 2010.

Luddene Perry and Dan Schultz — *A Field Guide to Buying Organic.* New York: Bantam, 2007.

Michael Pollan — *In Defense of Food: An Eater's Manifesto.* New York: Penguin, 2009.

Jill Richardson — *Recipe for America: Why Our Food System Is Broken and What We Can Do to Fix It.* Brooklyn, NY: Ig Publishing, 2009.

Michele Simon — *Appetite for Profit: How the Food Industry Undermines Our Health and How to Fight Back.* New York: Nation, 2006.

Karl Weber, editor   *Food Inc.: A Participant Guide: How Industrial Food Is Making Us Sicker, Fatter, and Poorer, and What You Can Do About It.* Philadelphia, PA: Public Affairs, 2009.

Periodicals

Glenn Baker   "Green Monkey See, Green Monkey Do," *NZ Business*, December 2009.

J. Steven Bird   "A Small Green Food Machine," *Natural Life*, July–August 2010.

Alan Borst   "Organic Farmers Increasingly Turn to Cooperative Business Model," *Rural Cooperatives*, May–June 2010.

Linda Buchwald   "Learning from Labels," *Scholastic Choices*, November–December 2009.

Claire Connors   "The Health That Got Me Fit," *Shape*, February 2009.

Corn & Soybean Digest   "Are Organic Foods Over-Hyped?" July 30, 2010.

James Delingpole   "Eat Local Organic Food If You Like, But Don't Kid Yourself That It's Green," *Spectator*, September 18, 2010.

Catherine Elton   "Home Delivery," *Time*, August 30, 2010.

Meagan Francis   "Healthy Eats for Kids," *Natural Health*, September 2009.

Julia M. Gallo-Torres	"Fortified Junk Food?" *Prepared Foods*, February 2009.
Just-Food	"Ethical Food: A Complicated Picture," September 13, 2010.
Jeffrey Kluger	"What's So Great About Organic Food?" *Time*, August 30, 2010.
Stephanie Liberatore	"Health Wise," *Science Teacher*, September 2008.
Alex MacEachern and Dan Zdzieborski	"Organically Entertaining: Having Company?" *Natural Life*, May–June 2010.
David Orgel	"Warning Signs for Organic/Natural in New Data?" *Supermarket News*, July 12, 2010.
Janet Oswald	"Planning for Urban Agriculture," *Plan Canada*, Summer 2009.
Josh Ozersky	"Farm vs. Supermarket," *Time*, August 30, 2010.
Mark Pendergrast	"Going Organic for Good," *Wine Spectator*, March 31, 2010.
Andrew Purvis	"The Organic Dilemma," *Grocer*, July 10, 2010.
Merritt Watts	"Ready, Set, Grow!" *Self*, April 2010.

Index